MODERNITIES & OTHER WRITINGS

Of all the avant-garde writers, Blaise Cendrars (1887–1961) was the one most attuned to our age; hence the title of this collection of his short prose works. In these seven essays, Cendrars considers modern artists, many of them his friends and associates, and their altered relations to a new world of communications technology, advertising, and mass politics.
French Modernist Library series. $19.95
Available at bookstores.

University of Nebraska Press 901 N 17 • Lincoln, NE 68588-0520 • 800-755-1105

FARRAR STRAUS GIROUX

POETRY

Fall/Winter 1992–93 Poetry

Derek Walcott
Winner of the 1992 Nobel Prize in Literature
OMEROS
Hardcover 374-22591-5
Paperback 374-52350-9
Available now

Seamus Heaney
Photographs by Rachel Giese
SWEENEY'S FLIGHT
Hardcover/September
374-27219-0

Gjertrud Schnackenberg
A GILDED LAPSE OF TIME
Hardcover/November
374-16226-3

Les Murray
DOG FOX FIELD
Hardcover/January
374-14314-5

Joseph Brodsky
TO URANIA
Paperback/April '92
374-52333-9

Christopher Logue
KINGS
An Account of Books 1 and 2 of Homer's *Iliad*
Paperback/October
374-52368-1

Aleksandr Kushner
APOLLO IN THE SNOW
Selected Poems 1960–1987
Paperback/November
374-52321-5

Heberto Padilla
A FOUNTAIN, A HOUSE OF STONE
Paperback/December
374-52364-9

Farrar Straus Giroux

Now at your bookstore, or call 1-800-631-8571
To receive a current catalogue of all our titles, please write:
Farrar, Straus & Giroux
19 Union Square West New York, New York 10003

GRAND STREET

44

Cover: William Christenberry, *Southern Monument VI* (detail), 1987.

Keith Haring mural copyright © 1992 The Estate of Keith Haring.

Jasper Johns lithograph copyright © 1993 Jasper Johns/U.L.A.E./V.A.G.A.

Minor White photographs copyright © 1982 Trustees of Princeton University.

Grand Street is set in ITC New Baskerville by Crystal Graphics, Houston, Tex., and printed by W. E. Barnett & Associates, Houston, Tex. Color separations and halftones are by Color Separations, Inc., Houston, Tex.

Grand Street (ISSN 0734-5496; ISBN 0-393-30955-X) is published quarterly by Grand Street Press (a project of the New York Foundation for the Arts, Inc., a not-for-profit corporation), 131 Varick Street, #906, New York, N.Y. 10013. Contributions and gifts to Grand Street Press, a project of the New York Foundation for the Arts, Inc., are tax-deductible to the extent allowed by law.

Volume Eleven, Number Four (*Grand Street* 44). Copyright © 1993 by New York Foundation for the Arts, Inc., Grand Street Press. All rights reserved. Reproduction, whether in whole or in part, without permission is strictly prohibited.

Unsolicited material should be addressed to the editors at *Grand Street,* 131 Varick Street, #906, New York, N.Y. 10013. Manuscripts will not be returned unless accompanied by a stamped, self-addressed envelope.

Second-class postage at New York, N.Y., and additional mailing offices. Postmaster: Please send address changes to Subscription Service, Dept. GRS, P.O. Box 3000, Denville, N.J. 07834.

Subscription orders and address changes should be addressed to Subscription Service, Dept. GRS, P.O. Box 3000, Denville, N.J. 07834. Subscriptions are $30 a year (four issues). Foreign subscriptions (including Canada) are $40 a year, and must be payable in U.S. funds. Single-copy price is $10 ($12.99 Canada). *Grand Street* is distributed to the trade by W. W. Norton & Company, 500 Fifth Avenue, New York, N.Y. 10110, and to newsstands only by B. DeBoer, Inc., 113 E. Centre St., Nutley, N.J. 07110 and Fine Print Distributors, 6448 Highway 290 E., Austin, Tex. 78723.

GRAND STREET

Editor
Jean Stein

Managing Editor	*Art Editor*
Esther Allen	Walter Hopps
Poetry Editor	*Designer*
Erik Rieselbach	Don Quaintance
Assistant Editors	*Production Assistant*
Howard Halle	Elizabeth Frizzell
Sebastian Thomas	
	Interns
Editorial Assistant	Stephanie Koven
Allison Marshall	Heather O'Donnell

Copy Editor
Kate Norment

Contributing Editors

Hilton Als, Morgan Entrekin, Raymond Foye,
Jonathan Galassi, Andrew Kopkind, Alberto Manguel,
Olivier Nora, Edward W. Said, Robert Scheer, Jean Strouse,
Jeremy Treglown, Katrina vanden Heuvel,
Shelley Wanger, Drenka Willen

Publishers

Jean Stein & Torsten Wiesel

CONTENTS

Edmund White
Reprise — *10*

Seamus Deane
Four Poems — *26*

Theodor W. Adorno
Wagner's Relevance for Today — *32*

Lyn Hejinian
from *Sleeps* — *60*

Pham Thi Hoai
Nine Down Makes Ten — *66*

Albert Mobilio
Talus Slope — *78*

Andrew McCord
Frames of a Coptic Funeral — *80*

William Christenberry
Klan Dolls   *(portfolio)* — *81*

Andrei Platonov
from *Happy Moscow* — *96*

Rodney Jones
Shame the Monsters — *118*

Martin Duberman
The Night They Raided Stonewall — *120*

Michael Krüger
from *Idylls and Illusions* — *148*

Fred Wilson
Mining the Museum   (*portfolio*)   *151*

Nance Van Winckel
Ghost Pig   *173*

Mei-Mei Berssenbrugge
Sphericity   *174*

Andrew Kopkind
Slacking Toward Bethlehem   *176*

James Haining
The Rose Chapel   *189*

Bernadette Mayer
Ice Cube Epigrams   *190*

Georges Perec
Backtracking   *194*

Edvard Kocbek
Two Poems   *203*

Gerald Burns
Atalanta in Cleveland   *206*

David Searcy
from *Ordinary Horror*   *208*

Sharon Olds
Two Poems   *246*

About the Cover   *249*

Contributors   *250*

Illustrations   *256*

EDMUND WHITE

Reprise

A novel I'd written, which had flopped in America, was about to come out in France, and I was racing around vainly trying to assure its success in translation. French critics seldom give nasty reviews to books, but they often ignore a novel altogether, especially one by a foreign writer, even one who like me lives in Paris.

In the midst of these professional duties I suddenly received a phone call. A stifled baritone voice with a Midwestern accent asked if I was "Eddie." No one had called me that since my childhood. "It's Jim Grady. Your mother gave me your number."

I hadn't seen him in almost forty years, not since I was fourteen and he twenty, but I could still taste the Luckies and Budweiser on his lips, feel his powerful arms closing around me, remember the deliberate way he'd folded his trousers on the crease rather than throwing them on the floor in romantic haste as I'd done.

I met Jim through our parents. My mother was dating his father, an arrangement she'd been falling back on intermittently for years although she mildly despised him. She went out with him when there was no one better around. She was in her fifties, fat, highly sexed, hard-working, by turns bitter and wildly optimistic (now I'm all those things, so I feel no hesitation in describing her in those terms, especially since she was to change for the better in old age). My father and she had divorced seven years earlier, and she'd gone to work partly out of necessity but partly to make something of herself. Her Texas relations expected great things from her and their ambitions had shaped hers.

Before the divorce she'd studied psychology, and now she worked in the public schools of suburban Chicago, traveling from one to another, systematically testing all the slow learners, problem cases, and "exceptional" children ("exceptional" meant either unusually intelligent or retarded). She put great stock in making an attractive, even stunning appearance at those smelly cinderblock schools and rose early in the morning to apply her makeup, struggle into her girdle, and don dresses or suits that followed the fashions better than the contours of her stubby body.

In the gray, frozen dawns of Chicago winters she would drive her new Buick to remote schools, where the assistant principal would install her in an empty classroom and bring her one child after another. Shy, dirty, suspicious kids would eye her warily, wag their legs together in a lackluster parody of sex, fall into dumb trances, or microscopically assay the hard, black riches they'd mined from their nostrils, but nothing could dim my mother's glittering determination to be cheerful.

She never merely went through the motions or let a more appropriate depression muffle her performance. She always had the highly colored, fatuously alert look of someone who is listening to compliments. Perhaps she looked that way because she was continuously reciting her own praises to herself as a sort of protective mantra. Most people, I suspect, are given a part in which the dialogue keeps running out, a supporting role for which the lazy playwright has scribbled in "Improvise background chatter" or "Crowd noises off." But my mother's lines had been fully scored for her (no matter that she'd written them herself), and she couldn't rehearse them often enough. Every night she came home, kicked off her very high heels, and wriggled out of her orthopedically strong girdle, shrinking and filling out and sighing "Whooee!"—something her Ranger, Texas, mother would exclaim after feeding the chickens or rustling up some grub in the summer heat.

Then my mother would pour herself a stiff bourbon and water, first of the many highballs she'd need to fuel her through the evening. "I saw fifteen patients today: twelve Stanford-Binets, one Wexford, one House-Tree-Person. I even gave a Rorschach to a beautiful little epileptic with high potential." On my mother's lips "beautiful" meant not a pretty face but a case of grimly classic textbook orthodoxy. "The children loved me. Several of them were afraid of me—I guess they'd never seen such a pretty, stylish lady all smiling and perfumed and bangled. But I put them right at ease. I know how to handle those backward children, they're just putty in my hands."

She thought for a moment, regarding her hands, then became animated. "The assistant principal was so grateful to me for my fine work. I guess she'd never had such an efficient, skilled state psychologist visit her poor little school before. She accompanied me to my automobile, and boy, you should have seen her eyes light up when she realized I was driving a fine Buick." Mother slung her stocking feet over the arm of the upholstered chair. "She grabbed my hand and looked me right in the eye and said, 'Who *are* you?'" This was part of the litany I always hated because it was obviously a lie. "'Why, whatever do you mean?' I asked her. 'You're no ordinary psychologist,' she said. 'I can see by your fine automobile and your beautiful clothes and your fine mind and lovely manners that you are a real lady.'" It was the phrase "fine automobile" that tipped me off, since only Southerners like my mother said that. Chicagoans said "nice car." Anyway I'd never heard any Midwesterner praise another in such a gratifying way; only in my mother's scenarios were such heady scenes a regular feature.

As the night wore on and my sister and I would sit down to do our homework on the cleared dining room table, as the winter pipes would knock hypnotically and the lingering smell of fried meat would get into our hair and heavy clothes, our mother would pour herself a fourth highball and put on her glasses to grade the tests she'd administered that day or to write up her reports in her round hand, but she'd interrupt her work and ours to say, "Funny, that woman simply couldn't get over how a fine lady like me could be battling the Skokie slush to come out to see those pitiful children." The note of pity was introduced only after the fourth drink, and it was, I imagine, something she felt less for her patients than for herself as the telephone stubbornly refused to ring.

At that time in my mother's life she had few friends. Going out with other unmarried women struck her as a disgrace and defeat. She was convinced couples looked down on her as a divorcée, and those single men who might want to date a chubby, penniless, middle-aged woman with two brats hanging around her neck were, as she'd say, scarce as hen's teeth.

That's where Mr. Grady came in. He was forty-five going on sixty, overweight, and utterly passive. He too liked his drinks, although in his case they were Manhattans; he fished the maraschino cherries out with his fingers. He didn't have false teeth, but there was something weak and sunken around his mouth as he mumbled his chemically bright cherries. His hairless hands were liver-spotted, and the nails were flaky, bluish, and unusually flat, which my mother, drawing on her fragmentary medical knowledge, called "spatulate," although I forget which malady this symptom was supposed to indicate. His wife had left him for another man, much richer, but she considerately sent Mr. Grady cash presents from time to time. He needed them: he lived reasonably well and he didn't earn much. He worked on the city desk of a major Chicago daily, but he'd been there for nearly twenty years, and in that era, before the Newspaper Guild grew strong, American journalists were badly paid unless they were flashy, opinionated columnists. Mr. Grady wrote nothing and had few opinions. He occasionally assigned stories to reporters, but most of the time he filled out columns that ran short with curious scraps of information. These items were called, for some reason, "boilerplate" and were composed weeks, even months in advance. For all I knew they were bought ready-made from some Central Bureau of Timeless Information. Although Mr. Grady seldom said anything interesting and was much given to dithering over the practical details of his daily life, his work furnished him with the odd bit of startling knowledge.

"Did you realize that Gandhi ate meat just once in his life and nearly died of it?" he'd announce. "Did you know there is more electric wire in the Radio City Music Hall organ than in the entire city of Plattsburgh?"

He was capable of going inert, like a worm that poses as a stick to escape a bird's detection (I have my own stock of boilerplate). When mother would hector him for not demanding a raise or for not acting like a man, his face would sink into his jowls, his chin into his chest, his chest into his belly, and the whole would settle lifelessly onto his elephantine legs. His eyes behind their thick glasses would refuse all contact. In that state he could remain nearly indefinitely until at last my mother's irritation would blow over and she would make a move to head off for Miller's Steak House, a family restaurant with a menu of sizzling T-bones, butter and rolls, French-fried onions, and hot fudge sundaes, which would contribute to Mr. Grady's early death by cardiac arrest.

In September 1954 the Kabuki Theater came from Tokyo to Chicago for the first time, and my mother and Mr. Grady bought tickets for themselves and me and Mr. Grady's son Jim, whom we had never met (my sister didn't want to go—she thought it sounded "weird," and the prospect of meeting an eligible young man upset her).

The minute I saw Jim Grady I became sick with desire—sick because I knew from my mother's psychology textbooks, which I'd secretly consulted, just how pathological my longings were. I had looked up "homosexuality" and read through the frightening, damning diagnosis and prognosis so many times with an erection that finally, through Pavlovian conditioning, fear instantly triggered excitement, guilt automatically entailed salivating love or lust or both.

Jim was tall and tan and blond with hair clipped soldier-short and a powerful upper lip that wouldn't stay shaved and always showed a reddish gold stubble. His small, complicated eyes rapidly changed expression, veering from manly impenetrability to teenage shiftiness. He trudged rather than walked, as though he were shod with horseshoes instead of trim Oxford lace-ups. He wore a bow tie, which I usually associated with chipper incompetence, but in Jim's case seemed more like a tourniquet hastily tied around his large, mobile Adam's apple in a makeshift attempt to choke off its pulsing maleness. If his Adam's apple was craggy, his nose was small and thin and well made, his bleached-out eyebrows so blond they shaded off into his tanned forehead, his ears small and neat and red and peeling on top and on the downy lobes.

He seemed eerily unaware of himself—the reason, no doubt, he left his mouth open whenever he wasn't saying "Yes, ma'am" or "No, ma'am" to my mother's routine questions, although once he smiled at her with the seductive leer of a lunatic, as though he were imitating someone else. He had allergies or a cold that had descended into his larynx and made his monosyllables sound becomingly stifled—or maybe he always talked that way. He could have been a West Point cadet, so virile and impersonal did his tall body appear, except for that open mouth, those squirming eyes, his fits of borrowed charm.

Someone had dressed him up in a hairy alpaca suit jacket and a cheap white shirt that was so small on him that his red hands hung down out of the cuffs like hams glazed with honey, for the backs of his hands were brushed with gold hair. The shirt, which would have been dingy on anyone less tan, was so thin that his dark chest could be seen breathing through it like a doubt concealed by a wavering smile. He wasn't wearing a T-shirt, which in those days was unusual, even provocative.

Mr. Grady was seated at one end, my mother next to him, then Jim, then me. My mother took off her coat and hat and combed her hair in a feathery, peripheral way designed to leave the deep structure of her permanent intact. "You certainly got a good tan this summer," she said.

"Thank you, ma'am."

His father, heavily seated, said tonelessly, without lifting his face from his chin or his chin from his chest, "He was working outside all summer on construction, earning money for his first year in med school."

"Oh, really!" my mother exclaimed, suddenly fascinated, since she had a deep reverence for doctors. I too felt a new respect for him as I imagined the white surgical mask covering his full upper lip; "I want you on your hands and knees," I could hear him telling me, "now bend forward, cross your arms on the table, turn your face to one side, and lay your cheek on the back of your forearm. Arch your back, spread your knees still wider." He was pulling on rubber gloves and from my strange, sideways angle I could see him dipping his sheathed finger into the cold lubricant . . .

"Have you chosen a specialty already?" my mother asked as the auditorium lights dimmed.

"Gynecology," Jim said—and I clamped my knees together with a start.

Then the samisens squealed, kotos thunked dully, and drums kept breaking rank to race forward faster and faster until they fell into silence. A pink spotlight picked out a heavily armored and mascaraed warrior frozen in midflight on the runway, but only the scattered Japanese members of the audience knew to applaud him. The program placed a Roman numeral IV beside the actor's name, which lent him a regal importance. Soon Number Four was stomping the stage and declaiming something in an angry gargle, but we hadn't paid for the earphones that would have given us the crucial simultaneous translation since my mother said she always preferred the gestalt to the mere details. "On the Rorschach I always score a very high W," she had coyly told the uncomprehending and uninterested Mr. Grady earlier over supper. I knew from her frequent elucidations that a high W meant she saw each inkblot as a whole rather than as separate parts, and that this grasp of the gestalt revealed her global intelligence, which she regarded as an attribute of capital importance.

A mincing, tittering maiden with a homely, powdered white face and an impractical hobble skirt (only later did I read that the performer was a man and the fifth member of his improbable dynasty) suddenly metamorphosed into a sinister white fox. With suicidal daring I pressed my leg against Jim's. First I put my shoe against his, sole planted squarely against sole. Then, having staked out this beachhead, I slowly cantilevered my calf muscles against his, at first just lightly grazing him. I even withdrew for a moment, proof of how completely careless and unintended my movements were, before I sat forward, resting my elbows on my knees in total absorption, leaning attentively into the exotic squealing and cavorting on stage—an intensification of attention that of course forced me to press my slender calf against his massive one, my knobby knee against his square, majestic one.

As two lovers rejoiced or despaired (one couldn't be sure which) and tacky paper blossoms showered them, Jim's leg held fast against mine. He didn't move it away. I stole a glance at his profile, but it told me nothing. I pulsed slightly against his leg but still didn't move away. I rubbed my palms together and felt the calluses that months of harp practice had built up on my fingertips.

If I kept up my assaults, would he suddenly and indignantly withdraw—even, later, make a remark to his father, who would feel obliged to tip off my mother about her son the fairy? I'd already been denounced at the country club where I'd worked as a caddie the previous summer. While waiting on the benches in the stifling hot caddie house for golfers to arrive, I'd pressed my leg in just this way against that of an older caddie named Mikey, someone who until then had liked shooting the shit with me. Now he stood up and said, "What the hell are you, anyway, some sort of fuckin' Liberace?" He'd tried to pull away several times, but I'd ignored his hints.

This time I'd wait for reciprocal signals. I wouldn't let my desire fool me into seeing mutual longing where only mine existed. I was dreading the intermission because I didn't know if I could disguise my tented crotch or the blush bloom that was slowly drifting up my neck and across my face.

I flexed my calf muscle against Jim's and he flexed back. We were football players locked into a tight huddle or two wrestlers each struggling to gain the advantage over the other (an advantage I was only too eager to concede). We were about to pass over the line from accident into intention. Soon he'd be as incriminated as I. Or did he think this dumb show was just a joke, indicative of other intentions, anything but sexual?

I flexed my calf muscles twice and he signaled back twice; we were establishing a Morse code that was undeniable. On stage, warriors were engaged in choreographed combat, frequently freezing in midlunge, and I wondered where we would live, how I would escape my mother, when I could kiss those full lips for the first time.

A smile, antic with a pleasure so new I scarcely dared to trust it, played across my lips. Alone with my thoughts but surrounded by his body, I could imagine a whole long life with him.

When the intermission came at last, our parents beat a hasty retreat to the bar next door, but neither Jim nor I budged. We had no need of highballs or a Manhattan; we already had them and were already in New York or someplace equally magical. As the auditorium emptied out, Jim looked at me matter-of-factly, his Adam's apple rising and falling, and he said, "How are we ever going to get a moment alone?"

"Do you have a television set?" I asked (they were still fairly rare).

"Of course not. Dad never has a damn cent; he throws his money away with both hands."

"Why don't you come over to our place on Saturday to watch the Perry Como show, then drink a few too many beers and say you're too tight to drive home and ask to stay over. The only extra bed is in my room."

REPRISE

"Okay," he said in that stifled voice. He seemed as startled by my efficient deviousness as I was by his compliance. When our much livelier parents returned and the lights went back down, I wedged a hand between our legs and covertly stroked his flexed calf, but he didn't reciprocate and I gave up. We sat there, knee to knee, in a stalemate of lust. I'd been erect so long my penis began to ache, and I could feel a pre-come stain seeping through my khakis. I turned bitter at the prospect of waiting three whole days till Saturday. I wanted to pull him into the men's room right now.

Once at home, my mother asked me what I thought of Jim, and I said he seemed nice but dumb. When I was alone in bed and able at last to strum my way to release (I thought of myself as the Man with the Blue Guitar), I hit a high note (my chin), higher than I'd ever shot before, and I licked myself clean and floated down into the featherbed luxury of knowing that big tanned body would soon be wrapped around me.

Our apartment was across the street from the beach and I loved to jump the Lake Michigan waves. Now I'm astonished I enjoyed doing anything that athletic, but then I thought of it less as sport than as opera, for just as in listening to 78 records I breasted one soaring outburst after another by Lauritz Melchior or Kirsten Flagstad, so was I thrilled by the repeated crises staged by the lake in September—a menacing crescendo that melted anticlimactically away into a creamy glissando, a minor interval that swelled into a major chord, all of it as abstract, excited, and endless as Wagner's *Ring,* which I'd never bothered to dope out motif by leitmotif, since I too preferred an ecstatic gestalt to tediously detailed knowledge. We were careless in my family, careless and addicted to excitement.

Jim Grady called my mother and invited himself over on Saturday evening to watch the Perry Como show on television. He told her he was an absolute fanatic about Como, that he considered Como's least glance or tremolo incomparably cool, and that he especially admired his long-sleeved golfer's sweaters with the low-slung yoke necks, three buttons at the waist, coarse spongy weave, and bright colors. My mother told me about these odd enthusiasms; she was puzzled by them because she thought that fashion concerned women alone and that even over women its tyranny extended only to clothes, certainly not to ways of moving, smiling, or singing. "I wouldn't want to imitate anyone else," she said with her little mirthless laugh of self-congratulation and a disbelieving shake of her head. "I like being me just fine, thank you very much."

"He's not the first young person to swoon over a pop star," I informed her out of my infinite world-weariness.

"Men don't swoon over men, dear," Mother reminded me, peering at me over the tops of her glasses. Now that I unscramble the signals she was emitting, I see how contradictory they were. She said she admired the sensitivity of a great dancer such as Nijinsky, and she'd even given me his biography to make sure I knew the exact perverse composition of that sensitivity: "What a tragic life. Of course he ended up psychotic with paranoid delusions, martyr complex, and degenerative ataxia." She'd assure me, with snapping eyes and carnivorous smile, that she liked men to be men and a boy to be all boy (as who did not), although the hearty heartlessness of making such a declaration to her willowy, cake-baking, harp-playing son thoroughly eluded her. Nor would she have tolerated a real boy's beer brawls, bloody noses, or stormy fugues. She wanted an obedient little gentleman who would sit placidly in a dark suit when he wasn't helping his mother until, at the appropriate moment and with no advance fuss, he would marry a plain Christian girl whose unique vocation would be the perpetual adoration of her *belle-mère*.

At last, after our dispirited Saturday night supper, Jim Grady arrived, just in time for a slice of my devil's food cake and the Perry Como show. My sister skulked off to her room to polish her hockey stick and read through fan-magazine articles on Mercedes McCambridge and Barbara Stanwyck. Jim belted back the six-pack he'd brought along and drew our attention with repulsive connoisseurship to every cool Como mannerism. I now realize that maybe Como was the first singer who'd figured out that the TV lens represented twenty million horny women dateless on Saturday night; he looked searchingly into its glass eye and warbled with the calm certainty of his seductive charm.

As a homosexual, I understood the desire to possess an admired man, but I was almost disgusted by Jim's ambition to imitate him. My mother saw men as nearly faceless extras who surrounded the diva, a woman; I regarded men as the stars; but both

REPRISE

she and I were opposed to all forms of masculine self-fabrication, she because she considered it unbecomingly narcissistic, I because it seemed a sacrilegious parody of the innate superiority of a few godlike men. Perhaps I was just jealous that Jim was paying more attention to Como than to me.

Emboldened by beer, Jim called my mother by her first name, which I'm sure she found flattering, since it suggested he saw her as a woman rather than as a parent. She drank one of her many highballs with him, sitting beside him on the couch, and for an instant I coldly appraised my own mother as a potential rival, but she lost interest in him when he dared to shush her during a bit of the singer's studied patter. In those days before the veneration of pop culture, unimaginative highbrows such as my mother and I swooned over opera, foreign films of any sort, and "problem plays" such as *The Immoralist* and *Tea and Sympathy*, but in spite of ourselves we were guiltily drawn to television with a mindless, vegetablelike tropism best named by the vogue word of the period, *apathy*. We thought it beneath us to study mere entertainment.

Jim was so masculine in the way he held a Lucky cupped between his thumb and middle finger and kept another unlit behind his ear, he was so inexpressive, so devoid of all gesture, that when he stood up to go, shook his head like a wet dog, and said, "Damn! I've had one too many for the road," he was utterly convincing. My mother said, "Do you want me to drive you home?" Jim laughed insultingly and said, "I think you're feeling no pain yourself. I'd better stay over, Delilah, if you have an extra bed."

My mother was much more reluctant to put Jim up than I'd anticipated. "I don't know, I could put my girdle back on . . ." Had she picked up the faint sex signal winking back and forth between Jim and her son? Or was she afraid he might sneak into her bedroom after lights out? Perhaps she worried how it might look to Mr. Grady: drunk son spends night in lakeside apartment—and such a son, the human species at its peak of physical fitness, mouth open, eyes shifting, Adam's apple working.

At last we were alone, and operatically I shed my clothes in a puddle at my feet, but Jim, undressing methodically, whispered, "You should hang your clothes up or your mother might think we were up to some sort of monkey business." Hot tears sprang to my eyes, but they dried as I looked at the long torso being revealed, with its small, turned waist and the wispy hairs around the tiny brown nipples like champagne grapes left to wither on a vine gone pale. His legs were pale because he'd worn jeans on the construction site, but he must have worn them low. For an instant he sat down to pull off his heavy white socks, and his shoulder muscles played under the overhead light with all the demonic action of a Swiss music box, the big kind with its works under glass.

He lay back with a heavy-lidded, cool expression I suspected was patterned on Como's, but I didn't care, I was even pleased he wanted to impress me as I scaled his body, felt his great warm arms around me, tasted the Luckies and Bud on his lips, saw the sharp focus in his eyes fade into a blur. "Hey," he whispered, and he smiled at me as his hands cupped my twenty-six-inch waist and my hot penis planted its flag on the stony land of his perfect body. "Hey," he said, hitching me higher and deeper into his presence.

Soon after that I came down with mononucleosis, the much-discussed "kissing disease" of the time, although I'd kissed almost no one but Jim. I was tired and depressed. I dragged myself with difficulty from couch to bed, but at the same time I was so lonely and frustrated that I looked down from the window at every man or boy walking past and willed him to look up, see me, join me, but the will was weak.

Jim called one afternoon, and we figured out he could come by the next evening when my mother was going somewhere with my sister. I warned him he could catch mono if he kissed me, but I was proud that after all he did kiss me long and deep. Until now the people I'd had sex with were boys at camp who pretended to hypnotize each other or married men who cruised the Howard Street Elevated toilets and drove me down to the beach in station wagons filled with their children's toys. Jim was the first man who took off his clothes, held me in his arms, looked me in the eye, and said, "Hey." He who seemed otherwise so stiff and ill at ease became fluent in bed.

I was bursting with my secret, all the more so because mononucleosis had reduced my world to the size of our apartment and the books I was almost too weak to hold (that afternoon it had been Oscar Wilde's *Lady Windermere's Fan*). In the evening my mother was washing dishes and I was drying, but I kept sitting down to rest. She said, "Mr. Grady and I are thinking of getting married."

The words just popped out of my mouth: "Then it will have to be a double wedding." My brilliant repartee provoked not a laugh but an inquisition, which had many consequences for me over the years, both good and bad. The whole story of my homosexual adventures came out, my father was informed, I was sent off to boarding school and a psychiatrist—my entire life changed.

My mother called up Jim Grady and boozily denounced him as a pervert and child molester, although I'd assured her I'd been the one to seduce him. I did not see him again until almost forty years later in Paris. My mother, who'd become tiny, wise, and sober with age, had had several decades to get used to the idea of my homosexuality (and my sister's, as it turned out). She had run into Jim Grady twice in the last three years and warned me he'd become maniacally stingy to the point he'd wriggle out of a drinks date if he thought he'd have to pay.

And yet when he rang me up from London, where he was attending a medical conference, he didn't object when I proposed to book him into the pricey hotel next door to me on the Ile St. Louis.

He called from his hotel room, and I rushed over. He was nearly sixty years old, with thin gray hair, glasses with clear frames he'd mended with black electrician's tape, ancient Corfam shoes, an open mouth, a stifled voice. We shook hands, but a moment later he pulled me into his arms. He said he knew, from a magazine interview I'd given, that this time I was infected with a virus far more dangerous than mononucleosis, but he kissed me long and deep, and a moment later we were undressed.

Over the next four days I had time to learn all about his life. He hadn't become a gynecologist after all but a sports doctor for a Catholic boys' school, and he spent his days bandaging the bruised and broken bodies of teenage athletes. His best friend was a fat priest nicknamed "The Whale," and they frequently got drunk with one of Jim's soldier friends who'd married a real honey, a little Chinese gal. Jim owned his house. He'd always lived alone and seemed never to have had a lover. His father had died from an early heart attack, but Jim felt nothing but scorn for him and his spendthrift ways. Jim himself had a tricky heart, and he was trying to give a shape to his life. He was about to retire.

It was true he'd become a miser. He bought his acrylic shirts and socks in packs of ten. His glasses came from Public Welfare. At

REPRISE

home he went to bed at sunset to save on electricity. We spent hours looking for prints that cost less than five dollars as presents for The Whale, the army buddy, and the Chinese gal. He wouldn't even let me invite him to a good restaurant. We were condemned to eating at the Maubert Self, a cafeteria, or nibbling on cheese and apples we'd bought at the basement supermarket next to the Métro St. Paul. He explained his economies to me in detail. Proudly he told me that he was a millionaire several times over and that he was leaving his fortune to the Catholic church, although he was an atheist.

I took him with me to my literary parties and introduced him as my cousin. He sat stolidly by like an old faithful dog as people said brilliant, cutting things in French, a language he did not know. He sent every hostess who received us a thank-you letter, which in America was once so common it's still known as a "bread-and-butter note" although in France it was always sufficiently rare as to be called a *"lettre de château."* The same women who'd ignored him when he sat at their tables were retrospectively impressed by his New World courtliness.

On his trip to Paris I slept with him just that first time in his hotel room; as we kissed, he removed his smudged, taped welfare glasses and revealed his darting young blue eyes. He undressed my sagging body and embraced my thirty-six-inch waist and bared his own body, considerably slimmer but just as much a ruin with its warts and wattles and long white hair. And yet, when he hitched me into his embrace and said, "Hey," I felt fourteen again. "You were a moron to tell your mom everything about us," he said. "You made us lose a lot of time." And if we had spent a life together, I wondered, would we each be a bit less deformed now?

As his hands stroked my arms and belly and buttocks, everything the years had worn down or undone, I could hear an accelerating drum and see, floating just above the rented bed, our young, feverish bodies rejoicing or lamenting, one couldn't be sure which. The time he'd come over when I had mono, my hot body had ached and shivered beside his. Now each time I touched him I could hear music, as though a jolt had started the clockwork after so many years. We watched the toothed cylinder turn under the glass and strum the long silver notes.

SEAMUS DEANE

The Siege of Derry

It began as an exodus, like people
Leaving their houses under threat,
Abandoning, abandoned, queuing
At a turnstile of weapons that
Slid their safety catches on and
Off in clicks and counter-clicks.
Such were my feelings as I waited
For permission to feel them.
Thronging, not getting through,
Beginning to hear the stridor
Of flames behind me, the tremor
Of hot air warping, panic
Exalting itself as it spread
Insinuations out in hairline
Cracks in the voices of people
Who had become leaden-heavy
As the dread stole like time
Passing up from their feet.
So it began. The back-up got
Worse and the inertia so deep
That it swallowed tomorrows
And yesterdays in the zero
Of its now and forever, amen.
The surrender of feeling
To those with the weapons
Came next. Then I got through.
Soon after, the houses fell in,
An unrecognizable world

Burned on the far side and I
With some others hunkered
Down out of the line of the fire,
Glad to be under orders at last,
The besieging and beseeching
Over, the city relieved and breathing,
The sigh of the conquered.

The Winter That Succeeded

In the winter that succeeded
That balmy summer of lemon
And white evenings when moons
Let a lax and fragrant sky
Outshine them until near midnight,
People said the war of the worlds,
That had ended a short time ago,
Was going to come again, in bursts,
That everything usual would become
Grotesque every so often and for
Long periods, just as the ice turned
The harbor into a grotto and the cold
Froze babies like fish in their cribs.
When we streaked downhill on sleighs
From the Creggan, wearing the gas masks
From the time of war, our goggled heads
Reconnoitered like insects magnified
And our crashes left us all over the snow
Like figures in a massacre. It was
So bad, they told us, that only the dead
Would be able to watch. Yet the winters
That came after were mild enough.
Hardly anything became estranged
By the wind, the ice, the cold.
But it was the winter that succeeded
The lemon summer that was left untold.

Love Poem

My hope lay sleeping in your arms
While houses became obedient
In rain. I heard the dying street
Alarms and the lenient strokes
Of small morning hours, the surf
Of stations off the air, the fridge
Remembering to shudder, the stark
Profile of a rifle shot emerging
Right behind the noise, as though
Your face were coming up from
An instant photo's blur. When quiet
Reigns like this, the streets
Hiss with the sodium of the lights,
The alleys and the lanes embrace
Their local darkness as a precious
Right and I start driving quickly
In the stacked rain, wishing
It had the penetration to come
Singing in and extinguish
These blazing rays of lifted
And of dipping lights. It is so
Inconvenient to be abroad
While my hope lies sleeping
Like a mole in the soft sudor
Of those unsuspecting dreams
From which it is outlawed.

The Sense of an Ending

The anchors were chatting and he
held a pump-action shotgun
up to my face and said he didn't
give diddly-squat about my troubles;
if the money was in the briefcase
and no shitting around with old
newspapers or detonator locks
then he probably wouldn't blow
my face into ribbons and brains
that they'd have to pick up
with a spoon. Just to show
he was serious he let the TV
have it with one barrel just as
the anchors gave way to the weather
and the whole fucking country
with its pat little clouds and
threatening fronts disappeared
as the set flew out of the wall
in a thunderflash that impressed
me no end. If I give you the money
how do I know, you don't, he replied.
I let that one ride and said okay
but how did he expect to get off
with a trail of corpses leading
straight to him and imagine
he wouldn't be fried, no matter
they couldn't do a ballistics
on the modified Thirty-nine

Smith I knew he had used
to blow all the others away.
That's when he smiled and I
thought that at least he would
tell me now before I brought up
the forty-four Mag and put
a hole between the stripes
of his tie. Then it all went
wrong, she came to the door
and blew the top of his head
all over my goddamned shirt.
I took two inches of hundreds
out of the case, let her look,
told her that was my fee,
including the shirt,
and walked out that door
and never looked back,
not even when she called
me every name but my own.
All I wanted was a cold beer
being able to ride the barstool
in my own time and no more
getting paid out of yuppie
briefcases flecked with
the blood and the bone
of the bad guys. Later,
I knew, I'd drink myself
silly, like a dumb shit,
just to forget her, and I'd
be down there making love
to the toilet bowl, more than
once, before I was really free.

THEODOR W. ADORNO

Wagner's Relevance for Today

This essay is drawn from a lecture given in September 1963 during the Berliner Festspielwochen.

Of the countless aspects with which Wagner's work presents us, I select one at random, as is unavoidable for the lecture form: the question of Wagner's relevance for today, of the perspective of present-day consciousness toward his work—assuming that one can speak generally of such a perspective. What is meant is advanced consciousness: consciousness that is equal to the Wagnerian oeuvre and that itself occupies an advanced standpoint in its development. Almost thirty years ago I wrote a book, *In Search of Wagner,** of which four chapters appeared in the *Zeitschrift für Sozialforschung* in 1939. The entire book did not appear until much later, in 1952, shortly after my return to Germany. Today I would formulate many things in the book differently. Its central problem, that of the relation between societal aspects on the one hand and compositional and aesthetic aspects on the other, might have to be argued more profoundly within the subject matter than it was then. But I am not distancing myself from the book, nor am I abandoning the conception. With regard to Wagner the situation has changed generally. Therefore,

---

* A translation by Rodney Livingstone was published in 1981 (London: NLB). [All footnotes are the translator's.]

Tannhäuser, Hoftheater Munich, 1861; drawing by Michael Echter

I would like to present—not as a revision of what I once thought, but as a way of taking into account what has newly come to our attention about Wagner—some divergences from the old text.

We have gained distance over the past thirty years. Wagner no longer represents, as he did in my youth, the world of one's parents, but that of one's grandparents instead. A rather commonplace symptom: I can still remember quite well from my childhood how my mother lamented the demise of Italian vocal art that was caused by the Wagnerian style of singing. Today that style is itself beginning to die out; it is exceedingly difficult to locate any singers who are up to it. The well-known and hypocritically criticized system of guest singers, by which a handful of the most famous Wagner singers are lent around, so to speak, from one new production to the next, is not just an aberration. The opera is beginning to regress to precisely that phase that had shown itself, in light of Wagner, to be outdated. Wagner no longer possesses the boundless authority of the earlier time. But what rose up against that authority was not so much a critically interventionary consciousness, in disagreement with the triumphal lord, as a reactive one: the ambivalence one feels toward a formerly beloved object that must now be consigned to the past, whatever the cost. At any rate, we have gained much freedom toward Wagner as an object of consideration: the affective tie to him has loosened.

If, thanks to this freedom, I may now make some comments about the historical changes in the attitude toward Wagner's art, I cannot ignore the political aspect. Too much catastrophe has been visited on living beings for a consideration that purports to be purely aesthetic to close its eyes to it. Yet the position of consciousness toward Wagner may also change politically. The form of nationalism that he embodied, especially in his work, exploded into National Socialism, which could draw on him, via Chamberlain and Rosenberg,* for its rationalization. With the integration of nations into blocs this is no longer so immediately threatening; therefore it also begins to recede in the work. However, one must not overestimate this. As the National Socialist potential continues to smolder within the German reality, now as then, so it is still present in Wagner. This begins to touch on the most serious difficulty he affords for present-day consciousness. The stormy applause that one may still encounter following a performance of, say, *Die Meistersinger,* the self-affirmation of the public, which it hears from within Wagner's music, still has something about it of the old virulent evil; the question of whether and how Wagner should be performed can be separated only wrenchingly from the acknowledgment of such demagogy. At an earlier time I attempted to localize this demagogy precisely in the purely musical-aesthetic form. But, if I am allowed to express myself so personally, perhaps my criticism has now earned me the right to emphasize what has outlasted it. My own experience with Wagner does not exhaust itself in the political content, as unredeemable as the latter is, and I often have the impression that in laying it bare I have cleared away one level only to see another emerge from underneath, one, admittedly, that I was by no means uncovering for the first time. At any rate, the private objections to Wagner's person and way of life

---

* Houston Stewart Chamberlain (1855–1927), author of the racialist *Die Grundlagen des 19. Jahrhunderts* [Foundations of the Nineteenth Century]; Alfred Rosenberg (1893–1946), anti-Semitic ideologue and author of *Der Mythos des 20. Jahrhunderts* [The Myth of the Twentieth Century]. In 1930s Germany, Rosenberg's book was second in popularity only to *Mein Kampf.*

that are still all the rage have something unspeakably subaltern about them; anyone who drags them out gets sweaty hands. If I, too, previously included his person among the subjects under discussion, it was because I was thinking of his social character—the private individual as the exponent and locus of social tendencies—not of the individual in his psychological arbitrariness, upon whom so many people imagine they are qualified to pass judgment. If the connection is not made between the power of artistic production that was concentrated in him and the society, whatever accusations are made against him are pure philistinism, not far removed from the contemptible genre of fictionalized biographies. It is well to remind ourselves, as a corrective, of the great biography by Newman*—anything but semi-official—which justifiably emphasized how dishonest was the indignation over Wagner's extravagance, for example, in view of the fact that during all the years he spent in emigration the theaters earned a fortune at his expense, while he had to do without.

The merely aesthetic anti-Wagnerianism rode the tide of the so-called neo-Classical movement—politically not at all progressive—which is linked primarily to the name of Igor Stravinsky. This movement is not only chronologically passé; it also suffers from internal exhaustion. As the perceptible sign of its capitulation, the late Stravinsky himself made use of the very technique against which his movement had originally honed its polemical edge: that of the Schoenberg school. This has to do not only with the mood of the times, but also with the deficiency that is intrinsic to neo-Classicism; its historical impossibility becomes a compositional defect. The tendency that is now emerging in opposition to neo-Classicism, and exposing by contrast the decorative weakness that is implicit in the latter, is producing many things that have more to do with Wagner than with those individuals who for the last thirty or forty years have enjoyed playing the role of his opponents. The second Vienna School, that of Arnold Schoenberg, which exercises a decisive influence on the most recent contemporary music, took Wagner as its immediate point of departure. This was precisely one of the things people used to like to criticize

---

* Ernest Newman, *The Life of Richard Wagner*, 4 vols., New York: Alfred A. Knopf, 1933–47.

Tristan und Isolde, Bayreuth, 1886; drawing by Carlo Brioschi

in the very early Schoenberg as a cheap way of discrediting the mature musician.

But what has changed about Wagner, in the interim, is not merely his impact on others, but his work itself, in itself. This is what forms the basis of his relevance; not some posthumous second triumph or the well-justified defeat of the neo-Baroque. As spiritual entities, works of art are not complete in themselves. They create a magnetic field of all possible intentions and forces, of inner tendencies and countervailing ones, of successful and necessarily unsuccessful elements. Objectively, new layers are constantly detaching themselves, emerging from within; others grow irrelevant and die off. One relates to a work of art not merely, as is often said, by adapting it to fit a new situation, but rather by deciphering *within* it things to which one has a historically different reaction. The position of consciousness toward Wagner that I experience as my own whenever I encounter him, and which is not only mine, is even more deserving of the appellation "ambivalent" than the earlier position—an oscillation between attraction and repulsion. This only points back to the Janus-like character of the work itself. Undoubtedly, every art of significance exhibits something like this, Wagner's especially. As progressive and regressive traits are intertwined in his work, so also in his reception. After what has occurred, it is self-evident that one assumes a defensive position toward him politically. This was true even beforehand and has remained so in view of the possibility of a reawakening of the powers that, like their patron goddess Erda, should better have gone on sleeping. In this regard, reality takes precedence over art. Still open is the question of how the appropriate defensiveness relates to the possibility of performing Wagner. One cannot, by the way—and here I touch on something central—simply imagine that it is possible to separate out the ideological element in Wagner and hold on to pure art as a kind of purified substrate. For the demagogic, the proselytizing, the collective-narcissistic gesture reaches right into the inner complexion of his music; here the suspect element is amalgamated with its opposite. But on the other hand—and this is a part of the ambivalence of the position of consciousness—among those resisting Wagner we find all those individuals, even today, who have simply not kept up musically. Among them is his greatest critic, Nietzsche. The anti-Wagnerian movement, the first large-scale incidence of *ressentiment* against modern art in Germany, has formed a fatal alliance with folk music (so-called) and young people's music, devotees of recorders and the like; their preferred tactic has been to compare him unfavorably with newly unearthed composers like Heinrich Schütz and to mobilize against him forces that would counter his highly differentiated and complex art with stupefaction. There is something like a right-wing, petit bourgeois opposition to Wagner. It may be that he was resisted by a good bourgeois element, namely, insistence on the responsibility and autonomy of the individual, but also by a bad one, a stuffy and dense narrow-mindedness to which Wagner is unalterably opposed. His music is free erotically to a degree shared by very few other things that were ever admitted into the German pantheon. Orthodox opinion, very early on, responded to this aspect of Wagner by committing the sin of self-righteous purity.

Ambivalence is a relation toward something one has not mastered; one behaves ambivalently toward a thing with which one has not come to terms. In response to this, the first task at hand would be, quite simply, to experience the Wagnerian work fully—

Tannhäuser, Bayreuth, 1891; Cosima Wagner, director; Max Brückner, set designer

something that to this day, despite all the external successes, has not been accomplished. *Tristan, Parsifal,* the most significant elements of the *Ring* are always more praised than truly appreciated. It is grotesque that in the *Ring,* then as now, *Die Walküre* still plays the most prominent role, on account of such selections as "Winterstürme wichen dem Wonnemond," or Wotan's farewell and the firestorm—in other words, on account of what in Vienna are called *Stückerl,* or little numbers. As such, they fly in the face of the Wagnerian idea. The incomparably greater architecture of *Siegfried,* in contrast, has never quite found its way into the public consciousness. At best, the opera-going public suffers through it as a cultural monument. The works of Wagner that have failed to win the appreciation of the public are precisely the most modern ones, those the most boldly progressive in technique and therefore the farthest removed from convention. Their modernity should not be misconceived as superficial, as a matter of the means they employ, simply because they make greater use of dissonances, enharmonic and chromatic elements, than the others. Wagnerian modernity is of a different order; it towers decisively over everything it leaves in its wake. Wagner is the first case of uncompromising musical nominalism, if I may use the philosophical term: his work is the first in which the primacy of the individual work of art and, within the work, the primacy of the figure in its concrete, elaborated reality, are established fundamentally over any kind of scheme or externally imposed form. He was the first to draw the consequences from the contradiction between traditional forms, indeed the traditional formal language of music as a whole, and the concrete artistic tasks at hand. The contradiction had already made itself felt, rumblingly, in Beethoven, and in essential ways generated his late style. Wagner, then, realized without reservation that the binding, truly general character of musical works of art is to be found, if at all, only through the medium of their particularity and concretion, and not by recourse to any kind of general types. Therefore, contrary to the opinion of the mass-distributed book on Wagner by Hans Gál,* Wagner's criticism of the opera carries very great weight, both theoretically and artistically. It must not be trivialized by the simplistic assertion that Wagner was just another opera composer, basically no different from others, who had come up with some secondary theories to use for his private propagandistic purposes. His verdict that opera was childish, his desire that music should finally come of age, cannot be repealed. Opera, as a form, is something historically emergent and transitory. Merely to locate Wagner's place within the genre is to deny the dynamic that is inherent in the history of this form. It is no accident that number operas, when they occur today, as in the *Rake* of Stravinsky, are possible only in a refracted mode, as stylization. Even anti-Wagnerians who return, in this manner, to the number operas recognize or acknowledge, in the irony with which they resurrect the numbers and set pieces, that the verdict Wagner imposed on such categories remains in force. He clearly faced the contradiction between the general and the particular in music, which until then had been crystallizing in mere unconsciousness, and his *ingenium* made its incorruptible decision that nothing general should exist, except in the extreme of particularity.

---

* Hans Gál (1890–1987), Austrian composer and teacher. An English translation (by Hans-Hubert Shonzeler) of Gál's *Richard Wagner* was published in 1976 (London: Stein & Day).

Tannhäuser, Landestheater Darmstadt, 1930; Renato Mordo, director

This, however, touches not only the form but also the content of Wagner's art. In him, the artistic consciousness of an antagonistic, internally contradictory world was radicalized. The traditional forms are as poorly adapted to this artistic consciousness as fossilized relations are to critical insight. In this sense, what he did was productive. More than that. In the introduction to Hegel's philosophy of history, which has become popular under the title *Reason in History*,* I found this sentence: "Mere desire, the wildness and brutality of the will, has no place in the theater and the sphere of world history." This theorem of Hegel's, who was not only aesthetically but also philosophically a classicist, is one to which Wagner did not adhere. In this, Wagner, who in his youth, before he converted to the ideas of Schopenhauer, is known to have been decisively influenced by Feuerbach, was quite the revolutionary Young Hegelian. His music shudders with the unrelieved violence that lives on today

---

* Volume 1 of Georg Wilhelm Friedrich Hegel's *Vorlesungen über die Philosophie der Geschichte* [Lectures on the Philosophy of History] was titled *Die Vernunft in der Geschichte: Einleitung in die Philosophie der Weltgeschichte* [Reason in History: Introduction to the Philosophy of World History]. It is not identical to the compilation published in English by Liberal Arts Press as *Reason in History* (New York, 1953).

in the world order. One can raise all imaginable sorts of objections to the Wagnerian mythology, exposing it as cheap and phony, as a romanticism of false beards and bull's-eye windows. Nevertheless, in comparison to all more moderate, detachedly realistic or classicist art, his work—especially the *Ring*—retains its decisive truth in this mythological moment: that in it violence breaks through as the same law that it was in the prehistoric world. In these thoroughly modern works, prehistory persists as modernity itself. This splinters the facade of the bourgeois surface, and through the cracks there shines enough of what has only now become fully evolved and recognizable to suffice as proof of Wagner's relevance for today. Admittedly, his gesture, the thing his music is arguing for— and Wagner's music, not merely his texts, is always arguing for something—is a gesture in favor of mythology. He becomes, one might say, an advocate of violence, just as his principal work glorifies Siegfried, the man of violence. But when, in his work, violence expresses itself in pure form, unobscured, in all its terror and entrapment, then the work, despite its mythologizing tendency, is an indictment of myth, willingly or not. This is shown by Siegmund's indescribable emigré-music in the opening passages of the second act of *Die Walküre*. Richard Strauss is the source of the divinatory statement that Wagner strove to deliver us from myth by means of the leitmotif. One might conclude from this that the leitmotif—quasi-rational, identifying, unity-creating—brings to a halt the blind, diffuse, and deadly ambiguity of myth, which Wagner's surging sound reproduces. Through self-consciousness, myth becomes something qualitatively different; the imaginative recollection of destruction marks its boundary.

That Wagner makes the case for myth, but accuses it through his creation, may provide the key to his dual character. His immediate relevance for today is not of the species of merely artistic renaissances. It approaches us from the vicinity of something unfinished, like many things from the nineteenth century, a prime example being Ibsen. This can be illustrated by a series of examples, several of which I shall adduce. First, Wagnerian harmony. Gál's book denies its relationship to modern harmony, to atonality, in stark contradiction to the fact that modern harmony was developed by Schoenberg, after *Verklärte Nacht,* as a continuation of Wagner's. It is self-evident that Wagner was not atonal, and it

Siegfried, Bayreuth, 1952; Wieland Wagner, director and set designer

would never have occurred to me to assert anything of the kind. All the tones and their combinations, even at their most daring, for example in *Tristan* and *Parsifal*, can be explained in accordance with the traditional teachings of harmony. At issue is a tendency, a potential—not what one finds literally in the notes, but what they tend toward—and this, indeed, has decisively to do with atonality. The preponderance of each particular harmonic event over harmonic reference points, over triads and seventh chords, presages what will later come into its own as a consistent atonality that completely does away with the reference points. In Wagner dissonance preponderates qualitatively, if not yet quantitatively. It has more power, more substantiality than consonance, and this points compellingly in the direction of the new music. On various occasions, Heinrich Schenker,* in his books, accused Wagner, whom

---

* Heinrich Schenker (1868–1935) was the author of several works on harmony and counterpoint. His *Harmonielehre* was first published anonymously in 1906. There is an English translation by Elisabeth Mann Borgese (Chicago: University of Chicago Press, 1954).

he could scarcely abide, of having destroyed the *Urlinie*, the basic line, despite his use of correct harmonic procedures. Schenker, in his odd terminology, means only that the skeletal structure of the entire musical progression along orderly steps within the usual functional harmony of thoroughbass and corresponding melody is lacking. The observation is correct, but Schenker's emphasis is wrong. As a retrograde proponent of the power of skeletons, of abstract generalities in music, he failed to hear precisely in the supposed destruction, the emancipation of music from its merely skeletal, abstract organization toward an organization located in its specific forms, the irresistibly new element that was the precondition of everything that was to come. The feeling of leaving solid ground behind, of drifting into uncertainty, is precisely what is exciting and also compelling about the experience of Wagnerian music. Its innermost composition, the thing one might, by analogy to painting, call its *peinture,* can in fact be apprehended only by an ear that is willing to cast itself, as the music does, into uncertainty. Here we may state that what is relevant for today is precisely what went unrecognized then and was therefore neither understood nor appreciated.

I would like to elaborate on this principle by means of a technical detail; for it is impossible to speak—rather than gossip—about artistic phenomena if one does not at least provide a perspective on their concrete technical complexion. It has become customary to emphasize the principle of the sequence in the mature works of Wagner; I myself did so at one time. By sequence is meant the repetition of abbreviated motifs—in Wagner the leitmotifs—on a higher level, generally with dynamic, intensifying effect. The spinning out of the music, its essential fiber or texture, thus works more or less with the repetition of given elements, in contrast to the essential technique of Viennese Classicism, which, borrowing Arnold Schoenberg's term, can be called the technique of developing variation. But however many sequences there are in Wagner, they by no means represent the sole principle; and above all, they themselves are already varied, frequently and with great subtlety, in themselves. A perfect example would be the famous beginning of *Tristan,* two sequencings of one model. By the third extension of the sequence, it is already varied—minimally, but in a harmonic-modulatory sense decisively—in comparison with the original model, and only thus is it led back to the *forte*-entry in the reformulated dominant of the tonic A-minor. The sequence principle in Wagner is by no means a crutch. It follows from the chromaticism, the prevalence of the minor second that pervades the entire musical material, at least in the works of the type to which I am referring. On the one hand, the sequence principle is intended to create the context that has vanished as a result of chromaticism, i.e., the abandonment of articulation by harmonic steps that carry a different weight. But on the other hand—and this shows the close and modern way in which Wagner conforms to his own material—chromaticism itself embodies something not altogether dissimilar to the sequential principle; the repetition of the smallest intervals corresponds to the repetition of individual musical events as they follow each other within the sequence. The identity of the elements in the sequence, which follow one another, is very closely related to the identity of the chromatic steps. Thus even the principle of the sequence is not a mechanical thing, as we musicians may conclude all too hastily; it is much more profoundly connected to the problems and tasks of the internal organization of Wagner's music than I was capable of comprehending thirty years ago.

In other of Wagner's works, it is true, things work quite differently; in these—the less chromatic works—the sequential principle plays no central role at all. The understanding of Wagner that is due and would be relevant for today would have to inquire into their structure. In *Die Meistersinger,* extensive musical differentiation is combined with a general absence of chromaticism, and frequently with a deemphasizing of sequences in favor of a colorful variety of individual forms. The continuity is created, over long stretches, by an unconstrained redrawing of the dramatic curve from moment to moment. The intact diatonic tonal structure makes it possible to dispense with surface links. In this way, the music achieves a concreteness of the irregular that traditional music never dreamed of. This would remain prototypical for Schoenberg, for Berg, and for the most recent tendency: the trend toward structures that are free, yet dense. The idea of a unity of constantly changing situations, which in Wagner still oriented itself to the requirements of the dramatic action, has, to this day, not been fully realized. It would provide the ideal model for a truly informal

Götterdämmerung, Staatstheater Kassel, 1974; Ulrich Melchinger, director

process of composition utilizing characteristic models that would be both differentiated from each other and necessarily complementary. In Wagner, naturally, nothing of the kind is yet present in pure, developed form, nor is it intended. The dramatic action was more important to him than the constructive structure, but the objective tendency toward the latter is unmistakable.

These complicated structural matters, which I have barely touched upon, bring me to the problem of so-called form in Wagner. It would be good to start with a bit of terminological order, without, however, overemphasizing it in a pedantic way. Many musical concepts, including the concept of rhythm, but particularly that of form, are used ambiguously and are often twisted to such a degree that they come to mean everything and nothing. If Wagner did away with given, familiar forms in opera such as the aria, recitative, or ensemble, it does not therefore follow that his music has no form, that it is, as the nineteenth century stridently complained, formless. This objection remains petty and reactionary, even if validated by the authority of Nietzsche. What is true about it is that peculiar sensation of floating—that the music has, so to speak, no solid ground under its feet. In Wagner, form grows aerial roots; he reacted allergically to that element within it that the restorationist language of the twentieth century would call ontological. But music that appears to swing back and forth in the air, as if held in the hand of an invisible puppeteer, has something static about it, just as Wagner's supposedly so dynamic sequential principle terminates in a feeling of eternal sameness. In the most recent music, which draws so near to painting and the graphic arts, the trend toward the static becomes quite marked—here, too, something is fully realized that Wagner had envisioned earlier.

The accusation of formlessness misses the point by confusing everything that is not oriented toward traditional forms with lack of organization. In fact, without following any abstract scheme, Wagner's music is organized, articulated, architectonically thought through in the highest degree. It was the great accomplishment of Alfred Lorenz,* who is undeservedly forgotten, to have been the first to see this. To deny that there is a formal problem in Wagner, as Gál does, is simply an expedient way of eliminating, or resolving, the problem by ignoring it. No sooner had the orientation toward given formal norms disappeared than the task of organizing music compellingly in and of itself became inescapable. True, the formal types that Lorenz proposed, the bow or arch form and the concept of the bar†—to which he surely gave too much emphasis, even if it is not completely unimportant in Wagner—are themselves much too abstract: mathematical, graphlike outlines that fall short of Wagner's developmental principle and thus of a material theory of musical forms. As a particular case in point, the art of transitions, which Wagner equated with the art of composition, cannot be adequately explained by diagrams. The task of the Wagner interpretation that is needed would be to describe, down to the details, how his forms, without borrowing, express, develop, and create themselves with compelling necessity from within. This occurs perhaps most splendidly in *Siegfried*—an unbroken ascending curve, further articulated so that each of the three acts contains

---

* Alfred Lorenz (1868–1939) is the author of *Das Geheimnis der Form bei Richard Wagner* [The Secret of Form in Richard Wagner], 4 vols., Berlin: Hesse, 1924–34.

† Lorenz's term *Bogenform* (bow or arch form) denotes a musical form that is roughly symmetrical, i.e., ABA or ABCBA. The "bar" stanza is the formal strophic design, AAB, based on German medieval Minnesang. Lorenz's analysis of the extended use of this form in *Die Meistersinger* was influential in reestablishing its importance for later composers as well.

an additional ascent, the strongest of these in the third act: altogether, probably the high point of Wagner's oeuvre. I would like to make the heretical suggestion that someone should attempt a separate production of the third act of *Siegfried* by itself, so that viewers could devote themselves to it with complete concentration; not until then will we be able fully to comprehend the riches it contains.

In connection with form I would like to say a few things about color and orchestration. Wagner's mastery as an orchestrator is unquestioned even by his opponents. The idea of extended instrumentation* has long been recognized in Wagner: translating the most delicate network of the composition into a correspondingly delicate network of instrumental colors and clarifying it in the process. The orchestration, the tone colors, become a means of making the course of the musical events visible down to its most subtle details. To this extent it already creates form. But this must be further elaborated. Wagner's art of orchestration does not exhaust itself in small-scale effects; it also answers the large-scale formal problem I have described above. Perhaps one can say that whatever Wagner did away with, in terms of general schemes, he replaced with the wholly new, thoroughly individualized dimension he gave to orchestration. Color itself became architectonic. For this, too, *Siegfried* offers perhaps the best example. Even the pitch levels, high and low, are articulated in the course of the music in such a way that in the individual acts, as in the work as a whole, an uplift in the music corresponds to a rise in the pitch level. What Wagner achieves in the differentiation of color through its dissolution into the tiniest elements, he complements by combining the smallest values constructively to create something like integral color. His tendency is to take the tone, once it has been broken down into minimal units, and create great tonal surfaces, like unbroken fields; to take the fragments into which the sword has been shattered, as Siegfried says in the enigmatic sword songs, and forge them back together into great homogeneous units. Only infinitesimally small elements can be combined flawlessly into such wholes. Anyone who is familiar with the formal problems of painting will have no trouble recognizing the relationship this musical duality

---

* *Ausinstrumentieren,* also translated as "integrated instrumentation."

Götterdämmerung, Bayreuth, 1976; Patrice Chéreau, director

of differential and integral techniques bears to impressionism. The unbroken tonal surface based on the breaking down of tones is one of the most important characteristics of Wagner's method: the creation of totality by means of its reduction to minute models of the particular, which then, because they approach liminal values, can be combined continuously into one another; indeed, properly speaking, they actually generate the great dense tonal surfaces. This is what lends Wagnerian sound its rounded, enveloping quality, the phenomenon that I have referred to, using a philosophical term, as totality, and that one might, from a technical point of view, better call the tonal surface. No other composer knows it in as unbroken and richly nuanced a way as Wagner. The integral tonal surface, the melding of differentiated tones into fields, is another thing that has attained its first full realization today in the idea of the incorporation of tone into the total musical construction.

Wagner's orchestration also makes evident how many of the prevalent objections against him either always missed the mark or have been rendered obsolete by history. Our parents accused him of being noisy; the complaint, oddly enough, has continued to accompany the history of the development of modern music. As it happens, word has gotten around that the covered orchestra in Bayreuth was hardly meant to encourage noise. But here, too, it would be better to begin at the extreme, with the noise itself, to emphasize the creative brilliance of Wagner's sound in those instances where it stands in opposition to the mean of moderate enjoyment, and simply cannot be listened to with delectation. At times, Wagner mobilizes extremes of loudness. Not often; anyone who knows the scores knows how sparing he is with the *fortissimo*. But when it does turn *fortissimo*, then in fact something happens resembling a protest against the moderate cultural consensus Wagner denounced in the knights of *Tannhäuser* and ridiculed in the guilds of *Die Meistersinger*. Barbarism can no more be equated with loudness, in his music, than the representation of myth can be equated with the direct expression of barbarism. Barbarism ceases to be barbaric through its reflection in great art; it becomes distanced, is even, if you will, criticized. Where Wagner goes to the extreme, it has a precise function: the objectification of the chaotic, undomesticated element that his works confront unreservedly. The violence of Wagnerian sound, where it occurs, is the violence of its content.

Wagner's peculiar transcendence vis-à-vis culture—he always stands simultaneously above and below it—is one of his eminently German characteristics. But anything that has such an integral aesthetic function as the sound described above finds in this its inner justification, becomes intrinsically beautiful. On recent occasions (for example, at a compellingly melodious performance of *Die Götterdämmerung* by Karajan in Vienna), I have noticed something remarkable: in the final act of the *Ring*, the only passages that seem noisy are those that are not resolved compositionally, in which the musical events do not fully correspond to the volume of sound—such as, for example, the overextended and compositionally uneventful climax of Siegfried's funeral march. The latter would seem altogether problematic; it is not coincidental that it recalls Liszt. The conquest, following Wagner, of extreme positions of musical expression and construction has, as it were, justified his loudness after the fact; it is no accident that works on the threshold of the new music, such as Schoenberg's *Gurrelieder* and Strauss's *Elektra*, with their tendency to triple *fortissimos*, show an affinity to Wagner. At the same time, however, his own art of orchestration is never heavily applied. Everywhere the phrase is transparent, everything can be heard, in contrast to a number of works from Strauss's middle period. If it is true that in Wagner the art of orchestration and tonal color is subordinated to the creation of the compositional fiber, then this implies that its goal is not murkiness or overblown sound but the clear representation of the musical events, which, because they are no longer self-explanatory within an overall scheme, require additional means for their clarification. Only by hearing Wagner from this perspective does one hear him correctly. He is already guided by the instrumentational ideal of clarity, which later led via Mahler to Schoenberg and the new music. It follows from the principle of the tonal realization of the musical structure. The *Siegfried Idyll*, which introduces the themes of the third act in *Siegfried* in a soloistic, chamber music setting, provides the proof by example. Light is even shed on certain eccentricities of Wagner's composition that arouse displeasure nowadays: for example, the overly long narratives, the tendency toward musical loquaciousness. In view of the difficulty inherent in reducing the rich content of the *Edda* Siegfried narrative to theatrical form, the repetition of things that occurred beforehand and are already known (in narratives like Wotan's lengthy excursus in the second act of *Die Walküre,* or the repetition of long-familiar items in the riddle scene between Wotan and Mime in the first act of *Siegfried,*) seem superfluous. Nor can we ignore the bothersome and discomfiting quality of certain long speeches, including Gurnemanz's tale of Amfortas and Klingsor, which are perhaps necessary from a dramatic point of view. There should be no prejudging the question whether contemporary Wagner interpretation should not finally decide to edit passages such as these when the harmonic structure allows it, despite the collective howls of the cultural keepers of the Grail. But if, in the process, such extraordinary things as that speech of Wotan's to Brünnhilde were to be sacrificed to the red pencil, it would only confirm the difficulty of the position of present-day consciousness toward Wagner: namely, that as I have said, what is magnificent in his work cannot be cleanly divided from what is questionable. One can scarcely be had without the other; his truth content and those elements that legitimate criticism has found questionable are mutually interdependent. The uncertainty with which a self-conscious performance practice approaches him is caused, not least of all, by the fact that there is no way around this interweaving of the true and the false in his work. In any case, it was Wagner's profound sense of form that created those narratives. The fundamental conception of the *Ring* is not actually dramatic, but correlative, narrative, like the original from which it was taken. If one wanted to draw out the paradox, one might speak, in regard to the entire *Ring* and other works of the mature Wagner, of epic theater—although the rabid anti-Wagnerian Brecht would not have wanted to hear this and would be at my throat. Wagner's instinct sensed clearly that epics—in which subjectivity, the free individual human being, does not yet exist but arises only as the antithesis to fate—do not permit dramatization in the true sense. In this Wagner was cleverer than Hebbel, who thought himself so much cleverer and was so much better educated. But the epic tendency does not merely follow from the content. One could, after all, object that Attic tragedy also concerned itself with epic materials and that it succeeded in translating them wholly into the dramatic form. The entirety of the *Ring,* which was conceived after all as a chef d'oeuvre and which one must begin by accepting as such, has something predecided, predetermined about it—a consequence of the Schopenhauerism in which its entire musical fiber is steeped. Step by step, what was to be expected and cannot happen otherwise is fulfilled. If in Hegel history meant progress in the consciousness of freedom, then in Wagner, who sided with Hegel's antipode, Schopenhauer, the *Ring* was a phenomenology of the spirit as fate. Consequently his work lacks the element of freedom, of openness, that constitutes drama. From Senta's ballad to the great narrative of Gurnemanz, the work is therefore interlarded with reports and ballads, sometimes in the manner of the great lieder art of the earlier nineteenth century. (I note only in passing that so far as I know the extremely productive inquiry into a relationship between Wagner and certain songs of Schubert has not been undertaken.) The narratives signify that what is occurring is reported truthfully, that it already existed as something predetermined. This points once more to the insight that Wagner's music, which—in contrast to traditional music that works with solid, extant forms—defines itself as dynamic, as continually in a state of becoming, ultimately turns static, in the final

WAGNER'S RELEVANCE FOR TODAY

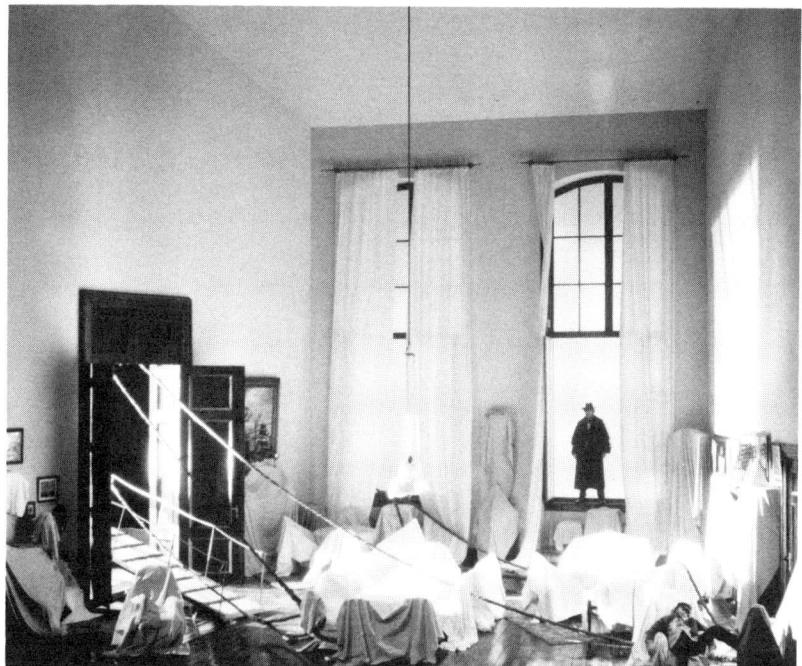

Der fliegende Holländer, Bayerische Staatsoper, 1981; Herbert Wernicke, director and set designer

analysis because its absolute dynamism lacks the other, antithetical element against which it could become genuinely dynamic. One would have some difficulty identifying, in Wagner's music, contrasting themes in the sense of Beethoven. A related element is the music's organization into fields. We know from studying logic that without solidity there can be no dynamics, that where everything flows nothing happens; the peculiar convergence between the philosophy of Heraclitus and that of his antipodes, the Eleatics, speaks to this fact.

In Wagner unceasing change—both an asset and a liability—ends in constant sameness. This is already embodied in his most striking musical material. For chromaticism—the principle par excellence of dynamics, of unceasing transition, of going further—is in itself nonqualitative, undifferentiated. One chromatic step resembles another. To this extent, chromatic music always has an affinity to identity. If a bit of speculation in the mode of the philosophy of history is allowed—and I would be the last to gainsay

Das Rheingold, Frankfurt, 1985; Ruth Berghaus, director

it—one might go so far as to surmise that Wagner's compositional process prophesied the dawning horror of the transition from a society that had reached the apogee of its dynamism to one that had again turned rigid, become utterly reified: a new feudalism, to use Veblen's term.

Also in this context, I would like to treat another dubious element in Wagner that again substantiates the close relationship between what is inadequate and what is grandiose in his work. I am again thinking of *Die Götterdämmerung*. It can hardly be denied that its final act is weak, falls short of its subject. Wagner conceives no music of world destruction adequate to the one he prophesies. It falls off, fails to fulfill the expectation of the maximal catastrophe that it has aroused, despite the gruesomeness of passages like Gutrune's scene before the corpse is brought back. Thus, for example, to take only the most obvious example, Brünnhilde's final song is infinitely weaker, somehow fractured, when compared to the fairly analogous one of Isolde. I used to explain this evident weakness as a result of the leitmotif-machine, the necessity of working with the preexisting, decades-old motival material, which the fully developed compositional style of the late Wagner has left far behind. But that is too superficial. The circular, inescapable nature of the conception of the tetralogy—already indicated by the word *ring* in the title—excludes from the start everything qualitatively different, even where it would have been required aesthetically at the critical juncture. Something similar was already going on in the *Meistersinger* quintet, where Wagner's sense of form tells him he needs to break out of the circle, so he launches into an indescribably melodic thought that does not derive from the machinery; however, he does not spin out the new idea in a logical manner, doesn't pursue it along the lines of its dynamic force, but instead busies himself once more with the already rather shopworn themes from the complex surrounding the *Preislied*. The same things that I have just described for you a bit sketchily in the third act of *Die Götterdämmerung* are quite literally valid for great philosophy, specifically Hegel's *Phenomenology of Spirit*, to which I have referred elsewhere. The last chapter of this work is called "Absolute Knowledge." The unwitting reader, who has chewed his way through the *Phenomenology*, hopes that in the end absolute knowledge will actually be revealed in the identity of subject and object, and there he will finally have it. But when one reads the chapter, one is sorely disappointed and, what's more, can imagine the scorn Hegel felt for such extravagant hopes even when kindled by his own philosophy. Absolute knowledge proves to be little more than a kind of recapitulation of the foregoing book; the quintessence of that motion of the spirit in which it purportedly came to itself without the absolute itself ever having been expressed, since, if one follows Hegel, the latter was, in fact, never capable of being expressed as a result. In short, musically speaking, it is a reprise, with the element of disappointment that characterizes all reprises. So, too, in *Die Götterdämmerung*. The absolute, redemption from myth, even when it takes the form of catastrophe, is possible only as a reprise. Myth is catastrophe in permanence. What does away with it brings it to fulfillment, and death, which is the end of the bad infinite, is at the same time absolute regression.

Parsifal, Hamburg Staatsoper, 1991; Robert Wilson, director and set designer

If I have succeeded in giving at least some sense of the fact that the aesthetic weakness here is bound up with the core conception, which is of something circling within itself, fatefully self-contained, foreclosing the realization of the thing it nonetheless promises, then it is possible to understand why Wagner's so-called aesthetic errors are not correctable at will. It is not an individual weakness of Wagner's that is responsible for them. They can be criticized only by stepping outside the bounds of aesthetics. To talk about errors may sound pedantic, but as soon as one speaks of truth, in regard to artworks of the highest order, one must also speak of error: otherwise one takes them to be nonbinding. Wagner's aesthetic weaknesses spring from the metaphysics of repetition, from the idea that "This is the way things are, and always will be; you don't escape, there is no way to escape." This leads to the problem of performing Wagner today, about which I would like to say a few words at least. The problem is antinomical. What is true of the narrative passages and of the third act of *Die Götterdämmerung* is true of everything that is hard to bear in Wagner. The problem is deeply embedded in the heart of the thing itself. If one removes the bothersome element, one violates the work, is forced to go beyond it, and with every step one takes this leads to discrepancies, friction, unsatisfying effects. But if one does not remove it, one is not only succumbing to antiquarianism, but is compelled to show all sorts of things—and by things I mean not only lilac bushes,* but music, from sequences to entire formal elements—that are no longer possible as they stand. Finally, attempts to flee from such antinomies into the timeless—the idea of which, it is true, is suggested by Wagner's mythology—are hopeless. Everything in Wagner has its temporal core. Like a spider, his mind sits amidst the powerful web of nineteenth-century exchange relationships. Even the subtly seductive Spitzwegian† quality of the second act of *Die Meistersinger* has its function within the whole; it belongs to the almost irresistible but contaminated attempt to invent a mythological recent past for the German people, on which they could then become intoxicated. For this reason the surrealistic attempts at a resolution are perhaps adequate after all, despite the outdated character of the surrealism of the '20s and '30s. They attempt not to mythologize Wagner in the sense of timelessness, but to explode his temporal core, to show Wagner himself as in the grip of history or, as we nowadays say all too readily, to alienate him. I like Max Ernst's idea: to have King Ludwig II amusing himself in the cave of the Venusberg. The latest parodistic and aggressive interpretation of the second act of *Die Meistersinger* in Bayreuth— I have not seen the production myself—seems to be in a similar vein. If it is true about Wagner that no matter what one does, it is wrong, the thing that is still most likely to help is to force what is false, flawed, antinomical out into the open, rather than glossing over it and generating a kind of harmony to which the most profound element in Wagner is antithetical. For that reason, only experimental solutions are justified today; only what injures the Wagner orthodoxy is true. The defenders of the Grail shouldn't get so worked up about it; Wagner's precise instructions exist and will continue to be handed down for historians. But the rage that is unleashed by such interventions proves that they strike a nerve, precisely that layer where the question of Wagner's relevance for

---

* A reference to the lilac monologue in the second act of *Die Meistersinger*.

† Carl Spitzweg (1806–1885), painter of grotesque characters.

today is decided. One should also intervene without question in conspicuously nationalistic passages like the final speech of Hans Sachs. In the same way, one should liberate the musical dramas from the stigma of the disgraceful Jewish caricatures Mime and Beckmesser—at least through the accents set by the production. If Wagner's work is truly ambivalent and fractured, then it can be done justice only by a performance practice that takes this into account and realizes the fractures instead of closing them cosmetically.

It should be asked whether Wagner's relevance for today, as I have attempted to illuminate it from widely divergent angles, isn't, in the familiar phrase, merely artistic, something that is ultimately confined to technical matters. The concept that is implied here of a technique separable from truth content is shallow. But I would like to address the truth content directly. If there is a formula to be found for it, it would be a music that is dark despite all its color and that points to the calamitous fate of the world by representing it. Even the barbaric aspects of Wagner's work are an expression of this: the culture that is shattered there the way Siegfried breaks the anvil of Mime's smithy is not yet a culture at all. Truly the world spirit behaved like the Wagnerian unfolding of total negativity. Even today there is nothing of more serious concern than this; this is why Wagner remains a serious matter. This is affirmed, for the last time perhaps, by the profound affinity between the poetic texts—whether or not one considers them successful—and their compositional realization. Such affinity has not been achieved by any art in the grand style since then. Music became specialized, and it is music's curse, from the point of view of the philosophy of history, that the process of specialization cannot be reversed at will, and yet impairs the relevance and authenticity of the resulting works. The fractures in the Wagnerian work are themselves already the consequence of a claim to totality that is not contented with the specialized artwork, in which Wagner, too, participated through technology. His artistry, his craft, those traits that already enchanted Nietzsche, should be held up in contrast to dull handiwork in order that we might again learn everything from them. In Wagner they serve a vision of the whole that criticizes not only the opera of former times, with its division into different jurisdictions, but also society, with its division of labor, its guilds and orders, as it exists down to the present day. When the whole of history is shown as circling within itself, as something within which history has not yet begun, it protests wordlessly against this very fact. His friend Bakunin heard this within him when he listened to the *Holländer* and said: "That was only water, what must this music become when one day it deals with fire!" That Wagner could not succeed equally in the representation of fire is itself a piece of metaphysics; driven by its own metaphysics, his music took itself back into itself. But because it does not, in the end, realize what it has promised, it is therefore fallible, given into our hands incomplete, as something to be advanced, unfinished in itself. It awaits the influence that will advance it to self-realization. This would seem to be its true relevance for our time.

Translated by Susan Gillespie

LYN HEJINIAN

from *Sleeps*

6

We have come on our own and we'll stay
But let's demand something now to know of where we
    are
The knowledge is embodied—and the body is
    trembling, terrified because it's unprepared
It forgot to get ready, it forgot to pack, it
    forgot to read

Lost memory, empty thought
A person who loves can't let itself sink
    like a rock
Nor are persons clouds apart floating in the
    sallow
A person who loves thinks like a clock

But as a result of not testing the real for
    activity one comes to wonder who lives
I am not saying that personal generosity will
    solve everything—a person can't even solve
    today by midnight
By its anonymity
And it couldn't take itself as an animal
And so to believe it to be what we truly believe
    it to be we must open it

So tomorrow I will torture myself
But I would be more than necessary
The consummation of what I'm going to sadden
The segments of my life in separation and laid
    side by side
Cruelty is always turning kindly aside
It creates a clinical situation—I, a body,
    turning for speculation

But love exalts only truths that are
    undemonstrable
They turn true by demanding some activity
So I will say "I" and sleep—sleep for pressure
    and sleep for sprawl

35

The first hour of this arrangement of thought
    objects is deathlike
Then as sleep deals with nature it attracts
    pensive wandering
The westward-moving "I" follows the sun but too
    slowly so that it loses ground

"I" dream of telling a man to be precise
I want him to discern the ideological form and
    function of the term "watering hole"
His name is Jack but his face is Sam
I wake, turn, think of turning, widen, until
    dehumanized I'm something congenial in brain
    beyond control
The wide gap between world and mind is sleepable

The concept of "same time" serves as an invitation
    to attend while things assimilate, mutate, or
    aesthetically vacillate

Just as the second hour meets the first I want to
    explain and explanation ramifies
I extrapolate and that's conditional
There is nothing unconditional—there is always
    room
It spreads like the shadow of knowledge over a
    sleeping person
Immortal before, immortal after, but mortal now as
    I say so
Or sleep so
Sleep late

39   *The Polar Circle*

The world is between tips
We say so to know
We go to look over or out to its pivot, to its
    wobble and drift
Terrible
We are leaving
There's nothing to come to there but
    transformation and tint
Seductions
So we can't be repeating
What one knows in this state can't be known in
    another
Time matches nothing

People don't circle, certainly not unless they are
    responsible
But sleeps pine or eagle or tide to gratify
And thousands depend on one
Repeated
And all that's repeated is mediated
Thought
The order is such that it situates
At the farthest extent of a scene are its
    reachings
Night life is search of its kind
Hands open and fingers shuffle
I could gesture not of persons but of crevice,
    preface, and prelude
I imagine without standpoint poised at loss point
At pole
I easily sleep in its entered light but don't
    write
It doesn't behoove me to make myself smaller than
    I am
And the horizon doesn't hold there
It isn't grained
Its gaping point of contact spreads the latitudes
The pole is interminable, coming and going as if
    solely on rock
But it isn't singular
It shares the mobility of an oblivion I want to
    witness

The world looks like
The pole draws the whirlpools
And to express scope one turns the top of one's
    head

In time the berries unfold of nothing but gold
    cloud
Every color is gathered and then flown
We were even in the red bogs—everything is always
    even
The rivers were amber as tea
And I didn't want to tell, though I seemed to
I always wanted what has no beginning but not what
    has no end
There must be point and it might be tide
Time—North
I think of reason everywhere and it overlaps
Reasonable eventuality and long partition—
    grammar, supper, and sleep ideas are chasing
To pole
It says the dog joined in and tore off the whole
    of a man's face while the man, his arms
    clasped round its back, broke every bone in
    the dog's body, and there the pair of them
    lay, dead, seizing what seemed to be the only
    chance

We dream with our limbs on our heads
As Poe says, It is a happiness to wonder
Our ankles are the hottest
It is happiness to dream
The men ask me where is the charred pot and I say
    it is in the car trunk
The men deny that the slopes have walked into the
    creek
They are probably right and keep consuming
Fire they need—they who come in and fall to their
    knees
To ground

SLEEPS

Human curiosity contradicts the human will to
    believe
Before going north I almost had been stopping
But what's the denial of solving
Night visions rhyme—peaks, language, sleep,
    light, tundra, lichen
Because of the obscurity of such phenomena Nature
    seems uncanny
It lets us mock and destroy the utterly complete
Sleep is what remains of Nature
That merely mathematical recognition of equality,
    Poe says, which seems to be the root of all
    beauty
With night thoughts like these, are we not
    logicians
The lower teeth fall out and point saying,
    "Ourselves!"
We are barbarian, recalcitrant, in sleep
Probably we sleep beyond our strength
But what has happened?
As herself at the Arctic limit I would leave
    myself
Still I ask, "Am I contributing something?"
A sleeper leaning over more than ever to make
    contact with reality
Everything is scattered beyond the face
Detached
But persons have their immortality to sacrifice—
    and why stop?

                                            for Lauri Nykopp

PHAM THI HOAI

Nine Down Makes Ten

The first man in my unhappy life was slender and gentle with an honest face. His was an honesty easy to find at any time, especially in people who have lived continually and without interruption in a sheltered environment. From an ordinary and uneventful childhood, to a college life, really no more than an extension of high school, and on to years as a government-employed technician, he displayed diligence, trustworthiness, and benevolence. It seemed that his was a kind of innate goodness, God-given and protected. It seemed that he had always been righteous and good, but in a modest way, throughout a life untouched by self-doubt. I often thought of his goodness as a small thimble of fire, incapable of contributing much heat to the world, but occasionally heartwarming, though only in a symbolic way. And everyone, especially me, would strain toward this warmth; this effort would eventually become a habit and, later on, a moral imperative. Actually, by his side I could perhaps have lived the most suitable kind of life for a woman, in an apartment somewhere with that small flame. I'd give birth to well-fathered children and sit nightly clutching a ball of colorful wool, knitting colorful clothes, oblivious to self-doubt. Moreover, I would never fear unfaithfulness from him, as he could barely conceptualize adultery. But then I was too young, and I saw him as a sort of precious chessman, fortunate to have been moved by some unseen hand toward the safe squares and away from the violent battles. It seemed he would remain like this until a natural death finally seized him—and of course he'd remain honest, even in death. At that time, I considered my own birth some kind of cruel prank. I underestimated the size of his thimble of fire and failed to realize that his conventional honesty was no less believable than other things in life. Lacking skepticism, how could he understand science, art, or religion, and in short, how could he understand love, which I considered the most fundamental craving for such a person as myself? I grew dissatisfied because he was too respectable and secure with his own respectability.

The second man was frivolous and merry, an urban child who had yet to go through the period of spiritual crisis characteristic of civilized society. He was crazy about music from Beethoven to the Beatles and possessed a good singing voice, but couldn't bear to practice. He also loved soccer and had a decent kicking foot but no concentration for workouts. Generally speaking, he had no concentration for anything, not even love. It's difficult to trust such a man, since it's never clear where the vectors of his personality are going. He seemed on first impression someone tremendously frivolous, one who possessed rare and peculiar notions of life, often puzzling to those who met him. His face was so natural it provoked suspicion, and I believed that under that wonderful skin lay hidden an extraordinary nature. How else to explain the perfect harmony existing between him and his environment, a final symbol of his capacity to live so deeply and so freely? But after only three sentences had been uttered from his lovely smiling mouth, this first impression quickly evaporated. He was one of a countless number of fortunate young men who live an unexamined life, not because of some conscious principle, but simply owing to circumstance—frivolity as a habit, as a way of life. He was frivolous in all details, and only details concerned him. His frivolity manifested itself in the care he took in striking a relaxed pose, and in the attention he devoted to celebrations, to feasting, and to appearing knowledgeable; this all in the context of a larger existence that was not at all frivolous, but serious and substantial. At a certain age, those as extroverted and unaffected as he sink into the cloudy chaos of life's problems. Nevertheless, he was a person who brought me many pleasant hours, almost my happiest ever. I learned several important things from him, namely the discovery that I have a body and that it has a voice, a voice initially timid, then passionate, sometimes daring and profane, and progressively harder to please. He was the first man to show me that I am a woman, and for a long while after, how long I'm not sure, I remained grateful to this ordinary man. Life would certainly be impoverished if it lacked such merry and superficial men. Furthermore he loved good food, and that truly is a worthwhile quality.

Man number three was around for less than a week but made me the most miserable. He was extremely handsome, so handsome that expressions of envy clogged the throats of those who met him. I immediately forgot who I was and experienced my first near-death state. After that I remained struck by a sensation both dangerous and seductive. This feeling has stayed with me throughout the remainder of my life, flooding and overwhelming smaller emotions, causing them to shrink and shrivel up. Recovery would demand a very large dose of optimism and an ability to adjust to new extremes. I knew that he was an inarticulate dullard, useless except for giving pleasure to the eyes, overreliant on his unusually gorgeous appearance, and frightfully uninteresting. But in his presence I completely forgot and forgave everything, even though he was genuinely uncouth, foul, and cruel. After one week, I abandoned my urge not to indulge my self-pity and cried like a child whose toy has been stolen before she gets a chance to play with it. He would continue to be so gorgeous and useless for his entire life, and I, throughout my life, would flee from the desire to give myself to him, tormented by the absurdity of God and of myself even more. That affair was perhaps my only experience with true platonic love, especially the time I timidly ran my fingers through tufts of hair so beautiful they seemed not to belong to him and then abruptly jerked away as if stung by an electric shock.

After that I had an old man, experienced and worldly. He was born into a family whose members had participated for many generations in great historical events. They were thoughtfully educated, upwardly mobile, skilled at rubbing shoulders wherever they went, and never ruffled by callous twists and turns of fate. His handsomeness had a majestic air, and his every gesture suggested a profound awareness of his own value. I lived with him the longest, more than two years, and I grew much during this period. He knew how to answer all of my questions, whether about politics, love, religion, or the psychological taboos of bygone eras. He knew the way to sit cross-legged, drinking and composing poetry with literary friends; he was dignified and serious with academic friends, simple and easygoing with old women and children in the neighborhood, and brutish and cocky with the scum of the street. Many women revered him as some sort of idol. Old people found him loving and affectionate: he never said anything to hurt them. I enjoyed his generosity until it gradually became like a solid gold chain clamped around my neck. "What right do you have to be so generous?" I protested. And his answer suggested, "Just carry on with your life, little girl. You are still so small." Perhaps his brand of perfection was like a perfectly baked earthenware vase, adorned with brightly colored and well-proportioned designs; but its basic components, earth and rocks, originally loose, dirty, and unformed, would remain essentially unchanged forever. In describing him, it's important to emphasize that he seemed profoundly satisfied with himself. Due to his advanced age and precious experience, plus a certain humorlessness, he did not dare or perhaps was unable to reject any part of the status quo. He gave me many things, or he almost gave me many things: affection to a nearly affectionate extent, warmth to a degree almost heartwarming. The whole of his perfect existence symbolized the limitless limitations of mankind. Not only did he unconditionally accept these limitations, but he used them to justify his behavior. He adroitly maintained a cozy family life while simultaneously offering his generosity to me. He explained that people are truly small creatures, fettered by their environment at birth and by various obligations as an adult. Thus they can maneuver only in a limited way and within the confines of some predetermined grid. I hated those grids and harshly mocked the way he struggled with his limitations. Up until the final moments, he still offered me a generous smile, and it really seemed that compared with other men, he cared about me the most. Countless times thereafter, I longed to abandon my high-pressure work and relationships and run back to him, hiding my face in his solid chest and conceding that he had always been right. But I clicked my tongue and decided against it. This flexible man was considered exemplary by the successful members of society, but who really cares what they think?

Man number five was an idealist. He belonged to that breed of men not born for women, money, or pleasure, and this made me curious. My curiosity, however, did not last long, for contrary to my expectations, he was insipid and shallow. His ideal world—to be brought about by a struggle either to reform educational science, protect the environment, or reestablish a tradition of sarong wearing among ethnic minorities (what a big deal)—perhaps could really exist someday. I never doubted its attractiveness, and sometimes, in a highly inspired state, he could transmit a bit of his passion and emotion to the nonbelievers. But in general his view of life suggested a narrow corridor that was periodically repainted but nevertheless remained cramped and dreary. In a calculating way, I studied and applied tactics of love, and bearing the costs of lost time and more annoyance than happiness, I contrived to probe the bulwarks of his idealism, to test its endurance. This plunged him into an overwhelming spiritual crisis. Friends took him to the emergency room, where his deeply self-tortured soul was injected with tens of thousands of units of antibiotics, and just because he could not choose between his love and his ideals. He was the kind of person who possesses only enough internal strength to devote himself to one thing at a time. Leaving the hospital, he embarrassingly thanked me and disappeared down one of his mysterious corridors, this one concerned with the public reform of morning exercises for people too physically unfit to work. However, my calibrated burst of love had misfired, and his ideals gave him an easy way out. That was the only affair in which I actively played the role of seductress from beginning to end, and after he was gone I was genuinely sad and regretful. After thinking a while, it became clear that he had chosen his dreary and narrow world over me. A lesson for simple curiosity. But I must admit he was the purest man I have ever met.

The sixth man was extremely complex, almost irrationally so, in the context of this most poor and backward society. When I met him, he had achieved an undeniable level of prestige in the diminutive intellectual world of Hanoi, a place where one can meet the most famous people without a prior appointment and use intimate terms of address within the first moments of striking up a conversation. I immediately surrendered before him—this human labyrinth, this infinitely dimensional zone cluttered with the disorder of contradictions, ideology, experience, and ambition. But I couldn't help wondering: Do all these interesting and complicated things really exist, or are they only an expensive and ultimately meaningless drama that people feel compelled to stage in order to cope with their fellow men and themselves? Conventional geniuses never seem to have personalities; who would dare say that Shakespeare, for example, was melancholy, bitter, or sharp-tongued? Therefore I concluded that my sixth man was no genius. He had too much personality and was too worried about his own originality. His complexity seemed the natural outgrowth of the uncontrolled interaction between two currents. On the one hand was the traditional educational system, in which the value of everything—romanticism, historical method, even the slipping of cushions under the bed before a night of lovemaking—is fixed according to a guaranteed standard of truth, goodness, and beauty. And on the other hand was real life: vivid, crowded, subverting all conventions regardless of tradition, undermining all ideologies, and naturally overturning all values. Because he was sensitive, he found it hard to overlook clashes between the two, but because he was at the same time intelligent, he refused to take sides. Gradually he found that the best way out was to situate himself somewhere above the fray and contentedly gaze down. Consequently, people who participated in increasingly public discussions claimed that in fact he systematically rejected everything. They were wrong. He was too complicated and lost in his own complexity to reject everything. However, he did become a somewhat legendary and original figure, and as people stood anxious and sweaty in his presence, time passed, and I grew tired. During the time I lived with him, I tended to dwell obsessively on my own sadness. I uttered strange and often contradictory phrases, ate and dressed on purpose in a slovenly manner, and lavished praise on only those books that no one understood. When we broke up, I felt the world to be shallow and its people superficial. It seemed that I never received from this famous man a soulful kiss, meaning one both natural and pure. Afterward, I heard that he had become a radical moralist, preaching about the nature of three distinct roads: the acceptance of, rejection of, and escape from conventional morality. Later on, he became a kind of popular sage, a dialectician who approached society's intricate problems through dialectical methods and by applying extracts of oriental and occidental knowledge. In the end he became a recluse, and in an unrelated development, the intellectual life of Hanoi contracted, and no one spoke further of him.

The seventh man brought me much excitement but also my moments of greatest uneasiness. He was not unusually attractive: short, with thinning hair and a small forehead. Only his voice was exquisite, deep, melodious, and full of unforeseen contingencies. Upon hearing his voice, difficult-to-please listeners, even those impressed only by outward appearance, would be riveted and believe that before them was, if not a genius in disguise, some sort of otherworldly species of man, a being who used this earth only as a temporary dwelling. Or perhaps they would feel that this small man must deeply understand the quintessence of life, as if his existence had spanned scores of generations and consequently could draw on the experience of both ghosts and men. It was said that he followed nihilistic principles, but I didn't understand what this meant. I speculated that it was a unique philosophical idea that could never be fully grasped, or perhaps the final foundation of all foundations, or a mode of behavior reserved especially for those without virtue, those both unhappy and very lonely. But this man refused to advertise his noble misery, the pain he felt for humanity, the loneliness in his blood, or the weariness with which he experienced the age. On the contrary, his expression suggested contentment and freedom from worry, the capacity to accept or reject circumstances with equal ease; and sometimes he was simply difficult to read. His one fascination was with the brevity of human existence, and the only being who provoked him to fits of anger and an enduring sensation of confusion and helplessness was God. He considered God to be his only worthwhile rival and lamented the fact that the great one so rarely showed himself. It was perhaps the complexity of his relationship with God that fundamentally distinguished him from the mass of nihilists in the movement. Their lazy activism was habitually insignificant, and they always seemed prepared to shout "I've found it!" after taking only half a step out the door. It was not easy to label him godless, immoral, or relativistic, and finally one could say only that he had a great sense of humor, his genius lying with his comic gifts. Many women went out with him. This small Don Juan was thoughtful and considerate toward them, and because of his skill in the various stages of love affairs, he earned a sultry reputation. After studying with him, many miserable women left and, turning on him, denounced what they had learned. I also left him, after admitting to myself that I was to remain a weak woman and would spend my entire life searching for strength outside of myself. In my present state of panic I dare not enter into his zone, a zone wonderful for creating poetry and philosophy but inappropriate for comforting the hearts of women. I'm afraid that I will forever grieve over this unhappy Don Juan, and I can drive away my sadness only by shrugging my shoulders and saying, "He was really pitiable: no emotion, no passion, no faith; in short, he didn't know what to live for."

The eighth man had the hair of a poet, the face of a poet, and a soul especially given to poetry. Such qualities are found only in people who have a lot of time and no concrete obligations toward life. When engrossed in the rising and falling of his watery waves, and once acquainted with his passionate love of writing—swiftly, without semicolons—I began to understand that the most worthwhile obsession is an obsession that is actually independent of the object of fixation. The object is only borrowed as a pretext, a means, an environment, through which or in which the obsessed person can project his own eternal and essential hunger, thus fulfilling the requirements of death—the dissolution of the ego for something, anything, that exists independently outside one's self. Perhaps that obsession should be controlled. At some point the most mundane catalyst, a skirt or a fallen leaf, is enough to provoke a series of captivating chain reactions, while at another time much more important objects will inspire only an absurd indifference. I did not know whether I was worthwhile or mundane, but this was not really the issue. I was grateful to this man and enjoyed the taste of his affection, despite a small stubborn girl within me who refused to cooperate. She said: According to this particular mode of obsession all objects are equal, and therefore I am no different from a potato or an ant, but if people like to manufacture an obsession by constantly stoking their own engine, then by all means they should go ahead. Gradually I learned to repress that obstinate girl and ignore my uneasiness with the difference between artificially produced obsession and primeval obsession. Let Proust distinguish between the two, or the column "Mothers Advise Daughters" in some women's magazine; I am interested only in my own obsession and its consequences. The most ironic aspect of its unforeseen consequences was that both he and I became pitiful victims of the obsession. It forced him to wait by every street on which I might pass, to pull me away from all activities, no matter how fundamental to existence: eating, sleeping, seeking work; it interfered with all my relationships, with my family, colleagues, and friends, and expanded into all areas and times that I liked to save for myself. I no longer had my own spaces, times, or life-style; my environment was upset, my psychological state was upset, my language went out of control. The obsession was like the third character in a love triangle leading him and poking me in the back; it followed its own dizzying trajectory and changed obstinate people into slaves, oblivious to their limited abilities. In short, it swallowed us without chewing: he failed his examinations, unable to resist the rush toward inertia, and I turned blind like a Chinese lantern at a festival. In this situation, people can't help but grate on and annoy each other. The demands of individual liberation eventually transform society into a mass of "I"s, each one desiring to control the others. This naturally provokes conflict. Exhausted after such a time-consuming conflict, he abandoned the relationship for the call of religion, but this new obsession exacted an even higher price. I returned to my original form of a potato, or maybe an ant, and heaved a sigh of relief. I feel sorry for God or Buddha, as this poet will certainly grate on them. But perhaps those two gentlemen understand the essence of life better than I and can look beyond him.

The ninth man was a man of action, few words, forthrightness, and pragmatism. He was intelligent, decently educated, and sensitive enough to appreciate the real value of such nonmaterial activities as wordplay, pipe dreams, fortunetelling, or making love. However, the road he chose for himself satisfied a predilection for certitude and controlled vigilance. He believed in no one, entrusted himself to no one, and struggled to force life itself to bend to his will. His profound desire to conquer life was impressive, vaguely like Don Quixote's, both desperate and dauntless. He had held down many jobs, for many different reasons, ranging from the desire to secure life's basic necessities to attempts to secure glory and power. But he was rarely satisfied, as work never quite met his expectations. The only measure he took seriously was that of practical advantage, immediate material gain being optimal and the forging of useful future connections merely acceptable. He was strict and prompt in the repayment of debts. While people found him useful, they were often cool toward him because he was completely lacking in false ethics, those gastric juices that allow for the digestion of the inedible components in the relations between people. He promised little, yet was so helpful with my unhappy life's most pressing problems (more so than all other men combined), that during those moments of satisfaction and gratitude I confusedly asked myself if this really could be love. And could women like myself have lost such confidence in themselves and in this difficult-to-understand era that we need such a love as this? He did grant me three things: First, because he was always so busy, he did not have the time to undergo a period of spiritual crisis, something that I had already been blessed with enough times before; second, as relations with women never took up his whole life, I enjoyed a notable degree of freedom; and third, with him, I suddenly felt a daily sensation of being deeply and snugly attached to my life, a sensation that I had thought about many times before but never actually experienced. I grew stronger and more contented, and began seriously to consider the prospect of marrying him. Life with such a thoroughly practical man would certainly promise a measure of success, like entering into a contract in which each side does not sap the other's vitality, as often happens with those claiming to be madly in love. There is certainly some advantage in avoiding excessive closeness and coolly carrying out contractual provisions. At our final meeting, he said, "In all areas including marriage, I am always faithful to a single measure of value: practical advantage." And on considering this measure, he determined that I was not to be the one to satisfy his requirements. Now he must bear responsibility for his heartlessness.

Enough. He was the ninth man.

Translated by Peter Zinoman

ALBERT MOBILIO

Talus Slope

Flat fire rains down. The grazed field,
a river veers through. Ravens swarm
on the face of church rock. Bruised smoke
cores the guttered zone of skylight as
I raise my hand to wake myself &
measure out a bandage for my eyes.
An incessant sun has washed away
the ore, the initials of my subplot.

Listen, there are seeds buried
in scrolling air. Rumors fill the watchtower;
their syllables decay with every echo.
No one who wears the body
can be sheltered here. Acreage thickens
around my waist. The waves below
are like those above. In the dark water
I've been fed, I begin to bathe.

Miles plowed within my marrow. A haven
among the cottonwoods where the climate
is intricate & pure enough to keep
intact the bridges of the earths.
Flood-carved chamber to which I'm drawn,
where my exhalation tumbles free.
Sight pockets outward, drifts through
mesa cliffs, works into the highway's
exhausted roots. Charred inscription
a scorpion feeds upon; stone's lineage

TALUS SLOPE

threads back to firmament. The air-
stream's now a trembling, unsought relic.
My tent pitched on a veil of sand,
what lock secures me, holds me fast?

Like charcoal to the disease, like spit to
the whetstone. Like gold rounded, like a ball
rounded, the canyon bursts with all
its dwellings. Plumes twist up from meteor city.
What's left are split-twig figures
of bighorn sheep, some inches of this much
xeroxed terrain. Blown through the geologic
sleeve, old dirt drowns my voice,
suffocates my eyes. The helmsman's
fear is swallowed blood & white crows
dizzy a scrap of shade thrown down
by gnarled junipers. I pry for a handhold
in teeth of broken slate. My lift,
a headlong fall against the talus slope.

ANDREW McCORD

Frames of a Coptic Funeral

after Sebastião Salgado

In a chiaroscuro cast by two great trees
The photographer finds what he is after—
A leopard light, two hundred refugees
Afraid of light—the picture of disaster.

To confound the helicopters overhead
These people flee at night. They wait by day,
Under the baobab trees, or sleep, or fray
A plastic sack into strands to bind the dead.

A child is laid out on the parched gray earth
Tied knee to knee, toe to toe, and thumb
To thumb—naked, ready for someone
To carry to a stray patch of quiet earth

Where there is nothing to make a cross above him.
His cairn is a shell that missed the ones that loved him.

WILLIAM CHRISTENBERRY

Klan Dolls

Klan Dolls

William Christenberry was born in Hale County, Alabama, in 1936, in the place and at the time that James Agee and Walker Evans were creating the American classic *Let Us Now Praise Famous Men*. In this work Agee calls for the use of the most humble materials to create a "lyric poetry" from everyday experience. Since the 1950s Christenberry has developed this principle more fully than any other artist, and has done so in an extraordinarily wide variety of media: painting, sculpture, drawing, and photography. He is best known for his pioneering work in color photography, which introduced the small-format Brownie snapshot camera to serious photography.

Over the past twenty years Christenberry has devoted considerable attention to one particular fringe element of the American South: the Ku Klux Klan. Christenberry's fascination with the Klan springs from a nightmarish encounter at the Tuscaloosa courthouse one evening when he was a young man. "I started climbing slowly . . . a very dimly lit stairwell. . . . About halfway up, this Klansman in full robe and hood suddenly stepped out on the top of the landing. . . . I froze for a moment. We both looked at each other. And then I turned and ran." Thomas Southall, of the Amon Carter Museum in Fort Worth, has written of Christenberry's Klan pieces: "This creation, like his other work, has a way of giving physical form to intangible feeling. We are left not with a simple polemic or documentary statement, but with a new sense of how complex and deeply rooted prejudice is." For Christenberry, a white Southerner, these fetishistic works seem to constitute a kind of exorcism of racism; nonetheless, they are rarely exhibited.

The artist recently created a new series of Klan dolls. These effigies—bound, tortured, and executed—are arranged against a background of Alabama red dirt or Confederate or American flags and photographed. The studies included in this portfolio were commissioned by *Grand Street*.

—Walter Hopps

ANDREI PLATONOV

from *Happy Moscow*

Young scientists, engineers, aviators, doctors, pedagogues, actors, musicians, and workers from the new factories gathered that evening at the district Komsomol club. None was more than twenty-seven years old, but each had already become famous throughout his motherland—throughout the new world—and each was a bit ashamed of his early fame, and that made life hard. The club's elderly employees, who had let their lives and talent slip away in the unlucky bourgeois period, with covert sighs of inner impoverishment arranged the furnishings in the two large rooms, in the one for a formal meeting and in the other for conversation and refreshments.

Among the first to arrive was the twenty-four-year-old engineer Selin, accompanied by the Komsomolka Kuzmina, a pianist ever pensive from imagining music.

"Let's grab a bite to eat!" Selin said to her.

"Let's," Kuzmina agreed.

They went over to the snack counter. There Selin, a powerful, ruddy trencherman, immediately consumed eight sausage sandwiches, while Kuzmina took only two pastries for herself. It wasn't digestion she lived for, but playing.

"Selin, why are you eating so much?" Kuzmina asked. "It may be good, but it's terrible to look at you!"

Selin ate indignantly. He chewed as he plowed, his trusty jaws making a persistent, diligent effort.

Soon afterward ten more people arrived all at once—the traveler Golovach, the mechanical engineer Semyon Sartorius, two girls who were friends and both in hydraulics, the composer Levchenko, the astronomer Sitsylin, the aviation meteorologist Vechkin, the designer of high-altitude aircraft Muldbauer, and the electrical engineer Gunkin and his wife. Behind them still others could be heard and a few more arrived. They were all acquainted with each other—from work, through social contact, or on the basis of information received.

Before the meeting started, each abandoned himself to his pleasure—some to friendship, some to food, some to questions about unsolved problems, some to music and dancing. Kuzmina found a small room with a new grand piano and there indulged herself in Beethoven's Ninth Symphony—all the movements, one after the other, from memory. Her heart was wrung by the profound freedom and inspired thought of the music and by egotistical sadness that she herself was incapable of composing the same way. The electrical engineer Gunkin listened to Kuzmina and pondered the high electrical frequencies with which the universe is shot through, the emptiness of the terrible lofty world that draws human consciousness into itself . . . Muldbauer saw in the music the representation of remote weightless countries up in the air where the black vault of heaven is located and, suspended in that vault, an unflickering sun of lifeless incandescence, the place where, far from the warm and darkly green earth, the truly serious cosmos begins—mute space burning with the occasional signal lights of stars—and he thought about the fact that the path there has long been free and clear . . . Let's be done with the tedious turmoil of the earth and allow good old Stalin to direct the velocity and thrust of human history beyond the bounds of earthly gravity—for the great instruction of the earth, for the great instruction of reason in a courageous act long destined for it.

A little while later Moscow Chestnova arrived as well and silently smiled from joy at seeing her comrades and hearing music that stirred her life to the implementation of a loftier fate.

The last of all to turn up at the club was the surgeon Sambikin.

He had just been at the clinic of the Institute for Experimental Medicine and had himself bandaged the boy he had operated on. He arrived oppressed by sorrow at the arrangement of the human body, which squeezes a great deal more suffering and death into its bones than life and movement. And it would have been strange for Sambikin to feel good, given the intensity of his concern and his sense of responsibility. His whole mind was filled with thought, and his heart beat calmly and truly, and he required no better happiness than that, yet at the same time his awareness of that enjoyment was beginning to make him feel ashamed . . . He already wanted to leave the club and work a while that night at the Institute on his research into death, but all of a sudden he saw Moscow Chestnova passing by. The vague charm of her appearance astonished Sambikin; he saw strength and luminous enthusiasm concealed behind the diffidence and even timidity of her face. A bell rang, signaling the start of the meeting. Everyone left the room in which Sambikin found himself, and only Chestnova remained behind to fasten one of her stockings. After taking care of the stocking, she noticed the solitary Sambikin staring at her. Out of embarrassment and awkwardness (to live in the same world, do the same thing, and yet not be acquainted) she bowed to him. Sambikin approached her, and they went in together to attend the meeting.

They sat down next to each other, and amid the speeches, glorification, and greetings, Sambikin clearly heard the pulsing of Moscow's heart in her breast.

He whispered a question in her ear: "Why is your heart pounding like that? I can hear it!"

"It wants to fly, and it's beating," Moscow whispered to Sambikin with a smile. "You see, I'm a parachutist!"

"The human body flew long ago in the now perished millennia," Sambikin thought. "The human rib cage represents folded wings."

He felt his warm head. Something was beating there too, something that wanted to fly out of its dark, lonely confinement.

After the meeting it was time for recreation and supper. The young guests went off to different rooms before sitting down at the table together.

The mechanical engineer Sartorius asked Moscow Chestnova

to dance, and she went off to twirl with him, curiously examining the great round face of the famous inventor in the field of precision industry, an engineer-designer of world importance. Sartorius held Moscow tightly, danced gravely, and smiled timidly, revealing his inhibited attraction to her. Moscow, however, looked at him like a woman in love. She quickly abandoned herself to her feeling, not resorting to the feminine policy of indifference. She liked that unattractive person who was shorter than she, with his kind and gloomy face, someone who had been unable to endure the promptings of his heart and had acted in a way that for him was extremely bold: he had approached a woman and asked her to dance. But before long the dancing had apparently started to bore him. His hands had already got used to the warmth of Moscow's body, ardent under her light dress, and he began to mumble something. On hearing it, Moscow at once took offense: "He's embracing me, he's dancing with me, but he's thinking about something completely different!" she said.

"That's how I am," Sartorius replied.

"Tell me right now just how that is!" Moscow frowned and stopped dancing.

Sambikin hurtled past them, producing a breeze. He too was dancing, having fallen in step with some Komsomolka of great prettiness. Moscow smiled at him: "Are you really dancing too? What a strange person you are!"

"You have to try everything!" Sambikin answered her as he moved.

"Is that how you feel?" Moscow called after him.

"No, I'm only pretending!" Sambikin answered her. "It's theoretical!"

The Komsomolka, offended now, deserted Sambikin at once, and he started laughing.

"Well, hurry up and say something!" Moscow turned to Sartorius with forced seriousness.

"Can she really be a fool? What a pity!" Sartorius thought. At that point the meteorologist Vechkin came over to them, and then Sambikin, and Sartorius failed to say anything to Moscow in reply. It was only an hour later that they saw each other again—when they all sat down to supper together.

A large table had been set for some fifty people. Flowers, which seemed pensive in their beauty, stood every half meter, and they gave off a posthumous fragrance. The wives of the designers and the young women engineers were arrayed in the republic's best silk; the government dressed up its finest people. Moscow Chestnova had on a tea dress that weighed two or three grams at most and was so skillfully sewn together that even the pulsing of her blood vessels was registered by the agitation of the silk. All the men, not excluding the careless Sambikin and the overgrown, melancholy Vechkin, had come in suits of choice material, simple and expensive. To dress badly and sloppily would have been to reproach with poverty the country that had nourished and clothed those present with its finest goods and was itself thriving on the strength and drive of that youth, on its labor and talent.

A small Komsomol orchestra was playing short pieces on the balcony beyond an open door. The spacious night air came through the door of the balcony into the hall, and the flowers on the long table breathed it in and gave off an even stronger fragrance, feeling alive in the lost earth. The ancient city roared and was lit up like a new building. Sometimes the laughter and voice of some passerby would reach the club from the street, and then Moscow Chestnova felt like going outside and inviting everybody in for supper: all the same, socialism will come! At times she felt so good that she wanted somehow to step out of herself, to step out of her body in its dress, and become another person—Gunkin's wife, Sambikin, the reservist she had met, Sartorius, a peasant woman on a kolkhoz in the Ukraine . . .

Chandeliers from the Electrodevice plant cast a pale and tender energy over the people and the expensive furnishings. Light appetizers stood on the table while the main supper was being heated on far-off kitchen ranges.

The assembled, who were beautiful by nature or thanks to their animation or their still-unfinished youth, long delayed taking their places as they sought out the best company, although in the end they sat down with whomever was close at hand.

Once those thirty or so people had taken their seats, their inner resources, stimulated by each other, multiplied, and among them was born the shared genius of lively candor and happy, intellectually amicable rivalry. But the highly tuned sense of mutual relations acquired in a difficult technical culture, where victory does not come by means of ambiguous play—that sense of conduct permitted neither foolishness nor sentimentality nor self-importance. Those present were aware of or guessed at the sullen dimensions of nature, the reach of history, the extent of future time, and the true scale of their own powers. They were rational, practical people uncorrupted by idle delusion.

Moscow Chestnova was more impatient and wilder than the rest. She had had a glass of wine to drink without waiting for the others and was flushed from happiness and from being unaccustomed to wine. Sartorius noticed it and smiled at her with his broad, inexact face that looked like the countryside. His father's last name was not Sartorius but Zhuyboroda, and his peasant mother had borne him in her entrails alongside warm, well-chewed rye bread.

Sambikin was also watching Chestnova and thinking about her: Should he love her or shouldn't he? In general, she was pretty, and she didn't belong to anyone, yet how much thought and feeling would have to be driven out of his body and heart in order to find room for an attachment to that woman? And even if he found it, Chestnova would not be faithful to him, nor could she ever trade life in all its clamor for the whisper of a single human being.

"No, I will not love her and I cannot!" Sambikin decided once and for all. "Especially since it would be necessary to spoil her body in a certain way, and it would grieve me to lie day and night about being excellent . . . I don't want to, it's too hard!" He forgot himself in the course of his reverie, no longer aware of the others. Those present, even though they were sitting at a lavish and inviting table, ate little or only a bit at a time. They felt bad about the expensive food obtained through the patient effort of the kolkhozniks in their calamitous struggle with nature and the class enemy. Only Moscow Chestnova didn't care and ate and drank like a predatory creature. She said a variety of foolish things, made fun of Sartorius, and felt a shame that made its way into her heart from her mendacious, vulgar mind, which was sadly aware of the shameful expanse within. No one insulted Chestnova or stopped her as long as her energy did not flag and she herself kept talking. Sambikin knew that foolishness is a natural expression of errant feeling that has not yet found its goal and passion, but Sartorius enjoyed Moscow regardless of her behavior. He already loved her as a living truth, and through his happiness he saw her vaguely and imperfectly.

In the din of the already late evening Viktor Vasilievich Bozhko inconspicuously entered the room and, not wishing to be noticed, took a seat on a couch by the wall. He caught sight of the flushed and merry Moscow Chestnova and shuddered in dismay. Some scientific young fellow went over to where she was sitting and began singing to her:

You go about drunk,
You are so pale,
So sweet,
Faithful friend of mine . . .

Hearing that, Moscow covered her face with her hands and either started crying or blushed with shame—it's not clear which. Sartorius at that moment was arguing with Vechkin and Muldbauer; he was proving that, after class-oriented man, the earth will be occupied by a passionate technical being who will, in a practical way, sense the whole world through his work . . . The ancient people who began history were technical beings too. The Greek cities, ports, labyrinths—even Mount Olympus—were built by the Cyclopes, the one-eyed workers who each had had an eye put out by the ancient aristocrats as a sign that they were a proletariat condemned to build countries, dwellings for the gods, and ships of the sea, and that for the one-eyed people there would be no salvation. Three or four thousand years, a hundred generations, have gone by, and the descendants of the Cyclopes have emerged from the gloom of the historical labyrinth into the light of nature. They have retained a sixth of the earth's surface for themselves, and the rest of the earth lives only in expectation of them. Even the god Zeus was probably the last of the Cyclopes, and worked on erecting the Olympic hill and lived in a shack on top of it and survived in the memory of the ancient aristocratic tribe. The bourgeoisie of those ancient times wasn't stupid; it promoted the dead of the great workers to the rank of gods, for, unable to understand creation without pleasure, it was secretly amazed that those who had perished had silently possessed the supreme power, the capacity for labor, and the soul of labor—technology.

Sartorius got to his feet and picked up a glass of wine. Of small stature with an ordinary face warmed by life, and now carried away by imaginative thought, he was happy and attractive. Chestnova, first name Moscow, stared at him and decided to kiss him sometime. To his now silent comrades he said, "Let us drink to the anonymous Cyclopes, to the memory of all our tormented and perished fathers, and to technology—the true soul of man!"

They all drank at once, and the musicians started playing an old song based on a poem by Yazykov:

Beyond the ninth wave of foul weather
There is a blessed country,
Where the vault of heaven does not darken,
Where the silence does not pass away.

Bozhko sat meekly and inconspicuously. He was happier than those taking part in the soirée; he knew that the foul weather was passing and that beyond the window lay a blessed country illuminated by the stars and by electricity. He loved that country sparingly and silently and picked up every crumb that fell from its bounty, so that the country would remain completely whole.

A lavish supper was served. They cautiously began to sample it, but Semyon Sartorius could not eat or drink anything else. The torment of his love for Chestnova, Moscow had suddenly taken complete possession of his body and heart, so that he opened his mouth and breathed with effort, as if something in his breast were making him uncomfortable. Moscow smiled mysteriously at him from a distance. Her secret life reached Sartorius as warmth and unease, and her penetrating eyes looked at him without attention, as at an ordinary fact. "Oh what a swine physics is!" Sartorius thought, grasping his situation. "Well, what's left for me now, except foolishness and personal happiness!"

The urban night gleamed in the outer darkness, sustained by the voltage of distant machines. The agitated air, warmed by millions of people, pierced Sartorius's heart with anguish. He went out onto the balcony, gazed up at the stars, and whispered some old words acquired secondhand: "My God!" Sambikin sat at the table as before without touching his food. He was carried away in thought further than the next morning and, as in a fog at sea, was dimly mulling over future immortality. He wanted to extract the power of long life or maybe its eternity from the corpses of perished beings. Several years before, while rummaging in the bodies of dead people, he had taken thin sections from their hearts, brains, and sex glands. Studying them under a microscope, he had noticed faint traces of some unknown substance on the sections. Afterward, testing those almost exhausted traces for chemical reactivity, electroconductivity, and photosensitivity, he had discovered that the unknown substance possessed the pungent energy of life, but that it only occurred inside the dead. There wasn't any of it in the living. In the living, long before they passed away, stains of death accumulated. Sambikin had been perplexed for several years then, and even now his perplexity remained: the corpse, it turned out, was a reservoir of intense life under great pressure, if only for a short time. Investigating more carefully, and thinking about it almost constantly, he reached the conclusion that at the moment of death a sort of secret sluice opens up in a person's body, and from it a special fluid flows through the organism, a fluid that is toxic to dead matter and washes away the remains of fatigue and is carefully retained all one's life, right up to the moment of ultimate peril. But where in the darkness, where in a person's bodily nooks, was that sluice that sparingly and reliably retained the last charge of life? Death, as it rushes through the body, breaks the seal on that extra, condensed life, so that it goes off inside the person for the last time like an unsuccessful shot and leaves vague traces on his dead heart . . . The fresh corpse is completely permeated with the traces of that secret substance, and every part of the dead person retains in itself creative strength for those who go on living. Sambikin proposed to transform the dead into a power that would sustain the longevity and health of the living. He understood the pristine character and potency of the primordial fluid that bathes a person's insides at the moment of his final breath. That fluid, when added to a living but enfeebled human being, was capable of rendering him straight, firm, and happy . . .

    Sartorius remained standing on the balcony a long time. Everything seemed unresolved and extraneous to him now. Alien people were riding down the street in the trolley, and the traffic noises and sound of conversation reached his hearing as if from far away. He listened to them without interest or curiosity, like someone sick and alone. He wanted to go home at once and lie down under a blanket and warm his sudden pain so that it would pass away by morning when it was time to go to work again.

Behind him his peers were enjoying both the consciousness of their success and their future technical dream. Muldbauer was talking about an atmospheric stratum somewhere between fifty and a hundred kilometers above the earth, where the electromagnetic, light, and temperature conditions are such that any living organism would not only not tire and die but would in fact be capable of everlasting existence in the middle of violet space. That was the "Heaven" of the ancients, and it will be the happy country of the men of the future: beyond the distant reaches of low-spreading foul weather there really is a blessed country. Muldbauer was predicting the imminent conquest of the stratosphere and the subsequent penetration of the dark blue altitudes of the world where the airborne country of immortality lies. Then man will take wing, and the earth will become the legacy of the animals and once again and forevermore will be covered with dense forests of primeval virginity. "And the animals have a presentiment of it!" Muldbauer said with conviction. "When I look in their eyes, it seems to me they are thinking, 'When will it all end, when will you finally leave us?' The animals are wondering when people will finally leave them alone so that they can follow their own destinies!"

Sartorius smiled a bored smile; he would have liked just then to remain in the very belly of the earth, even to take up residence in an empty grave, and live his life inseparably with Moscow Chestnova till death. Yet he would have been sorry to go away without a reply to those night stars that had gazed down at him since childhood, would have been sorry to be a nonparticipant in a communal life full of labor and a feeling of fellowship among people. He was afraid of mutely walking through the city with his head bent down concentrating on nothing but love, and he did not wish to grow indifferent to his desk crammed with ideas in draft form, or to the iron cot he lay on, or to his desk lamp, his patient witness in the darkness and silence of nights spent working . . . Sartorius rubbed his chest under his shirt and said to himself, "Go away, leave me alone again, foul element! I am a simple engineer and rationalist, I repudiate you, as I do womankind and love . . . Better for me to bow down before atomic dust and the electron!" But the world that was spread out before him in the form of noise and light was already beginning to grow still and to pass beyond the dark threshold of his heart, leaving alive behind it only the single most touching creature in the world. Could he really reject that creature in order to bow down to the atom, the dust particle, and ashes?

Moscow Chestnova came out to Sartorius on the balcony. She said to him with a smile, "Why are you so sad? Do you love me or not?"

She breathed the warmth of her smiling mouth on him, and her dress rustled, and Sartorius was seized by the boredom of spite and courage, and he replied, "No, I admire another Moscow—the city."

"Well, that's all right, then," Chestnova readily acquiesced. "Let's go have supper. Comrade Selin has eaten more than anybody else . . . He's completely stuffed and is sitting there flushed with eyes that are sad all the time. Do you happen to know why?"

"No," Sartorius quietly answered. "I'm sad myself."

Moscow peered through the darkness at his irregular face, down which tears were running from wide-open eyes.

"Better not to cry," Moscow said. "I love you too . . ."

"You're just saying that," Sartorius said, not believing her.

"No, it's true, absolutely true!" Chestnova exclaimed. "Let's go away from here right now . . ."

As they walked arm in arm among their celebrating friends, Sambikin gazed at them with eyes that had forgotten to blink and that were abstracted by reflection a long way from personal happiness. Near the exit Bozhko suddenly turned up in front of Chestnova and respectfully made a patient request of his own. Chestnova was so glad to see him that she grabbed a piece of cake from the table and treated him to it on the spot.

Bozhko now worked at the Trust for Industrial Weights and Measures and was utterly carried away by concern with weights and balances. He asked Moscow Ivanovna to introduce him to so famous an engineer, one who would be able to invent a simple and accurate balance that might be made at low cost for all the kolkhozes and sovkhozes and for the rest of Soviet commerce. Failing to notice Sartorius's melancholy, Bozhko informed them of the great untold disasters of the socialist economy, of the extra difficulties of socialism on the kolkhozes, of the deterioration of the standard workday, of kulak politics developed on the basis of the inaccuracy of weights, balances, and scales, and of the widespread, albeit involuntary, defrauding of working-class consumers in cooperatives and retail establishments . . . And all of it only because of the dilapidated condition of the state weighing inventory, its antiquated construction, and the shortage of metal and wood for the manufacture of new weighing machines.

"You'll excuse me for coming here in spite of myself," Bozhko said. "I realize I'm a bore. People were talking here, and I heard them, about how man will soon take to the air and be happy. I shall always listen to that sort of thing with pleasure, but there are a few things we need in the meantime . . . We need to weigh bread and flour accurately on the kolkhozes." Moscow smiled at him with the gentleness of her passing mood: "You are excellent, our very own Soviet man! Sartorius, go at once to their trust tomorrow and make them a blueprint for the cheapest, simplest balance—and let it be accurate!"

Sartorius grew thoughtful. "It's hard," he confessed. "It's easier to perfect a locomotive than a balance. Balances have been in use for thousands of years . . . It's the same as inventing a new water bucket. But I'll come to your trust and I'll help you if I can."

Bozhko gave him the address of his enterprise and happily set off for his room, where his usual task of international correspondence in Esperanto awaited him.

• • •

The enterprise was on the eve of liquidation. It took some time before Sartorius realized that what is intended for liquidation may sometimes prove to be not only durable but even doomed to perpetual existence. The enterprise was located in the Old Arcade on a mezzanine where goods vulnerable to dampness had once been kept. The stairway from the enterprise led down to the stone gallery that used to surround the old commercial courtyard. An iron sign had been placed on the door: REPUBLIC TRUST FOR BALANCES, WEIGHTS, AND MEASURES OF LENGTH—THE "STANDARD OF LABOR."

The headquarters of that half-forgotten and impoverished branch of heavy industry was a single large gloomy room with a low ceiling constructed in the form of an underground vault that reached so low at its edges that the employees sitting by the walls almost touched the ceiling with their heads. There were several desks in the room, each accommodating one or two people who wrote or did calculations on their abacuses. There were about thirty people, or at least no more than forty, although the noise of their work, their activity, questions, and exclamations, created the impression of an immense establishment of first-rate importance.

That same day Sartorius was given the position of engineer responsible for new weighing devices, and he took his seat at a flat desk opposite Victor Vasilievich Bozhko.

Thus his new life began. Over several nights Sartorius finished his final project at the Institute for Experimental Mechanical Engineering where he had been working, and then concentrated his attention on the oldest machine in the world, the balance. Nothing has changed so little in the course of the last five thousand years of history as the weighing machine. In the time of the Cyclopes, in ancient Greece and Carthage, in Persia destroyed under the blows of Alexander the Great—everywhere, in all times and in all places, the most universal and indispensable machine has been the balance. The balance is as old as the weapon, and it may be that they were once the same thing, the battle sword having been placed with its center on the point of a rock for use as a balance in the fair distribution of the spoils of victory.

Bozhko, unable to work without loving with his whole mind and heart the object of labor entrusted to him, expounded to Sartorius on the decisive importance of the balance in the life of mankind.

"The late Dimitri Ivanovich Mendeleev," he said, "cared more about balances than about anything else! Even more than about his periodic table of the elements. And why not? After all, the whole thing was based on the balance—the atomic weight and nothing else!"

Bozhko also knew why the weighing apparatus is the most inconspicuous and paltry of objects: because a person looks carefully only at what lies on top of it—at the sausage or bread—but he doesn't see what's underneath. Yet under that bread and sausage is the balance, the tool of honesty and justice, a simple, humble machine that counts and preserves the sacred bounty of socialism, measuring out nourishment for the worker and the collective farmer according to their creative labor and their need.

And with diligence and miserly concern for the crumbs of bread that fall by the wayside because of the inaccuracy of balances, Sartorius delved deep into his work. Hidden away from everyone else, two feelings came together within him and were conjoined—love for Moscow Chestnova and belief in the future of socialism. Pictured in his vague imagination were summer, the rye grown high, the voices of millions of people settled on the earth free for the first time of the burden of want and grief, and Moscow Chestnova coming toward him from far away to be his wife. She had been through life and experienced it along with countless other people, and had left the years of patient waiting and feeling behind in the darkness of youth now passed by. She was returning as the same person, only in a poor shift and barefoot, with her arms grown robust from work, and more cheerful and serene than she had been before. She had found contentment for her wandering heart . . .

The wandering heart! For a long time it trembles in a person from foreboding, wrung by the happenstance and calamity of everyday life, and at last it rushes forward, losing its warmth on cold and chilly roads.

Bent over his desk at the enterprise, Sartorius worked as quickly as possible on improving the construction of balances. The trust manager informed him of the danger of weight riots on the collective farms, as in the salt riots of the old days, for inadequate balances mean either a short weight of bread per workday ration, or else the issuance of extra bread, in which case there is a defrauding of the state. Moreover, the pan of the commercial balance, if that balance is inaccurate, may become an arena for kulak politics and class warfare. The weights problem is also fraught with danger—at many weighing stations, instead of using stamped weights, they have been putting awful trash like bricks and cast-iron bars on the balances, and in certain cases they have even seated pregnant women on them, paying out a workday ration for the hire of their bodies. All this will inevitably lead to the loss of hundreds of thousands of centners of grain.

Burning for Chestnova and afraid of remaining alone in his room, Sartorius sometimes spent the night at the enterprise. At

10:00 P.M. the watchman would take a preliminary nap in the chair by the doorway and then go into the manager's plywood office and lay himself down in the latter's soft armchair. The time passed on the big official clock, the empty desks called forth a yearning for their absent occupants, and sometimes mice came out to gaze at Sartorius with timid eyes.

 He sat alone working on the same problem that Archimedes, and later Mendeleev, had once pondered. The problem would not yield to him, however; the balance was fine as it stood, even though another and better one was needed that would use less metal in its manufacture. Sartorius covered whole sheets of paper with calculations of prisms, levers, and deformation tensions, with material costs, and with all sorts of other data as well. Suddenly tears spilled from his eyes of their own accord and began rolling down his face, and he was astonished by that phenomenon. Deep inside in his body lived something like a separate animal, and it was silently weeping, taking no interest in the weights and measures industry. After midnight, when the fragrance of distant plants and fresh wide-open spaces wafted over the entire city and came through the ventilation window in a wave, Sartorius, losing the thread of his meditations, would lay his head down on his desk. Chestnova had once given off that same fragrance of nature and goodness in his presence. He was not jealous of her now: let her eat well and in abundance, avoid sickness, be happy, love those who pass through her life, and then sleep somewhere in warmth and without remembering any sort of misfortune.

 Once or twice in the night the phone would suddenly ring, and then Sartorius would hasten to pick it up and listen, but it wasn't for him. It was a wrong number, and the other person would apologize and disappear into the silence forever. Of Sartorius's many friends, none knew where he had gone; he had long since abandoned the great road of technology and had forgotten about his fame as a mechanical engineer, which could have been worldwide.

 Once Sambikin came by to see him at home. The surgeon told Sartorius that the spinal cord in man possesses a certain capacity for rational reflection, so that it is not only the brain in the head that is able to think. Sambikin had recently verified this assumption in regard to a certain child on whom he had performed a secondary cranial trepanation. He had been forced to ablate.

"What's so wonderful about that?" Sartorius said without joy.

"It's the basic secret of life, and in particular the secret of the whole human being," Sambikin said thoughtfully. "It used to be claimed that the spinal cord works only for the sake of the heart and the purely organic functions, whereas the brain is the higher coordinating center . . . That's wrong: the spinal cord is capable of thought, and the brain takes part in the simplest instinctive processes . . ."

Sambikin was pleased with his discovery. He still believed that in one go you could ascend the mountain where time and space would become visible to man's usually gray gaze. Sartorius smiled a bit at Sambikin's naïveté: nature, by his reckoning, was more difficult than such a momentary victory implied and could not be confined in a single law.

"Well, what's next?" Sartorius asked.

Sambikin's entrails started to gurgle from the noise of his higher experiences.

"Here's what's next . . . It has to be experimentally checked a thousand more times. But it's entirely possible that it will turn out that the secret of life is to be found in man's dual consciousness. We always think two thoughts straightaway and are unable to think just one! After all, we have two organs for one object! They each think in opposite directions, although in regard to the same subject . . . This could be the basis, you realize, of a truly scientific, dialectical psychology, which doesn't yet exist in the world. The fact that the human being is capable of dual thought on every question has made him the best animal on earth . . ."

"What about the other animals?" Sartorius asked. "Don't they have heads and spines too?"

"True. But there's a trifling difference, although that difference has decided world history. It was necessary to get used to coordinating, to combining in a single impulse two thoughts, one coming up out of the earth itself, from the depths of one's bones, and the other coming down from the heights of the cranium. It was necessary for them to come together in a single instant and fall wave upon wave, each resonating with the other . . . Whereas with the animals, which also have two thoughts arising in response to each impression, those thoughts proceed separately and don't come together in a single stroke. That's where the secret of man's evolution lies, that's why he has outdistanced all the other animals! He took something almost as if it were nothing: he managed to train two feelings, two dark currents, to come together and to measure their strength against each other . . . And in coming together, they were transformed into human thought. Obviously, that nothing was imperceptible . . . Animals might have those states too, but rarely and accidentally. But man was cultivated by that event; he became a dual being . . . And sometimes in illness, in misfortune, in love, in terrible dreams, in anything, in fact, remote from the norm, we clearly sense that there are two of us: that is, I'm one person, there's somebody else in me as well. That somebody, that secret 'he,' frequently murmurs, occasionally weeps, wants to leave you for somewhere far away—he's bored, he's afraid . . . We become aware that there are two of us, and we're sick of each other. We sense a lightness, a freedom, the thought-free heaven of the animal, when our consciousness wasn't dual but unitary. A single instant separates us from the animals when we lose the duality of our consciousness, and very often we reside in the Archeozoic era, without understanding the meaning of it . . . But then our two consciousnesses are linked together once again, and once again we become people in the embrace of our 'equivocal' thought, and nature, organized on the principle of poor singularity, gnashes its teeth and draws away from the action of those terrible dual mechanisms that it did not give birth to but that came into being on their own . . . How awful it is for me to be alone now! That perpetual copulation of two passions that's heating my brain . . ."

Sambikin, who obviously hadn't slept for a long time, nor eaten, grew faint and sat down in despair.

Sartorius treated him to some canned meat and vodka. Gradually they both calmed down from weariness and fell asleep without undressing and with the electric light still on, while their hearts and minds continued to stir in a muffled way within them, hurrying to work through at their own pace their usual feelings and global tasks.

Midnight had already chimed on Spassky Tower and the music of the Internationale had long since fallen silent. Soon it would be dawn, and foreseeing it, the most delicate birds, those least given to visiting, began to rustle in the bushes and cultivated gardens, and then they rose up and flew off, departing that country where summer was already beginning to cool.

When daybreak came and the streetlights had turned yellow, lanky Sambikin and little Sartorius were still asleep on the same couch and breathing noisily like hollow men. Though hampered by sleep, their concern about the final arrangement of the world still gnawed at their consciences, and from time to time they muttered aloud in order to drive their disquiet away. Where was Moscow Chestnova, where was she sleeping now, what summer of life was she seeking for herself at the beginning of autumn, leaving her friends to wait behind?

Close to waking, Sartorius smiled. Timid in character, he felt as if he had died and been buried in the earth, in deep warmth, while up above, on the daylight surface of his tomb, only Moscow Chestnova was left to weep for him. There wasn't anybody else; he had died anonymously, like someone who really had completed all his tasks: the republic was now glutted with balances, and the whole arithmetical calculation of future historical time had been worked out, so that fate had been rendered harmless and would never again reach the point of despair.

He woke up satisfied and full of resolve to make and bring to perfection a whole technical support system that would automatically pump over to the human body from nature the basic everyday strength of nourishment. But from remembering Moscow, his eyes had already lost their morning luster, and from fear of suffering he woke up Sambikin.

"Sambikin!" Sartorius asked. "You're a doctor, you know the whole reason for life, after all . . . Why does it last so long, and how may it be consoled or made happy forever?"

"Sartorius!" Sambikin facetiously replied. "You're a mechanical engineer, you know what a vacuum is . . ."

"Well, of course: an emptiness into which something is drawn . . ."

"An emptiness," Sambikin said. "Come with me and I'll show you the cause of all life."

They went outside and set off on a trolley. Sartorius looked out the window and saw about a hundred thousand people or so, but nowhere did he see the face of Moscow Chestnova. She might even have died, since time moves on and accidents do happen.

They came to the surgical clinic of the Institute for Experimental Medicine.

"I'm dissecting four corpses today," Sambikin announced. "Three of us here are working on the same problem: to obtain a certain mysterious substance, the traces of which are found in every fresh corpse. That substance has great rejuvenating power for living but tired organisms. What it consists of is unknown! But we're trying to learn . . ."

Sambikin got ready the same way he usually did and then led Sartorius to the dissecting department. This was a large cold chamber where four dead people lay in boxes with ice between their double walls.

Sambikin's two assistants removed the body of a young woman from one of the boxes and placed it in front of the surgeon on a sloping table that looked like an enlarged musician's stand. The woman lay there with clear, wide-open eyes: the material of her eyes was so indifferent that it could shine even after death, at least until it decomposed. Sartorius started feeling bad. He resolved to run from the Institute back to his trust and appear before the trade union committee to ask for comradely assistance in dealing with the terror of his anguished heart.

"All right," Sambikin said, now ready for work, and gave Sartorius an explanation. "At the moment of death in the human body a last sluice opens up, although we have not been able to ascertain where. Behind that sluice, in some dark cranny of the organism, the final charge of life is sparingly and reliably retained. Nothing, save death, opens up that spring, that reservoir—it remains tightly sealed until the very moment of death . . . But I will find that cistern of immortality . . ."

"Look for it," Sartorius said.

Sambikin cut off the woman's left breast, removed the rib cage in its entirety, and then with extreme care proceeded to the heart. With the aid of his assistants, he removed it and, using special instruments, carefully transferred it to a glass cylinder for later investigation. The cylinder was then picked up and carried off to his laboratory.

"There are traces of the unknown secretion I was telling you about on this heart too," Sambikin informed his friend. "Death, as it rushes through the body, breaks the seal on that extra, condensed life, so that it goes off inside the person for the last time like an unsuccessful shot and leaves vague traces on his dead heart . . . But that substance is of the highest value by virtue of its energy. And it's odd: the most vital thing appears at the moment of final breath . . . Nature safeguards its measures well!"

After that Sambikin began turning the dead girl over, as if to show Sartorius how plump and chaste she was.

"She's good-looking," the surgeon muttered indistinctly. The thought passed through his mind of marrying the dead woman, a woman more beautiful, faithful, and lonely than many living women, and he carefully bandaged her ruined chest. "Now we'll have a look at the universal cause of life . . ."

Sambikin cut through the fatty membrane of the abdomen and then guided his scalpel along the intestine, revealing its contents: inside lay a compact column of still undigested food, but before long the food came to an end and the intestine was empty. Sambikin slowly passed through the section of emptiness until he reached the place where the excrement began, and there he stopped.

"You see!" Sambikin said, opening the empty section between the food and excrement wider. "The emptiness in the intestine draws all humanity into itself and moves world history. That's the soul. Take a sniff!"

Sartorius sniffed it. "It's all right," he said. "We'll fill that emptiness; then something else will become the soul."

"But what?" Sambikin smiled.

"I don't know what," Sartorius answered, feeling a pitiful humiliation. "First we need to feed people so they won't be drawn into that intestinal emptiness . . ."

"Without a soul, you can't feed anybody else or eat your own fill," Sambikin objected in a bored tone. "You can't do anything."

Sartorius bent over the entrails of the corpse where the empty human soul was located in the intestine . . . He touched the remnant of food and excrement with his fingers and carefully examined the poor, cramped arrangement of the whole body, and then he said, "This really is the best, the most ordinary soul. There isn't any other anywhere."

The engineer turned toward the exit from the department of corpses. He stooped low and went out, feeling Sambikin's grin behind him. He was saddened by the grief and poverty of life, so pitiful that it had to be almost continually distracted by illusion from awareness of its true condition. Even Sambikin seeks illusions in his thoughts and discoveries—he too is carried away by the complexity and great essence of the world in his imagination. But Sartorius saw that more than anything else the world consists of hapless matter it is virtually impossible to love but that must be understood.

Translated by Judson Rosengrant

Though praised by Ernest Hemingway and a few others, the work of Andrei Platonov has never received much attention in the United States. In his native Russia, however, Platonov is ranked among the very greatest writers. Although he was a Communist, Platonov ran afoul of the Soviet literary establishment from the beginning: the precepts of socialist realism do not govern either his style—a strange fusion of literary and spoken Russian, with a generous admixture of ideological jargon—or his subject matter, which emphasizes the disparity between Communism's utopian goals and the harsh reality of people's lives. Platonov was accused of pessimism, nihilism, petit bourgeois psychology, and other sins—in the margin of his story "Profit," printed in *Krasnaya Nov* in 1931, Stalin scrawled, in red pencil, the word "Scum!"—and for long periods was unable to publish at all. After the Second World War, in which he served as a war correspondent, he effectively gave up writing. At his death much of his work remained unpublished, including the remarkable novels *The Foundation Pit* and *Chevengur,* and the novel from which the preceding extract is drawn, *Shchastlivaia Moskva* [*Happy Moscow*].

Less a novel than, in the words of its translator, Judson Rosengrant, "a savage allegorical fantasy," *Happy Moscow* has little plot in the usual sense. Its central figure is Moscow Chestnova, a sexually vibrant young orphan, unfocused and impulsive, around whom the other characters revolve; the novel's thirteen chapters (two of which are translated here) portray their musings and interactions as they attempt to construct a meaningful life in the new Soviet world.

Over the last three decades, much of Platonov's writing has begun to see the light of day in what was until recently the Soviet Union. In the fall of 1991, the magazine *Novyi Mir* published *Happy Moscow* in its entirety. This excerpt is the first translation of any part of it into any language.

RODNEY JONES

Shame the Monsters

It is good, after all, to pause and lick one's genitalia
To hunch one's shoulders and gag, regurgitating lunch,
To mark one's curb and grass, to bay when the future beckons
      from the nose,
Not to exhaust so much of the present staring into the flat face
      of a machine,
Not to spend so much of the logic and the voice articulating a complex whimper
      of submission,
But to run with a full stomach under the sun, to play in the simple water
      and to wallow oneself dry in the leaves,
To take the teeth in the neck, if it comes to that,
If it comes to little and lean and silent, to take the position of the stone,
      even to hide under the stone,
But not to ride up the spine of the building with the acid scalding
      the gut,
Not to sit at a long table, wondering
How not to howl when the tall one again personifies the organization,
Speaking of the customs in remote precincts and the manufacture
      of weapons there,
Or the near Edens where the pitted balls fly over the tonsured lawns.

Dear mammals, help me, the argument with flesh is too fierce
      if it outrides time
And shocks numb the stubborn, beautiful muscles of the heart.
See, in the memorial gardens, how even the cry struggles in its trap
      under that black hat like a flower.
In the long rows of tombstones, the ones who were eaten betray nothing
      of the fear that brought them.

And it was their silence that marked them, day after oathless day
      until they were covered by the silent lawns.
Better to take the mud in the hands and holler for no reason,
      to praise the strange
Alchemy of mud and rain: there is sex; there is food.
It is good to say anything in the spirit of hair and breasts
      and warm blood,
And not to deny the private knowledge, not to wonder how
      not to speak of death,
And not to deny the knowledge of death, not to invent the silence,
Not to wonder how not to say the words of love.

MARTIN DUBERMAN

The Night They Raided Stonewall

Most of the employees at the Stonewall Inn in Greenwich Village, and some of the customers, did drugs, primarily "uppers." Desbutal—a mix of Desoxyn and Nembutal—was a great favorite (though later banned by the FDA), and the bar was also known as a good place to buy acid. The chief supplier was Maggie Jiggs, a famous drag queen who worked the main bar at Stonewall, along with her partner, Tommy Long. (Tommy kept a toy duck on the bar that quacked whenever someone left a tip.) They were a well-known team with a big following. Maggie, blond, chubby, and loud, knew everybody's business and would think nothing of yelling out in the middle of the crowded bar, "Hey, girl, I hear you got a whole new plate of false teeth from that fabulous dentist you been fucking!" But Maggie loved people, had good drugs, was always surrounded with gorgeous men, and arranged wonderful three-ways, so her outspokenness and even her occasional thievery were (usually) forgiven.

Maggie and Tommy were stationed behind the main bar, one of two bars in the Stonewall. But before you could get to it, you had to pass muster at the door (a ritual some of the customers welcomed as a relief from the lax security that characterized most gay bars). That usually meant inspection, through a peephole in the heavy front door, by Ed Murphy, "Bobby Shades," or muscular Frank Esselourne. "Blond Frankie," as he was known, was gay, but in those years not advertising it, and was famous for being able to spot straights or undercover cops with a single glance.

If you got the okay at the door—and for underage street kids that was always problematic—you moved a few steps to a table, usually covered by members of what one wag called the "Junior Achievement Mafia" team. That could mean, on different nights, two of the co-owners, Zucchi and Mario; Ernie Sgroi, who always wore a suit and tie and whose father had started the famed Bon Soir on 8th Street; "Vito," who was on salary directly from another co-owner, "Fat Tony" Lauria, and was hugely proud of his personal collection of S.S. uniforms and Nazi flags (he made bombs on the side); or "Tony the Sniff" Verra, who had a legendary nose for no-goods and kept a baseball bat behind the door to deal with them. At the table, you had to plunk down three dollars (one dollar on weekdays), for which you got two tickets that could be exchanged for two watered-down drinks. (According to Chuck Shaheen, *all* drinks were watered, even those carrying the fanciest labels.) You then signed your name in a book kept to prove, should the question arise in court, that Stonewall was indeed a private "bottle club." People rarely signed their real names: "Judy Garland," "Donald Duck," and "Elizabeth Taylor" were the popular favorites.

Once inside Stonewall, you took a step down and straight in front of you was the main bar, where Maggie held court. Behind the bar some pulsating gel lights went on and off—later exaggeratedly claimed by some to be the precursor of the innovative light shows at The Sanctuary and other gay discos that followed. On weekends, a scantily clad go-go boy with a pin spot on him danced in a gilded cage on top of the bar. Straight ahead, beyond the bar, was a spacious dancing area—at one point in the bar's history lit only with black lights. That in itself became a subject for camp, because the queens, with Murine in their eyes, all looked as if they had white streaks running down their faces. Should the police (known as "Lily Law," "Alice Blue Gown"—"Alice" for short—or "Betty Badge") or a suspected plainclothesman unexpectedly arrive, white bulbs instantly came on in the dance area, signaling everyone to stop dancing or touching.

The queens rarely hung out at the main bar. There was another, smaller room off to one side, with a stone wishing well in the middle, its own jukebox and service bar, and booths, that became headquarters for the more flamboyant contingent among Stonewall's melting pot of customers. There were the "scare drag queens" like Tommy Lanigan-Schmidt, Birdie Rivera, and Martin Boyce—"boys who looked like girls but who you knew were boys." And there were the "flame" (not "drag") queens who wore eye makeup and teased hair but essentially dressed in male clothes—if an effeminate version with fluffy sweaters and Tom Jones shirts.

Only a few full-time transvestites, like Tiffany, Spanola Jerry (a hairdresser from Sheepshead Bay), and Tammy Novak (who performed at the Eighty Two Club), were allowed to enter Stonewall in drag. (Tammy sometimes transgressed by dressing as a boy.) Not even "Tish" (Joe Tish), who regularly changed back into men's clothes after a performance, would be admitted in drag, though he had been a well-known drag performer since the early fifties and in the late sixties had a long-running show at the Crazy Horse, a nearby café on Bleecker Street. Tish *was* admitted into some uptown straight clubs in full drag; there, as he sniffily put it, his "artistry" was recognized.

The queens considered Stonewall and Washington Square the most congenial downtown bars. If they passed muster at the Stonewall door, they could buy or cajole drinks, exchange cosmetics and the favored Tabu or Ambush perfumes, admire or deplore somebody's latest Kanecalon wig, make fun of six-foot transsexual Lynn's size-twelve women's shoes (while admiring her fishnet stockings and miniskirts and giggling over her tales of servicing the firemen around the corner at the 10th Street station), move constantly in and out of the ladies room (where they deplored the fact that a single red light bulb made the application of makeup difficult), and dance in a feverish sweat till closing time at 4:00 A.M.

The jukebox on the dance floor played a variety of songs, even an occasional "Smoke Gets in Your Eyes" to appease the romantics. The Motown label was still top of the heap in the summer of 1969, and three of the five hit singles for the week of June 28—by Marvin Gaye, Junior Walker, and the Temptations—carried its imprint. On the pop side, the Stonewall jukebox played the "Love Theme" from *Romeo and Juliet* over and over, the record's saccharine periodically cut by the Beatles' "Get Back" or Elvis Presley's

"In the Ghetto." And all the new dances—the Boston Jerk, the Monkey, the Spider—were tried out with relish. If the crowd was in a particularly campy mood (and the management was feeling loose enough), ten or fifteen dancers would line up to learn the latest ritual steps, beginning with a shouted "Hit it, girls!"

The chinos-and-penny-loafer crowd pretty much stayed near the main bar, fraternizing with the queens, if at all, mostly on the dance floor. ("Two queens can't bump pussy," one of them explained. "And I don't care how beefy and brawny the pussy is. And certainly not for a relationship.") The age range at Stonewall was mostly late teens to early thirties; the over-thirty-five crowd hung out at Julius', and the leather crowd (then in its infancy) at Keller's. There could also be seen at Stonewall just a sprinkling of the new kind of gay man beginning to emerge—the hippie: long-haired, bell-bottomed, laid back, and likely to have "weird," radical views.

Very few women ever appeared in Stonewall. Sascha L. flatly declares that he can't remember *any*, except for the occasional "fag hag" (like Blond Frankie's straight friend Lucille, who lived with the doorman at One-Two-Three and hung out at Stonewall) or "one or two dykes who looked almost like boys." But Chuck Shaheen, who spent much more time at Stonewall, remembers— while acknowledging that the bar was "98 percent male"—a few more lesbian customers than Sascha does, and, of those, a number who were decidedly "femme." One of the lesbians who did go to Stonewall "a few times," tagging along with some of her gay male friends, recalls that she "felt like a visitor." It wasn't as if the male patrons went out of their way to make her feel uncomfortable, but rather that the territory was theirs, not hers. "There didn't seem to be hostility, but there didn't seem to be camaraderie."

• • •

"Sylvia" Ray Riviera had been invited to Marsha P. Johnson's birthday party on June 27, 1969, but she decided not to go. It's not that she was mad at Marsha; she simply felt strung out. She had been working as an accounting clerk in a Jersey City chain-store warehouse, keeping tally sheets of what the truckers took out—a good job with a good boss who let her wear makeup whenever she felt like it. But it was an eleven-to-seven shift, Sundays through Thursdays, all-night stints that kept her away from her friends on the street and decidedly short of the cash she had made from hustling.

Yes, she wanted to clean up her act and start leading a "normal" life. But she hadn't counted on missing the money so much, or on her drug habit persisting—and sixty-seven dollars a week in take-home pay just wasn't doing it. So she and her lover, Gary, decided to piece out their income with a side gig—passing bad checks—and on June 27 they had just gotten back from papering Washington, D.C. The first news they heard on returning was of Judy Garland's funeral that very day: how twenty thousand people had waited up to four hours in the blistering heat to view her body at Frank E. Campbell's Funeral Home on Madison Avenue and 81st Street. The news sent a melodramatic shiver up Sylvia's spine, and she decided to become "completely hysterical." "It's the end of an era," she tearfully announced. "The greatest singer, the greatest actress of my childhood is no more. Never again 'Over the Rainbow,'"—here Sylvia sobbed loudly—"no one left to look up to."

No, she was not going to Marsha's party. She would stay home, light her consoling religious candles (her grandmother, Viejita, had taught her that much), and say a few prayers for Judy. But then the phone rang, and her buddy Tammy Novak—who sounded more stoned than usual—*insisted* that Sylvia and Gary join her later that night at Stonewall. Sylvia hesitated. If she were going out at all—"Was it all right to dance with the martyred Judy not cold in her grave?"—she would go to her favorite, Washington Square. She had never been crazy about Stonewall, she reminded Tammy: Men in makeup were tolerated there, but not exactly cherished. And if she were going to go out, she wanted to *vent*—to be just as outrageous, as grief-stricken, as makeup would allow. But Tammy absolutely *refused* to take no for an answer and so Sylvia, moaning theatrically, gave in. She popped a Black Beauty, and she and Gary headed downtown.

Jim Fouratt's job at CBS required long hours, and he often got back to his apartment (after a stopover at Max's Kansas City) in the early morning. On the night of June 27 he had worked in the office until midnight, had gone for a nightcap at Max's, and about 1:00 A.M. had headed back to his apartment in the Village. Passing by the Stonewall Inn—a bar he despised, insisting it was a haven for marauding chicken hawks—Jim noticed a cluster of cops in front of the bar, looking as if they were about to enter. He shrugged it off as just another routine raid and even found himself hoping that *this* time (Stonewall had been raided just two weeks before) the police would succeed in closing the joint.

But as Jim got closer, he could see that a small group of onlookers had gathered. That was somewhat surprising, since the first sign of a raid usually led to an immediate scattering; typically, gays fled rather than loitered, and fled as quietly and as quickly as possible, grateful not to be implicated at the scene of the "crime." Jim spotted Craig Rodwell at the top of the row of steps leading up to a brownstone adjacent to the Stonewall Inn. Something was decidedly in the air.

Craig had taken up his position only moments before. Like Jim, he had been on his way home—from playing cards at a friend's—and had stumbled on the gathering crowd in front of the Stonewall. He was with Fred Sergeant, his current lover, and the two of them had scrambled up the brownstone steps to get a better view. The crowd was decidedly small, but what was riveting was its strangely quiet, expectant air, as if awaiting the next development. Just then, the police pushed open the front door of the Stonewall and marched in. Craig looked at his watch: it was 1:20 A.M.

Sylvia was feeling *very* little pain. The Black Beauty had hopped her up and the scotch had smoothed her out. Her lover, Gary, had come along; Tammy, Bambi, and Ivan were there; and rumor had it that Marsha Johnson, disgusted at all the no-shows for her birthday, was also headed downtown to Stonewall, determined to party *somewhere*. It looked like a good night. Sylvia expansively decided she did like Stonewall after all, and was just saying that to Tammy, who looked as if she were about to keel over—"that chile [Tammy was seventeen, Sylvia eighteen] could not control her intake"—when the cops came barreling through the front door. (The white warning lights had earlier started flashing on the dance floor, but Sylvia and her friends had been oblivious.)

The next thing she knew, the cops, with their usual arrogance, were stomping through, ordering the patrons to line up and get their IDs ready for examination. "Oh my God!" Sylvia shouted at Gary. "I didn't bring my ID!" Before she could panic, Gary reached in his pocket and produced her card—he had brought it along. "Praise be to Saint Barbara!" Sylvia shrieked, snatching the precious ID. If the raid went according to the usual pattern, the only people arrested would be those without IDs, those dressed in the clothes of the opposite gender, and some or all of the employees. Everyone else would be let go with a few shoves and a few contemptuous words. The bar would soon reopen, and they would all be back dancing. It was annoying to have one's Friday night screwed up, but it was hardly unprecedented.

Sylvia tried to take it in stride; she'd been through lots worse, and with her ID in hand and nothing more than makeup on, she knew the hassling would be minimal. But she was pissed; the good high she'd had was gone, and her nerve ends felt as raw as when she had been crying over Judy earlier in the evening. She wished she'd gone to the Washington Square, a place she preferred anyway. She was sick of being treated like scum: "I was just not in the mood," was how she later put it. "It had got to the point where I didn't want to be bothered anymore." When one of the cops grabbed the ID out of her hand and asked her with a smirk if she was a boy or a girl, she almost swung at him, but Gary grabbed her hand in time. The cop gave her a shove toward the door and told her to get the hell out.

Not all of the two hundred or so people who were inside Stonewall fared that well. Chico, a forty-five-year-old patron who looked sixty, was arrested for not having an ID proving he was over eighteen. Another patron, asked for "some kind of ID, like a birth certificate," said to the cop, "I don't happen to carry mine around with me. Do you have yours, Officer?" The cop arrested him. Eighteen-year-old Joey Dey had been dancing for a while with a guy in a suit but had decided he wasn't interested and had tried to get away; the man had insisted they go on dancing and then, just as the police came through the door, pulled out a badge and told him he was under arrest.

Harry Beard, one of the dance-floor waiters, had been coming off a ten-day amphetamine run and was crashed out in one of the side-room booths when the police arrived. He knew that the only way to avoid arrest was to pretend he was a customer, so he grabbed a drink off the bar, crossed his legs provocatively, and tried to act unconcerned. Fortunately for him, he had gone into one of the new unisex shops that very day and was wearing a soft pink blouse with ruffles around the wrists and down the front. One of the cops looked at him quizzically and said, "I know you. You work here." Harry was on welfare at the time, so, adopting his nelliest tone, he thrust his welfare card at the cop and replied, "Work here? Oh, don't be silly! I'm just a poor girl on welfare. Here's my welfare card. Besides, I wouldn't work in a toilet like this!" The cop looked skeptical but told Harry he could leave.

The Stonewall management had always been tipped off by the police before a raid was due to take place—this happened, on average, once a month—and the raid itself was usually staged early enough in the evening to produce minimal commotion and allow for a quick reopening. (Indeed, sometimes the "raid" consisted of little more than the police striding arrogantly through the bar and then leaving, with no arrests made.) Given the size of the weekly payoff, the police had an understandable stake in keeping the golden calf alive.

But this raid was different. It was carried out by eight detectives from the First Division (only one of them in uniform), and the Sixth Precinct had been asked to participate only at the last possible second. Moreover, the raid had occurred at 1:20 A.M.—the height of the merriment—and with no advance warning to the Stonewall management. (Chuck Shaheen recalls some vague tipoff that a raid *might* happen, but since the early-evening hours had passed without incident, the management had dismissed the tip as inaccurate.)

There have been an abundance of theories as to why the Sixth Precinct failed on this occasion to alert Stonewall's owners. One centers on the possibility that a payment had not been made on time or made at all. Another suggests that the extent of Stonewall's profits had recently become known to the police, and the Sixth Precinct brass had decided, as prelude to its demand for a larger cut, to flex a little muscle. Yet a third explanation points to the possibility that the new commanding officer at the precinct was out of sympathy with payoffs, or hadn't yet learned how profitable they could be.

But evidence has surfaced to suggest that the machinations of

the Sixth Precinct were in fact incidental to the raid. Ryder Fitzgerald, a sometime carpenter who had helped remodel the Stonewall interior and whose friends Willis and Elf (a straight hippie couple) lived rent-free in the apartment above Stonewall in exchange for performing caretaker chores, was privy the day after the raid to a revealing conversation. Ernie, one of Stonewall's Mafia team, stormed around Willis and Elf's apartment, cursing out the Sixth Precinct (in Ryder's presence) for having failed to provide warning in time. And in the course of his tirade, Ernie revealed that the raid had been inspired by federal agents. The Bureau of Alcohol, Tobacco and Firearms (BATF) had apparently discovered that the liquor bottles used at Stonewall had no federal stamps on them—which meant they had been hijacked or bootlegged straight out of the distillery. Putting Stonewall under surveillance, BATF had then discovered the bar's corrupt alliance with the Sixth Precinct. Thus, when the Feds decided to launch a raid on Stonewall, they deliberately kept the local police in the dark until the unavoidable last minute.

When the raid, contrary to expectations, did get going, the

previous systems put into place by the Mafia owners stood them in good stead. The strong front door bought needed time until the white lights had a chance to do their warning work: patrons instantly stopped dancing and touching; the bartenders took the money from the cigar boxes that served as a kind of cash register, jumped from behind the bar, and mingled inconspicuously with the customers. Maggie Jiggs, already known for her "two for the bar, one for myself" approach to cash, disappeared into the crowd with a cigar box full of money; when a cop asked to see the contents, Maggie said it contained her tips as a "cigarette girl," and they let her go. When later questioned by her employers, Maggie claimed that the cop had taken the box and the money. She got away with the lie.

The standard Mafia policy of putting gay employees on the door so they could take the heat while everyone else got their act together, also paid off for the owners. Eddie Murphy managed to get out ("of course," his detractors add, "he was on the police payroll"), but Blond Frankie was arrested. There was already a warrant outstanding for Frankie's arrest (purportedly for homicide—he was known for "acting first and not bothering to think even later"). Realizing that this was no ordinary raid, that this time an arrest might not merely mean detention for a few hours at Centre Street followed by a quick release, Frankie was determined not to be taken in. The owners, Zucchi and Mario, escaped through a back door connected to the office and were soon safely out on the street in front of the Stonewall. So, too, were almost all of the bar's customers, released after their IDs had been checked and their attire deemed "appropriate" to their gender—a process accompanied, as in Sylvia's case, by derisive, ugly police banter.

As for Fat Tony, at the time the raid took place he had still not left his apartment on Waverly Place, a few blocks from the Stonewall. Under the spell of methamphetamine, he had already spent three hours recombing his beard and agitatedly changing from one outfit to another, acting for all the world like one of those "demented queens" he vilified. He and Chuck Shaheen could see the commotion from their apartment window, but only after an emergency call from Zucchi could Tony be persuaded to leave the apartment for the bar.

Some of the campier patrons, emerging one by one from the

Stonewall to find an unexpected crowd, took the opportunity to strike instant poses, starlet-style, while the onlookers whistled and shouted their applause-meter ratings. But when a paddy wagon pulled up, the mood turned more somber. And it grew sullen when the police officers started to emerge from Stonewall with prisoners in tow and moved with them toward the waiting van. Jim Fouratt at the back of the crowd, Sylvia standing with Gary near the small park across the street from Stonewall, and Craig perched on top of the crowd—all sensed something unusual in the air, all felt a kind of tensed expectancy.

The police (two of whom were women) were oblivious to it initially. Everything up to that point had gone so routinely that they expected to see the crowd quickly disperse. Instead, a few people started to boo, and others pressed against the waiting van, while the cops standing near it yelled angrily for the crowd to move back. According to Sylvia, "you could feel the electricity going through people. You could actually feel it. People were getting really, really pissed and uptight." A guy in a dark red T-shirt danced in and out of the crowd, shouting "Nobody's gonna fuck with me!" and "Ain't gonna take this shit!"

As the cops started loading their prisoners into the van—among them, Blond Frankie, the doorman—more people joined in the shouting. Sylvia spotted Tammy Novak among the three queens lined up for the paddy wagon, and along with others in the crowd started yelling "Tammy! Tammy!"—Sylvia's shriek rising above the rest. But Tammy apparently didn't hear, and Sylvia guessed that she was too stoned to know what was going on. Yet when a cop shoved Tammy and told her to "Keep moving! Keep moving!" as he poked her with his club, Tammy told him to stop pushing, and when he didn't, she started swinging. From that point on, so much happened so quickly as to seem simultaneous.

Jim Fouratt insists that *the* explosive moment came when "a dyke dressed in men's clothing," who had been visiting a male employee inside the bar, started to act up as the cops moved her toward the paddy wagon. According to Jim, "the queens were acting like queens, throwing their change and giving lots of attitude and lip. But the dyke had to be more butch than the queens. So when the police moved her into the wagon, she got out the other side and started to rock it."

Harry Beard, the Stonewall waiter who had been inside the bar, partly corroborates Jim's account, though differing on the moment of explosion. According to Beard, the cops had arrested the cross-dressed lesbian inside the bar for not wearing the requisite three pieces of clothing "appropriate to one's gender" mandated by Section 887(7) of the New York Code of Criminal Procedure. As they led her out of the bar, so Beard's version goes, she complained that the handcuffs they had put on her were too tight; in response, one of the cops slapped her in the head with his nightstick. Seeing the cops hit her, people standing immediately outside the door started throwing coins at the police.

But Craig Rodwell and a number of other eyewitnesses sharply contest the view that the arrest of a lesbian was the precipitating incident, or even that a lesbian had been present in the bar. And they skeptically ask why, if she did exist, she has never stepped forward to claim credit; to the answer that she may long since have died, they sardonically reply, "And she never told another soul? And if she did, why haven't *they* stepped forward to claim credit for her?" As if all that isn't muddle enough, those eyewitnesses who deny the lesbian claimant themselves divide over whether to give the palm to a queen—Tammy Novak being the leading candidate—or to one of the many ordinary gay male patrons of the bar. Craig Rodwell's view probably comes as close as we are likely to get to the truth: "A number of incidents were happening simultaneously. There was no one thing that happened or one person, there was just . . . a flash of group—of mass—anger."

As the police, amid a growing crowd and mounting anger, continued to load prisoners into the van, Martin Boyce, an eighteen-year-old scare drag queen, saw a leg in nylons and sporting a high heel shoot out from the back of the paddy wagon into the chest of a cop, throwing him backward. Another queen then opened the door on the side of the wagon and jumped out. The cops chased and caught her, but Blond Frankie quickly managed to engineer another escape from the van; several queens successfully made their way out with him and were swallowed up in the crowd. Tammy Novak was one of them; she ran all the way to Joe Tish's apartment, where she holed up throughout the weekend. The police handcuffed subsequent prisoners to the inside of the van and succeeded in driving away from the scene to book them at the precinct house. Deputy Inspector Seymour Pine, the ranking officer, nervously told departing police to "just drop them off at the Sixth Precinct and hurry back."

From this point on, the melee broke out in several directions and swiftly mounted in intensity. The crowd, now in full cry, started screaming epithets at the police: "Pigs! Faggot cops!" Sylvia and Craig enthusiastically joined in, Sylvia shouting her lungs out, Craig letting go with a full-throated "Gay Power!" One young gay Puerto Rican went fearlessly up to a policeman and yelled in his face, "What you got against faggots?! We don't do you nuthin'!" Another teenager started kicking at a cop, frequently missing as the cop held him at arm's length. One queen mashed an officer with her heel, knocked him down, grabbed his handcuff keys, freed herself, and passed the keys to another queen behind her.

By now the crowd had swelled to a mob, and people were picking up and throwing whatever loose objects came to hand: coins, bottles, cans, bricks from a nearby construction site. Someone even picked up dog shit from the street and threw it in the cops' direction. As the fever mounted, Zucchi was overheard nervously asking Mario what the hell the crowd was upset about: the Mafia or the police? The *police*, Mario reassured him. Zucchi gave a big grin of relief and decided to vent some stored-up anger of his own: he egged on bystanders in their effort to rip up a damaged fire hydrant, and he persuaded a young kid named Timmy to throw the wire-mesh garbage can nearby. Timmy was not much bigger than the can (and had just come out the weekend before), but he gave it his all—the can went sailing into the plate-glass window (painted black and reinforced from behind by plywood) that stretched across the front of the Stonewall.

Stunned and frightened by the crowd's unexpected fury, the police, at the order of Deputy Inspector Pine, retreated inside the bar. Pine had been accustomed to two or three cops being able to handle with ease any number of cowering gays, but here the crowd wasn't cowering; it had routed eight cops and made them run for cover. As Pine later said, "I had been in combat situations, [but] there was never any time that I felt more scared than then." With the cops holed up inside Stonewall, the crowd was now in control of the street, and it bellowed in triumph and long-repressed rage.

Craig dashed to a nearby phone booth. Ever conscious of the

need for publicity—for visibility—and realizing that a critical moment had arrived, he called all three daily papers: the *Times*, the *Post*, and the *Daily News*, and alerted them that "a major news story was breaking." Then he ran to his apartment a few blocks away to get his camera.

Jim Fouratt also dashed to the phones—to call his straight, radical-left friends, to tell them that "people were fighting the cops—it was just like Newark!" He urged them to rush down and lend their support (as he had long done for *their* causes). Then he went into the nearby Ninth Circle and Julius' to try to get the patrons to come out into the street. But none of them would. Nor did any of his straight radical friends show up. It taught Jim a bitter lesson about how low on the scale of priorities his erstwhile comrades ranked "faggot" concerns.

Gary tried to persuade Sylvia to go home with him to get a change of clothes. "Are you nuts?!" she yelled. "I'm not missing a minute of this—it's the *revolution!*" So Gary left to get clothes for both of them. Blond Frankie, meanwhile—perhaps taking his cue from Zucchi—uprooted a loose parking meter and offered it for use as a battering ram against the Stonewall's door. At nearly the same moment somebody started squirting lighter fluid through the shattered glass window on the bar's facade, tossing in matches after it. Inspector Pine later referred to this as "throwing Molotov cocktails into the place," but the only reality *that* described was the inflamed state of Pine's nerves.

Still, the danger was very real, and the police were badly frightened. The shock to self-esteem had been stunning enough; now came an actual threat to physical safety. Dodging flying glass and missiles, Patrolman Gil Weisman, the one cop in uniform, was hit near the eye with a shard, and blood spurted out. With that, the fear turned abruptly to fury. Three of the cops, led by Pine, ran out the front door, which had caved in from the battering, and started screaming threats at the crowd, thinking to cow it. But instead a rain of coins and bottles came down, and a beer can glanced off Deputy Inspector Charles Smyth's head. Pine lunged into the crowd, grabbed somebody around the waist, pulled him back into the doorway, and then dragged him by the hair inside.

Ironically, the prisoner was the well-known—and heterosexual —folk singer Dave Van Ronk. Earlier that night Van Ronk had been in and out of the Lion's Head, a bar a few doors down from Stonewall that catered to a noisy, macho journalist crowd scornful of the "faggots" down the block. Once the riot got going, the Lion's Head locked its doors; the management didn't want faggots moaning and bleeding over the paying customers. As soon as Pine got Van Ronk back into the Stonewall, he angrily accused him of throwing dangerous objects—a cue to Patrolman Weisman to shout that Van Ronk was the one who had cut his eye and then to start punching the singer hard while several other cops held him down. When Van Ronk looked as if he were going to pass out, the police handcuffed him, and Pine snapped, "All right, we book him for assault."

The cops then found a fire hose, wedged it into a crack in the door, and directed the spray at the crowd, thinking that would certainly scatter it. But the stream was weak and the crowd howled derisively, while inside the cops started slipping on the wet floor. A reporter from *The Village Voice,* Howard Smith, had retreated inside the bar when the police did; he later wrote that by that point in the evening "the sound filtering in [didn't] suggest dancing faggots any more; it sound[ed] like a powerful rage bent on vendetta." By now the Stonewall's front door was hanging wide open, the plywood brace behind the windows was splintered, and it seemed only a matter of minutes before the howling mob would break in and wreak its vengeance. One cop armed himself with Tony the Sniff's baseball bat, the others drew their guns, and Pine stationed several officers on either side of the corridor leading to the front door. One of them growled, "We'll shoot the first motherfucker that comes through the door."

At that moment an arm reached in through the shattered window, squirted more lighter fluid into the room, and then threw in another lit match. This time the match caught, and there was a whoosh of flame. Standing only ten feet away, Pine aimed his gun at the receding arm and (he later said) was prepared to shoot when he heard the sound of sirens coming down Christopher Street. At 2:55 A.M. Pine had sent out emergency signal 10-41—a call for help to the fearsome Tactical Patrol Force—and relief was now rounding the corner.

The TPF was a highly trained, crack riot-control unit that had been set up to respond to the proliferation of protests against the Vietnam War. Wearing helmets with visors, carrying assorted weapons, including billy clubs and tear gas, its two dozen members all seemed massively proportioned. They were a formidable sight as, linked arm in arm, they came up Christopher Street in a wedge formation that suggested (by design) a Roman legion. In their path, the rioters slowly retreated but—contrary to police expectations—did not break and run. Craig, for one, knelt down in the middle of the street with the camera he'd retrieved from his apartment and, determined to capture the moment, snapped photo after photo of the oncoming TPF minions.

As the troopers bore down on him, he scampered up and joined the hundreds of others who scattered to avoid the billy clubs but then raced around the block, doubled back behind the troopers, and pelted them with debris. When the cops realized that a considerable crowd had simply re-formed to their rear, they flailed out angrily at anyone who came within striking distance. But the protesters would not be cowed. The pattern repeated itself several times: the TPF would disperse the jeering mob only to have it re-form behind them, yelling taunts, tossing bottles and bricks, setting fires in trash cans. When the police whirled around to reverse direction at one point, they found themselves face to face with their worst nightmare: a chorus line of mocking queens, their arms clasped around each other, kicking their heels in the air Rockettes-style and singing at the tops of their sardonic voices:

We are the Stonewall girls.
We wear our hair in curls.
We wear no underwear.
We show our pubic hair . . .
We wear our dungarees
Above our nelly knees!

It was a deliciously witty, contemptuous counterpoint to the TPF's brute force, a tactic that transformed an otherwise traditionally macho eye-for-an-eye combat and that provided at least the glimpse of a different and revelatory kind of consciousness. Perhaps that was exactly the moment Sylvia had in mind when she later said, "Something lifted off my shoulders."

But the tactic incited the TPF to yet further violence. As they were badly beating up on one effeminate-looking boy, a portion of the angry crowd surged in, snatched the boy away, and prevented the cops from reclaiming him. Elsewhere, a cop grabbed "a wild Puerto Rican queen" and lifted his arm as if to club him. Instead of cowering, the queen yelled, "How would you like a big Spanish dick up your little Irish ass?" The nonplussed cop hesitated just long enough to give the queen time to run off into the crowd.

The cops themselves hardly escaped scot-free. Somebody managed to drop a concrete block on one parked police car; nobody was injured, but the cops inside were shaken up. At another point, a gold-braided police officer who was being driven around to survey the action had a sack of wet garbage thrown at him through the open window of his car; a direct hit was scored and soggy coffee grounds dripped down the officer's face as he tried to maintain a stoic expression. Still later, as some hundred people were being chased down Waverly Place by two cops, someone in the crowd suddenly realized the unequal odds and started yelling, "There are two of 'em! Catch 'em! Rip their clothes off! Fuck 'em!" As the crowd took up the cry, the officers fled.

Before the police finally succeeded in clearing the streets—for that evening only, it would turn out—a considerable amount of blood had been shed. Among the undetermined number of people injured was Sylvia's friend Ivan Valentin; hit in the knee by a policeman's billy club, he had ten stitches taken at St. Vincent's Hospital. A teenager named Lenny had his hand slammed in a car door and lost two fingers. Four big cops beat up a young queen so badly—there is evidence that the cops singled out "feminine boys"—that she bled simultaneously from her mouth, nose, and ears. Craig and Sylvia both escaped injury (as did Jim, who hung back on the fringe of the crowd), but so much blood splattered over Sylvia's blouse that at one point she had to go down to the piers and change into the clean clothes Gary had brought back for her.

Four police officers were also hurt. Most of them sustained minor abrasions from kicks and bites, but Officer Scheu, after being hit with a rolled-up newspaper, had fallen to the cement sidewalk and broken his wrist. When Craig heard that news, he couldn't resist chuckling over what he called the "symbolic justice" of the injury. Thirteen people (including Dave Van Ronk), seven of them Stonewall employees, were booked at the Sixth Precinct on charges ranging from harassment to resisting arrest to disorderly conduct. At 3:35 A.M., signal 10-41 was canceled, and an uneasy calm settled over the area. It was not to last.

• • •

Word of the confrontation spread through the gay grapevine all day Saturday. Moreover, all three of the dailies wrote about the riot (the *Daily News* put the story on page one), and local television and radio reported it as well. The extensive coverage brought out the crowds, just as Craig had predicted (and had worked to achieve). All day Saturday, curious knots of people gathered outside the bar to gape at the damage and warily celebrate the implausible fact that, for once, cops, not gays, had been routed.

The police had left Stonewall a shambles. Jukeboxes, mirrors, and cigarette machines had been smashed; phones were ripped out; toilets were plugged up and overflowing; and shards of glass and debris littered the floors. (According to at least one account, moreover, the police had pocketed all the money from the jukeboxes, cigarette machines, cash register, and safe.) On the boarded-up front window that faced the street, anonymous protesters had scrawled signs and slogans: THEY INVADED OUR RIGHTS, THERE IS ALL COLLEGE BOYS AND GIRLS IN HERE, LEGALIZE GAY BARS, SUPPORT GAY POWER—and newly emboldened same-gender couples were seen holding hands as they anxiously conferred about the meaning of these uncommon new assumptions.

Something like a carnival, an outsized block party, had gotten going by early Saturday evening in front of the Stonewall. While older, conservative chinos-and-sweater gays watched warily, and some disapprovingly, from the sidelines, "stars" from the previous night's confrontation reappeared to pose campily for photographs. Handholding and kissing became endemic; cheerleaders led the crowd in shouts of "Gay Power"; and chorus lines repeatedly belted out refrains of "We are the girls from Stonewall."

But the cops, including Tactical Patrol Force units, were out in force, were not amused at the antics, and seemed grimfacedly determined not to have a repeat of Friday night's humiliation. The

THE NIGHT THEY RAIDED STONEWALL

TPF lined up across the street from the Stonewall, visors in place, batons and shields at the ready. When the fearless chorus line of queens insisted on yet another refrain, kicking their heels high in the air as if in direct defiance, the TPF moved forward, ferociously pushing their nightsticks into the ribs of anyone who didn't jump immediately out of their path.

But the crowd had grown too large to be easily cowed or controlled. Thousands of people were by now spilling over the sidewalks, including an indeterminate but sizable number of curious straights and a sprinkling of street people gleefully poised to join any kind of developing rampage. When the TPF tried to sweep people away from the front of the Stonewall, the crowd simply repeated the previous night's strategy of temporarily retreating down a side street and then doubling back on the police. In Craig's part of the crowd, the idea took hold of blocking off Christopher Street, preventing any vehicular traffic from coming through. When an occasional car did try to bulldoze its way in, the crowd quickly surrounded it, rocking it back and forth so vigorously that the occupants soon proved more than happy to be allowed to retreat.

Craig was enjoying all this hugely until a taxicab edged around the corner from Greenwich Avenue. As the crowd gave the cab a vigorous rocking and a frenzied queen jumped on top of it and started beating on the hood, Craig caught a glimpse inside and saw two terrified passengers and a driver who looked as if he were having a heart attack. Sylvia came on that same scene and gleefully cheered the queen on. But Craig realized that the cab held innocent people, not fag-hating cops, and he worked with others to free it from the crowd's grip so it could back out.

From that point on, and in several parts of the crowd simultaneously, all hell broke loose. Sylvia's friend Marsha P. Johnson climbed to the top of a lamppost and dropped a bag with something heavy in it on a squad car parked directly below, shattering its windshield. Craig was only six feet away and saw the cops jump out of the car, grab some luckless soul who happened to be close at hand, and beat him badly. On nearby Gay Street, three or four cars filled with a wedding party were stopped in their tracks for a while; somebody in the crowd shouted, "We have the right to marry, too!" The unintimidated and decidedly unamused passengers screamed back, angrily threatening to call the police. That produced some laughter ("The police are already here!") and more shouts, until finally the wedding party was allowed to proceed.

From the park side of Sheridan Square, a barrage of bottles and bricks—seemingly hundreds of them, apparently aimed at the police lines—rained down across the square, injuring several onlookers but no officers. Jim had returned to the Stonewall scene in the early evening; when the bottle-throwing started, he raced to the area where it seemed to be coming from and—using his experience from previous street actions—tried to persuade the bottle-tossers that they were playing a dangerous game, threatening the lives of the protesters more than those of the police.

They didn't seem to care. Jim identified them as "straight anarchist types, Weathermen types," determined "to be really butch about their anger" (unlike those "frightened sissies"), to foment as large-scale and gory a riot as possible. He thought they were possibly "crazies"—or police provocateurs—and he realized it would be ineffective simply to say, "Stop doing this!" So, as he tells it, he tried to temper their behavior by appealing to their macho instincts, suggesting that it would be even braver of them to throw their bottles from the front of the line; that way, if the police, taunted by the flying glass, charged the crowd, they could bear the brunt of the attack themselves. The argument didn't wash; the bottle-throwing continued.

If Jim didn't want people actually getting hurt, he did want to feed the riot. Still smoldering from the failure of his straight friends to show up the previous night (some of his closeted left-wing gay friends had also done nothing in response to his calls), he wanted this gay riot "to be as good as any riot" his straight onetime comrades had ever put together or participated in. And to that end, he carried with him the tools of the guerrilla trade: marbles (to throw under the hooves of the contingent of mounted police that had by now arrived) and pins (to stick into the horses' flanks).

But the cops needed no additional provocation; they had been determined from the beginning to quell the demonstration, and at whatever cost in bashed heads and shattered bones. Twice the police broke ranks and charged into the crowd, flailing wildly with their nightsticks; at least two men were clubbed to the ground. The sporadic skirmishing went on until 4:00 A.M., when the police finally withdrew their units from the area. The next day, the *New York Times* insisted that Saturday night was "less violent" than Friday (even while describing the crowd as "angrier"). Sylvia too considered the first night "the worst." But a number of others, including Craig, thought the second night was the more violent one, that it marked "a public assertion of real anger by gay people that was just electric."

When he got back to his apartment early Sunday morning, his anger and excitement still bubbling, Craig sat down and composed a one-page flyer. Speaking in the name of the Homophile Youth Movement (HYMN) that he had founded, Craig headlined the flyer, GET THE MAFIA AND THE COPS OUT OF GAY BARS—a rallying cry that would have chilled Zucchi. Using his own money, Craig printed up thousands of the flyers and then set about organizing his two-person teams. He had them out on the streets leafleting passersby by midday on Sunday. They weren't alone. After the second night of rioting, it had become clear to many that a major upheaval, a kind of seismic shift, was at hand, and brisk activity was developing in several quarters.

But not all gays were pleased about the eruption at Stonewall. Those satisfied by, or at least habituated to, the status quo preferred to minimize or dismiss what was happening. Many wealthier gays, sunning at Fire Island or in the Hamptons for the weekend, either heard about the rioting and ignored it (as one of them later put it: "No one [at Fire Island Pines] mentioned Stonewall") or caught up with the news belatedly. When they did, they tended to characterize the events at Stonewall as "regrettable," as the demented carryings-on of "stoned, tacky queens"—precisely those elements in the gay world from whom they had long since disassociated themselves. Coming back into the city on Sunday night, the beach set might have hastened off to see the nude stage show *Oh, Calcutta!* or the film *Midnight Cowboy* (in which Jon Voigt played a 42nd Street hustler), titillated by such mainstream daring while oblivious or scornful of the real-life counterparts being acted out before their averted eyes.

Indeed some older gays, and not just the wealthy ones, even sided with the police, praising them for the "restraint" they had shown in not employing more violence against the protesters. As one of the leaders of the West Side Discussion Group purportedly said, "How can we expect the police to allow us to congregate? Let's face it, we're criminals. You can't allow criminals to congregate." Others applauded what they called the "long-overdue" closing of what for years had been an unsightly "sleaze joint." There are even tales that some of the customers at Julius', the bar down the street from Stonewall that had long been favored by older gays ("the good girls from the fifties," as one queen put it), actually held three of the rioters for the police.

Along with Craig's teams, there were others on the streets of the Village that Sunday who had been galvanized into action and were trying to organize demonstrations or meetings. Left-wing radicals like Jim Fouratt, thrilled with the *lack* of leadership in evidence during the two nights of rioting, saw the chance for a new kind of egalitarian gay organization to emerge. He hoped it would incorporate ideas about gender parity and "rotating leadership" from the burgeoning feminist movement and build, as well, on the long-standing struggle of the Black movement against racism. At the same time, Jim and his fellow gay radicals were not interested in being subsumed any longer under anyone else's banner. They had long fought for every worthy cause other than their own and—as the events at Stonewall had proven—without any hope of reciprocity. They felt it was time to refocus their energies on themselves.

The Mattachine Society had still another view. With its headquarters right down the street from the Stonewall Inn, Mattachine was in 1969 pretty much the creature of Dick Leitsch, who had considerable sympathy for New Left causes but none for challenges to his leadership. Randy Wicker, himself a pioneer activist and lately a critic of Leitsch, now joined forces with him to pronounce the events at Stonewall "horrible." Wicker's earlier activism had been fueled by the notion that gays were "jes' folks"—just like straights except for their sexual orientation—and the sight (in his words) "of screaming queens forming chorus lines and kicking, went against everything that I wanted people to think about homosexuals . . . that we were a bunch of drag queens in the Village acting disorderly and tacky and cheap." On Sunday those wandering by Stonewall saw a new sign on its boarded-up facade, this one printed in neat block letters:

> WE HOMOSEXUALS PLEAD WITH
> OUR PEOPLE TO PLEASE HELP
> MAINTAIN PEACEFUL AND QUIET
> CONDUCT ON THE STREETS OF
> THE VILLAGE—MATTACHINE

The streets that Sunday evening stayed comparatively quiet, dominated by what one observer called a "tense watchfulness." Knots of the curious continued to congregate in front of Stonewall, and some of the primping and posing of the previous two nights was still in evidence.

The police seemed spoiling for trouble. "Start something, faggot, just start something," one cop repeated over and over. "I'd like to break your ass wide open." (A brave young man purportedly yelled, "What a Freudian comment, Officer!"—and then scampered to safety.) Two other cops, cruising in a police car, kept yelling obscenities at passersby, trying to start a fight, and a third, standing on the corner of Christopher Street and Waverly Place, kept swinging his nightstick and making nasty remarks about "faggots."

At 1:00 A.M. the TPF made a largely uncontested sweep of the area, and the crowds melted away. Allen Ginsberg strolled by, flashed the peace sign and, after seeing "Gay Power!" scratched on the front of the Stonewall, expressed satisfaction to a *Village Voice* reporter: "We're one of the largest minorities in the country—10 percent, you know. It's about time we did something to assert ourselves."

By Sunday, some of the wreckage inside the bar had been cleaned up, and employees had been stationed out on the street to coax patrons back in: "We're honest businessmen here. We're American-born boys. We run a legitimate joint here. There ain't nuttin' bein' done wrong in dis place. Everybody come and see." Never having been inside the Stonewall, Ginsberg went in and briefly joined the handful of dancers. After emerging, he described the patrons as "beautiful—they've lost that wounded look that fags all had ten years ago." Deputy Inspector Pine later echoed Ginsberg: "For those of us in public morals, things were completely changed . . . suddenly they were not submissive anymore."

On Stonewall

As revolutions go, the street-fighting that took place around Sheridan Square in Greenwich Village on the night of June 27, 1969, lacked the splendor of the Bastille or the sweep of the Finland Station. State power did not crumble, great leaders did not appear, no clear objective was advanced. A bunch of drag queens and their friends, pulled from the Stonewall gay bar in a police raid, refused to go docilely into the paddy wagons, and all hell broke loose along Christopher Street and the adjoining parks and alleys. Fighting between the queers and the cops resumed on the next night, but that was the extent of the violence. And yet the Stonewall riot must count as a transformative moment of liberation, not only for homosexuals, who were the street fighters, but for the entire sexual culture, which broke out of confinement that night as surely as gay people emerged from the closet.

Stonewall was a material metaphor for emergence, visibility, and pride, and its historic power has been its affirmation of gay identity rather than its establishment of a particular homosexual agenda. Unlike the "national days" of other communities, countries, and ethnic groups, the nationwide celebration of the anniversary of the riots memorializes an act of legitimization, not an act of parliament, a treaty, or a war. Gay Pride Week, the name for the observance, could hardly be more appropriate. Although Stonewall came at the very end of a decade of convulsive change and was profoundly informed by the struggles of black Americans, women, radical students, and insurgent movements throughout the Third World, it was in many ways the purest cultural revolution of them all and the precursor of the postmodern politics of identity that proliferated in the decades to follow. Lesbians and gays are surely today's children of Stonewall, but many more are stepchildren or close cousins. That June night almost a quarter of a century ago now belongs to everyone.

It has taken a generation—or is it now two?—for the crucial significance of Stonewall to emerge from its own gay closet and be seen in the light of the social history of its time. Because the event was so much a revolution of personal identity, it is natural that historians focus on details of personal experience, on the lives of the participants, on the hilarious, humdrum, and sad details of an utterly incongruous melee. In the preceding excerpt, Martin Duberman tells the story of the riot's beginnings through the accounts of the band of barflies, bartenders, and bouncers, the drags, spear-carriers, and politicos who just happened to be in the same place on the same night and think of themselves as a historic happy few way back on the eve of their own private Agincourt.

Lenin said somewhere that a revolution is a "festival of the oppressed," and although Stonewall wasn't remotely Leninist in any other regard, it was certainly festive, and the crowd that poured out of the bar was definitely low-down. The prominence of drag queens in the vanguard of the insurgency always made theoretical sense: as one of the most marginal, disdained, and isolated sectors of the homosexual world (it could not yet be called a "gay community"), the drags had the least to lose from acting out, or acting up—and perhaps the most to gain. But as much as "straight-appearing" gay men (an epithet that still appears in the personals columns) kept their distance from drag queens, or treated them only as camp objects of amusement, the "chinos-and-penny-loafers" boys, as Duberman calls them, could see that those qualities in the drags that were most despised by the straight world were hidden in all homosexuals in one form or another. The most untempered, outrageous, and flamboyant behavior—and the most oppressed—was thus the most liberating expression of all. In the gay liberation movement that exploded after Stonewall, young lesbians and gay men were urged to "get into their oppression," to comb the crannies of gay consciousness and sensibility, and to feel solidarity with those who suffered the most.

Stonewall was the beginning of something, but it was also the culmination of a long siege of conflict, during which protest had become a normal way of making politics, and all sorts and sizes of groups had bid for power. Many of the campaigns crossed communal lines, but there was a great deal of fear, a sense of threat, and sometimes an ardent "nationalism" that kept the groups apart. Stonewall is often described as a narrowly constructed, exclusively gay male "happening" (in the sixties sense), but lots of lines were crossed. As Duberman points out, the drag contingent, at least, was remarkably integrated in racial terms. Although the bar was not known as a lesbian hangout, lesbians were sometimes in attendance, and one story suggests that a butch lesbian cross-dresser might have been the instigator of the riot. Jim Fouratt, one of Duberman's witnesses, reported that he was unable to get his friends from "the Left" to join in the second-night fight, but if leftists didn't "get it" from the start, in less than a year gay liberation was on the agenda at every radical event, and Fouratt himself—as a gay politico—was a star speaker at the legendary "Free the Panthers" rally on the New Haven green on May Day, 1970.

Craig Rodwell, another witness, said in an earlier interview, for the documentary film *Before Stonewall*, that what was most magical about the Stonewall riot was that "everything came together that night." Somewhere in the existential depths of that brawl of screaming transvestites were all the antiwar marches, the sit-ins, the smoke-ins, the freedom rides, the bra-burnings, the levitation of the Pentagon, the endless meetings and broken hearts. Not only that, but the years of gay men and lesbians locking themselves in windowless, unnamed bars; writing dangerous, anonymous novels and articles; lying about their identity to their families, their bosses, the military; suffering silently when they were found out; hiding and seeking and winking at each other, or drinking and dying by themselves. And sometimes, not often, braving it out and surviving. It's absolutely astonishing to think that on one early summer's night in New York that world ended, and a new one began.

—Andrew Kopkind

MICHAEL KRÜGER

from *Idylls and Illusions*

As proof that he had existed there once,
he buried a whetstone under the wooden
threshold; set out. He saw the world, the blood
of the sun spurting vertically up into heaven, saw
the way a drop fell and killed the earth.
He also heard the mutters of dread as wolves drew near,
and also the cosmos' grinding grating. Matter
distended. Having outgrown his father's teachings,
he made his way back, and there at his side was a speckled pig.
The house, as was usual then, was a ruin. The whetstone alone
bore witness that he had existed there once.

Here on the edge of the forest, beneath the mendicant maple,
the boards for the dead, already half buried.
Wild cherries are casting a shadow
which keeps the brief path cool
between Herod's house and the house of the priest,
and raspberry, elder, and dog-rose
make the transition more easy.
Beetles are giving cryptic details
on how far wood has merged with earth.
Someone who wished to unite order and chaos
is sticking out of the ground here, head-down.

Alexandria missed, Sicily never arrived in,
Cheapside bypassed where the money broker's child
was born. There are candles at every window,
shepherd's purse in acid meadows, and fumes
staining the aprons, the spotted waistless jackets.

IDYLLS AND ILLUSIONS

Rifts in ground that is parched with too much history,
with philosophical filth. And repeatedly someone
who does not trim his mighty thousand-tongued beard
to the wind, who does not bemoan
the shortness of life, the unenlightened
state of things, as silly fools do.

You've lost your way in fairy tales. Your only escort:
crossbills that tried (in vain) to extract
the nails from the hands of the Lord. You pass
uninhabited villages by where ramblers
darken the doorjambs and lintels, where moss
has crawled its way over the roofs, carpet-thick.
Saints are sitting wearily on spotted clouds,
counting Poverty, Meekness, Charity
on their fingers, loaded down with privileges.
Skulls grow out of the loessial soil,
look at you, melt back into the mist.

No soul for miles around; the washing
is loudly reeling about on the line, and fungi are drying
away on the insides of weathered window cavities.
On the church—with its incompatible towers—
the crumbling doves are being fed seed,
al fresco, by some wrinkled fingers.
There on the corner, bleached: the black rat
from childhood, turned almost white by the dust
that is rising like smoke. I start, as though
I'd been under a spell, an evil spell,
and see the dove, a rusty nail held fast in its beak.

Winter closed over the land amidst the applause
of the sedge. Brownish ocher was brightly

lining the loamy bank, my heart
a watery sponge. The birds had taken to flying
underwater, invisible animals
dug communication trenches under the snow.
Foam on the stones, pulled to bits by the north wind.
Every winter, they pile a heap of stones
on the body, putting cranberries
on the top for the animals. Somewhere a fire,
and the feeling that Time is cracking, shattering, in the flames.

Behind the shed, where a scrawny lawn
covers the static scree, there has been growing,
since the snow melted and the ground—
a mix of loam and clay and sand and gravel—
appeared again, a plant never found
in these parts before. The postman too, who has
no interest in mail but knows his botany,
stares in disbelief at the hirsute stem,
shaggy and full of glands, at the capitate stigma;
he runs his fingers across a yellowy bulge
and says, as he hands me the bills, "expelled by culture."

And higher up now, closer to the sun,
he shows me plants with stiff hair on their leaves,
fine-veined, whose corollas, near the bottom,
are peppered with purple glands. "Only in Braunau,"
he says, "up to now," and the baa-baa of the lambs,
obliviously cropping the rarity, appears
to be agreement. "Plants are traveling faster,
chemistry's giving them wings; just look at these
three points on the corolla's lower lips.
Obstinate Bag, Obese Big-mouth,"
he says, and is gone with his mailbag.

FRED WILSON

Mining the Museum

"Mining the Museum" is an exhibition selected and installed by Fred Wilson. Wilson was invited by The Contemporary, Baltimore, to create the exhibition using the archives and resources of the Maryland Historical Society. The exhibition, organized by The Contemporary's curator, Lisa Corrin, was installed in the Society's museum in October 1992.

Wilson was responsible for all aspects of the exhibition, including arrangement of works, labeling, wall colors, graphics, film projections, and audio recordings. He was assisted by other artists, community historians, volunteers, and the staffs of The Contemporary and the Maryland Historical Society. The artworks and artifacts were displayed in a succession of rooms thematically arranged and differentiated by their wall colors of gray, green, red, and blue.

Benjamin Banneker, Harriet Tubman, and Frederick Douglass
Empty pedestals with names on labels

"Truth Trophy"
Industry award given for truth in advertising
c. 1913

Henry Clay, Napoleon Bonaparte, and Andrew Jackson
Pedestals with busts

153

Portraits of Unknown Cigar-Store Owner, Elizabeth Buckler, John Klein, and Bernard Faistenhamer
Cigar-store Indians labeled with names of merchants who commissioned them

Portraits of Native Americans
Photographs displayed on walls

Jenny Proctor and Jimmy Linkens

Photograph of Native Americans, c. 1930

Portrait of Henry Darnell III
Painting by Justus Kuhn, c. 1710
Spotlight illuminates enslaved child in dog collar

On the museum's sound system a child's voice asks,

"Am I your brother? Am I your friend? Am I your pet?"

Metalwork 1793–1880

Silver Service
Pitchers, steins, and goblets
Baltimore repoussé style, c. 1830–80

Iron Slave Shackles
c. 1793–1872

Mount Vernon Place

Photograph, c. 1900
African-American domestics with charges

"One of the Rebels, Geo. Washington"

Envelope engraved,
"The Southern Gentleman, and Slaveholder.
C.S.A. [Confederate States of America],"
c. 1861

Modes of Transport 1770–1910

Model of Baltimore Clipper
Of type converted to slavers (rigged as brig) after War of 1812

Maryland in 1750
Painting by Frank B. Mayer, c. 1856

Sedan Chair
Used by Governor Eden of Maryland, c. 1770

Baby Carriage
c. 1880, with Ku Klux Klan hood, c. 1900
Donated anonymously,

$200 REWARD.

Ran away from the subscriber, living eight miles from the city of Baltimore, on the Falls Turnpike Road, on

Friday, the 21st of May,
NEGROES
RICHARD & NED,

Richard aged about twenty-six years, five feet six or seven inches high, yellowish complexion, small beard, has a scar on his forehead, stutters a little in conversation, but when he is alarmed it is increased considerably: He is straight and well proportioned, except one leg which is a little crooked from having been once broken. His clothing not known, except a new wool hat, a dark grey broad-cloth surtout coat, and a blue uniform United States soldier's coat, both half worn, and two pair of new calf-skin shoes, one pair of which were right and left. Richard ran away from me in 1814; he was then taken up in Pennsylvania, at the house of a man named Gross, (near York Haven,) where he learned the distilling business----It is probable he will return to that state (and will call at Mr. Gross' house, as he left there a watch and some other articles) and engage with a distiller again.

NED, who was decoyed away by Richard, is about twenty years of age, quite black, five feet eight or nine inches high, stout and well formed, has a pleasant countenance, and generally smiles when spoken to, naturally slow in his motions and of an easy quiet disposition, he walks very erect and when in conversation has given himself the habit of spitting through his teeth. He has no particular marks recollected, except a scar on the back of his hand----His clothing like Richard's not particularly known, except a blue cloth coat with long skirts, a pair of greenish pantaloons, both half worn, and an old furred hat---Richard has provided himself with money by robbing Mr. Edmond T. Scarff of 75 dollars the night he ran away, and it is probable they will soon change their dress.

I will give FORTY dollars to any person that will give me information where they are so that I get them again, or ONE HUNDRED DOLLARS for each if brought home, and all reasonable charges paid.

Thomas Johnson.

N. B. They took with them two blankets, blue stripes, commonly called point blankets, 3 1-2 points.
MAY 25, 1819.

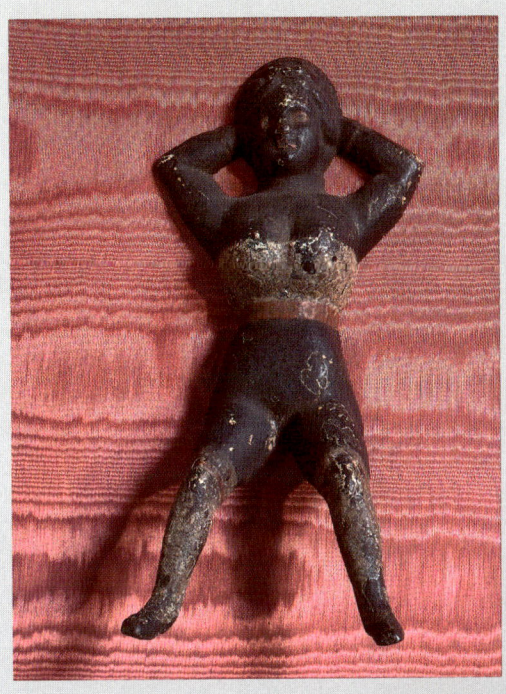

"Naughty Nellie" Bootjack

Cast iron, c. 1880

Zouave Soldier Doll

Dancing toy, c. 1882

Chesapeake Bay Decoys

Runaway Slaves Broadside

Printed in Baltimore, 1819

Cabinetmaking 1820–1960

Whipping Post
Baltimore City Jail, c. 1850

Side Chairs and Armchairs
Including one with logo
of Baltimore Equitable Society, c. 1820–96

African-Americans Who Resisted Slavery
Slide projections of names

The Gap at Harper's Ferry
Painting, artist unknown, c. 1880

Dollhouse *(above and right)*
Made by a child's father, c. 1904

Pikes from John Brown's Raid on Harper's Ferry
c. 1859

"The spirit of revolt spread throughout the Eastern Shore and in a County without police protection we were at the mercy of the slaves. The demon of massacre was at our door."

—from the autobiography of Mrs. Enoch Louis Lowe

Souvenirs of the Colony "Maryland in Liberia"

Artifacts from the African colony of freed American slaves, established by the American Colonization Society, c. 1870
Strip of ivory, beads, African comb, and beaded neck-rope with amulet

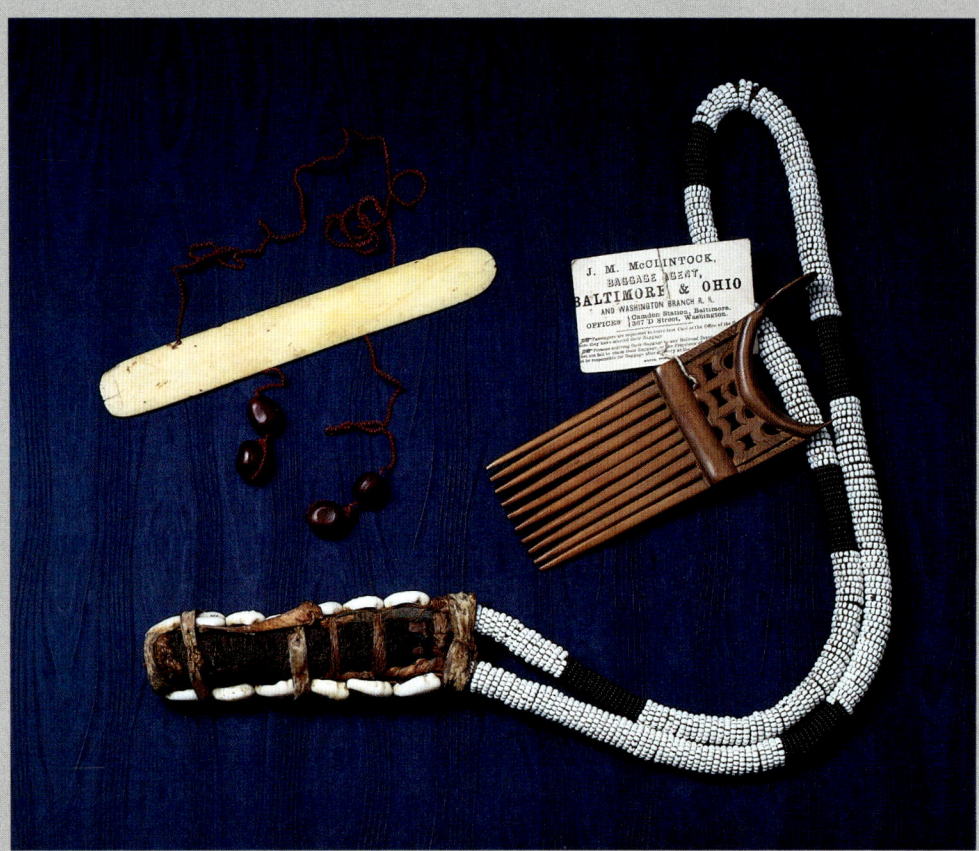

Objects Made by Enslaved African-Americans
Water jug by Melinda, Cockey Plantation
Woven basket, Woodlawn Plantation
Nursemaid's rocking chair, Snow Hill Plantation, c. 1825–50

Benjamin Banneker's Astronomical Journal
1790–1806; slide projection of his chart predicting eclipse of October 18, 1800; computer showing night sky of same day

Chippendale Table and Celestial Globe
c. 1776

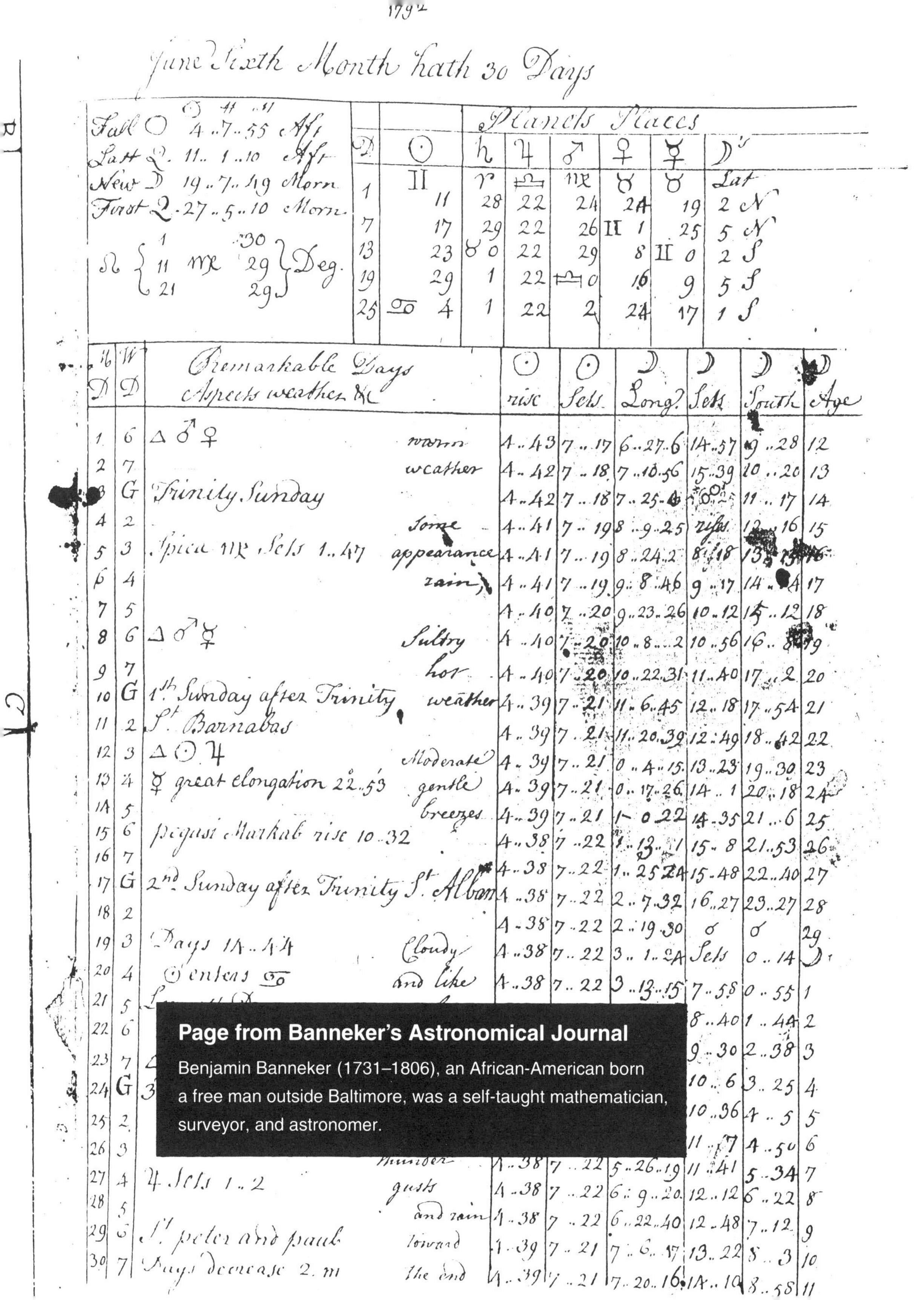

1792

June Sixth Month hath 30 Days

Full ○	4	7	55	Aft
Last ☾	11	1	10	Aft
New ☽	19	7	49	Morn
First ☽	27	5	10	Morn

☊ { 1 ♍ 30; 11 ♍ 29; 21 29 } Deg.

Planets Places

D	☉	♄	♃	♂	♀	☿	☽'s
	♊	♈	♎	♍	♉	♉	Lat
1	11	28	22	24	24	19	2 N
7	17	29	22	26	♊ 1	25	5 N
13	23	♉ 0	22	29	8	♊ 0	2 S
19	29	1	22	♎ 0	16	9	5 S
25	♋ 4	1	22	2	24	17	1 S

M D	W D	Remarkable Days Aspects weather &c		☉ rise	☉ Sets	☽ Long.	☽ Sets	☽ South	☽ Age
1	6	△ ♂ ♀	warm	4..43	7..17	6..27..6	14..57	9..28	12
2	7		weather	4..42	7..18	7..10..56	15..39	10..20	13
3	G	Trinity Sunday		4..42	7..18	7..25..4	16..2[illegible]	11..17	14
4	2		some	4..41	7..19	8..9..25	rises	12..16	15
5	3	Spica ♍ Sets 1..47	appearance	4..41	7..19	8..24..2	8..18	13..[illegible]	16
6	4		rain	4..41	7..19	9..8..46	9..17	14..4	17
7	5			4..40	7..20	9..23..26	10..12	15..12	18
8	6	△ ♂ ☿	Sultry	4..40	7..20	10..8..2	10..56	16..8	19
9	7		hot	4..40	7..20	10..22..31	11..40	17..2	20
10	G	1th Sunday after Trinity	weather	4..39	7..21	11..6..45	12..18	17..54	21
11	2	St Barnabas		4..39	7..21	11..20..39	12..49	18..42	22
12	3	△ ☉ ♃	Moderate	4..39	7..21	0..4..15	13..23	19..30	23
13	4	☿ great elongation 22°..53	gentle	4..39	7..21	0..17..26	14..1	20..18	24
14	5		breezes	4..39	7..21	1..0..22	14..35	21..6	25
15	6	pegasi Markab rise 10..32		4..38	7..22	1..13..1	15..8	21..53	26
16	7			4..38	7..22	1..25..24	15..48	22..40	27
17	G	2nd Sunday after Trinity St Alban		4..38	7..22	2..7..32	16..27	23..27	28
18	2			4..38	7..22	2..19..30	σ	σ	29
19	3	Days 14..44	Cloudy	4..38	7..22	3..1..24	Sets	0..14	☽
20	4	☉ enters ♋	and like	4..38	7..22	3..13..15	7..58	0..55	1
21	5	[illegible]					8..40	1..44	2
22	6						9..30	2..38	3
23	7	[illegible]					10..6	3..25	4
24	G	[illegible]					10..36	4..5	5
25	2						11..7	4..50	6
26	3		thunder	4..38	7..22	5..26..19	11..41	5..34	7
27	4	♃ Sets 1..2	gusts	4..38	7..22	6..9..20	12..12	6..22	8
28	5		and rain	4..38	7..22	6..22..40	12..48	7..12	9
29	6	St peter and paul	toward	4..39	7..21	7..6..17	13..22	8..3	10
30	7	Days decrease 2 m	the end	4..39	7..21	7..20..16	14..10	8..58	11

Page from Banneker's Astronomical Journal

Benjamin Banneker (1731–1806), an African-American born a free man outside Baltimore, was a self-taught mathematician, surveyor, and astronomer.

FRED WILSON

Mining the Museum

By excavating the site of institutional racism and retrieving forgotten African-American artifacts and heroes, Fred Wilson's "Mining the Museum" brings to light a history and a cultural presence that have been buried beneath layers of neglect and deliberate exclusion. Wilson has culled most of these objects from the permanent collection of the Maryland Historical Society and uses the museum itself as a locus for their presentation, which mimics the usual methods of curatorial selection and museum display: specially painted rooms, silkscreened wall texts, labels, audiovisual material, etc. The objects chosen, and the sly twists of Wilson's juxtapositions, call attention to the biases that normally underlie historical exhibitions, thus subverting and shattering them. In this way, "Mining the Museum" takes a place alongside other works that have focused on the meaning of the gallery or museum as both a formal space and an ideological construct. By adding the explosive element of racism, Wilson grafts a cold populist fury onto a now-familiar subgenre of conceptualism.

One antecedent of what has been referred to as "museumist art" and "institutional critique" is Yves Klein's 1958 Paris exhibition "Le Vide," in which he emptied the Galerie Iris Clert, transforming it into a "zone of immaterial pictorial sensibility." Whatever else Klein intended, the effect of this gesture was to call attention to the gallery space in and of itself. The idea was developed more explicitly in "Raid the Icebox 1 With Andy Warhol," a 1969 exhibition of objects from the art museum of the Rhode Island School of Design. Work in the 1970s by such artists as Marcel Broodthaers and Michael Asher continued to assail the perceived neutrality of institutions governing the cultural reception of art. Over time, the tenor of institutional critique has become increasingly radicalized, even as the practice itself has assumed a more entrenched—even conventional—position within contemporary art. Institutions, for example, have begun to invite artists to stage critiques within their own walls, as with Joseph Kosuth's "The Play of the Unmentionable" (1990) at the Brooklyn Museum. Yet in pite—or because—of this acceptance, "institutional critique" has assumed a preeminent role in redrawing the boundary between art and life. It is no accident that many of its practitioners, such as Louise Lawler, Judith Barry, Silvia Kolbowski, and Andrea Fraser, are women; others, like Wilson, are artists of color. At the heart of their projects is a struggle to redefine art history, erasing the demarcations of gender, race, and class. As such, their effort reflects the larger struggle being played out in society as a whole.

Indeed, "Mining the Museum" opened against the backdrop of a presidential campaign in which the looming threat of a reactionary *kulturkampf* was one defining issue. Notwithstanding the charged atmosphere in which it was presented, "Mining the Museum" succeeds in circumventing its own polemical potential; although it is a devastating indictment of racism, it is also—and chiefly—an optimistic act of consciousness-raising, and this hopeful note sets it apart from other, similar, works.

The exhibit begins with a sort of prologue that immediately challenges the assumptions that surround the ordering and presentation of history. The viewer is confronted with a Plexiglas case containing a gold-and-silver globe bearing the single word *Truth:* an old industry award given among advertising "clubs" in the first half of the century. This "Truth Trophy" is flanked on the left by three empty pedestals, labeled "Frederick Douglass," "Harriet Tubman," and "Benjamin Banneker," and on the right by three pedestals supporting marble portrait busts of Henry Clay, Napoleon Bonaparte, and Andrew Jackson. The missing historical figures are all African-American, and all at one point lived in Maryland, yet they are not represented in this ostensibly "local" institution. Meanwhile, the other figures, all white, and none from Maryland, are prominently displayed in appropriately colored stone. Wilson makes clear that the link between historical veracity and the portrayal of history is as tenuous as the connection between truth and advertising.

"Mining the Museum" is filled with such ironies: carved cigar-store Indians—as conceived by the nineteenth-century merchants who commissioned them—turn their backs on the viewer to gaze at photographs of actual Native Americans. Slave shackles are insinuated among period silverware. A Klan hood is secreted in a baby carriage, not far from a turn-of-the-century photograph that shows black domestics pushing prams that hold their infant charges (and future employers). A whipping post is encircled by staid Victorian furniture, pulled up as if for a performance. Wilson has also left "clues" alluding to the installation in other areas of the museum, such as a dog collar, similar to the collar worn by an enslaved child in a portrait of Henry Darnell III, placed where that painting normally hangs.

These objects are organized in a series of rooms, each painted a single color, signaling changes in thematic emphasis. The Green Room, for example, deals primarily with recovering the identity of African-Americans from examples of late eighteenth- and early nineteenth-century art and artifacts, while the Red Room deals with slave revolts and the battles for abolition. The last room of the exhibition is painted a deep and redemptive shade of blue. In one long, narrow space, Wilson juxtaposes artifacts made under slavery with others from Liberia. In a separate part of the room, he displays the astronomical journal of a free, self-taught African-American who was a prominent mathematician, surveyor, and astronomer, as well as a friend of Thomas Jefferson, to whom he once wrote, "Sir I freely and Chearfully acknowledge, that I am of the African race." This man was Benjamin Banneker, one of the figures absent from the show's initial tableau.

"Mining the Museum" thus ends by echoing its beginning, but adds a note of grace. After the relentless exposure of a complex, institutionally codified oppression, Wilson ends with the affirming portrayal of a courageous individual. In her upcoming book on "Mining the Museum," the exhibition's curator, Lisa Corrin, quotes James Baldwin: "The question of color takes up much space in these pages, but the question of color, especially in this country, operates to hide the graver question of self." With Banneker as an example, Wilson suggests that this question can be triumphantly confronted.

—Howard Halle

Ghost Pig

He has turned his back on the red pullets
pecking at a fallen fenceline. Gray pig
with white rings around his eyes. He steps
onto a nothing little gravel street
that'll soon veer off for the freeway.
I'd come to gather huckleberries
till the hour grayed up. So much dust, grit,
I've left behind me. A few wings are flapping
but the garbage-fed gulls are too full
to fly. The pig's tail was the last thing
to disappear from the road: flashed
like an inked question mark against the low
bushes. Once there was water down there,
yes, across the road, on the other
side, way over and farther back.

MEI–MEI BERSSENBRUGGE

Sphericity

1

Emphasizing not only the ground upon which her movement builds, but matter it forms, the idea
of movement is a material, also, like the transparency of light above a blue ridge *being* apricot,
though the ridge is not the blue color of air on it. This light like a space that's a passage
in time. There's movement when the space changes and in its state of being what it changed to.
The content of your focus on it, like an image, can start suddenly. The way my eye makes the horizon,
my state of mind is making the state of being of the space. The state of mind touches an object
by watching it against graduated lines in a reflection. "The ridge grows bluer," instead of coordinating
a change from patches of contacts. The mystery of a color can diminish without the ridge becoming opaque.
Every other moment of an experience must push to extravagance or sphericity, of horizon, not magnitude.

2

The time of having her becomes an absorptive surface, instead of when the person was alive.
There was an inseparable light of the event for each place, like a birthplace. The horizon
represented a passage in time *and* light, a one-way membrane she thinks is the edge of a shadow,
like a medical procedure into her body. Then color crosses back from a petal. I can correlate

SPHERICITY

my sensation of reddening with changes in the sky. I can't graph my sense of this position
    of my body,
which has no degree, but is more like time on either side of you. Each point of the space
marks the center of a sphere, as if your eyes were a point. As if a person being were like
    hearing.
Her time is the center of increasing disorder, an arrow in the space.

3

It is finite in extent, yet has no edges, like the surface of the earth. On the horizon,
an apricot seam is not the content of a concept of you. Knowing this light, like knowing
    home,
is not a content, but seeing it is a content of my consciousness. If it's an image, it
can have content, i.e., telling something to me, or if you were telling the content of your
    dream.

4

The image of an apricot band of light in my memory does not block out the impression
    of this band,
now. I can see your shoes on red dirt that covers blue hills and the pulsating band turn
    redder.
I define red by pointing to dirt, not like the shadow of a petal, a place in time, not a
    thing
with closeness or distance, as if I were walking instead of looking or remembering. The
    use I speak
of seeing is a form of use. Light releases events and things away from the thing to the
    culture
of the person or presence, as if a pivot between the necessity of relation among human
    beings,
called agreement in the form of life, and the lack of this necessity between time and a
    collapsed star.

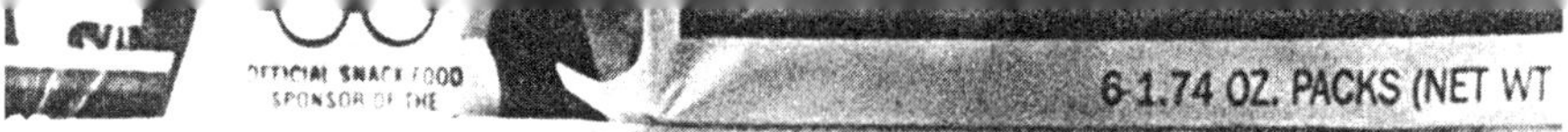
OFFICIAL SNACK FOOD
SPONSOR OF THE
6-1.74 OZ. PACKS (NET WT

York
PEPPERMINT
SLACKERS
ONE
FREE
BAR
6 FULL SIZE BARS

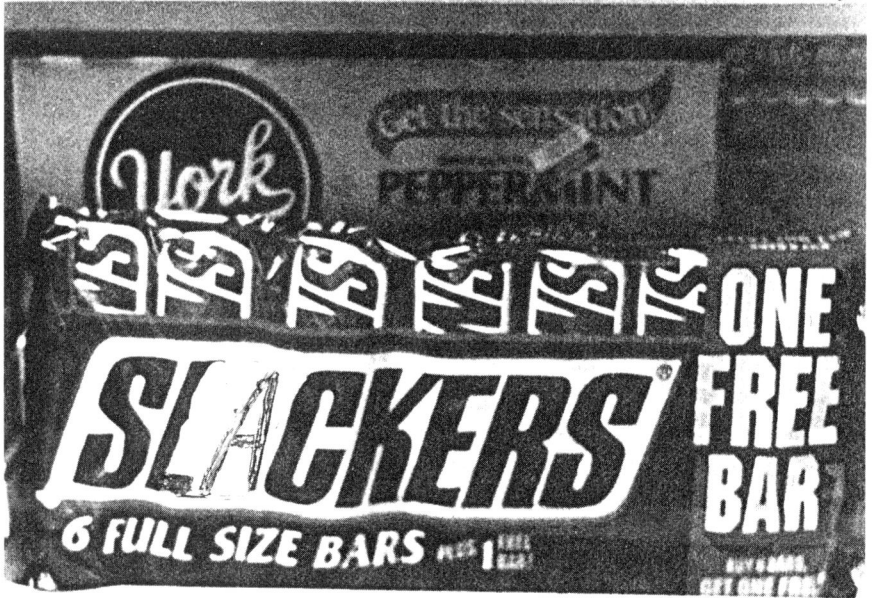

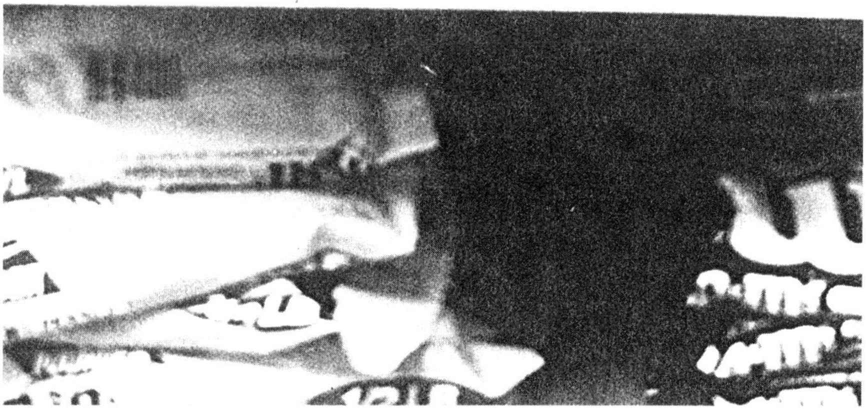

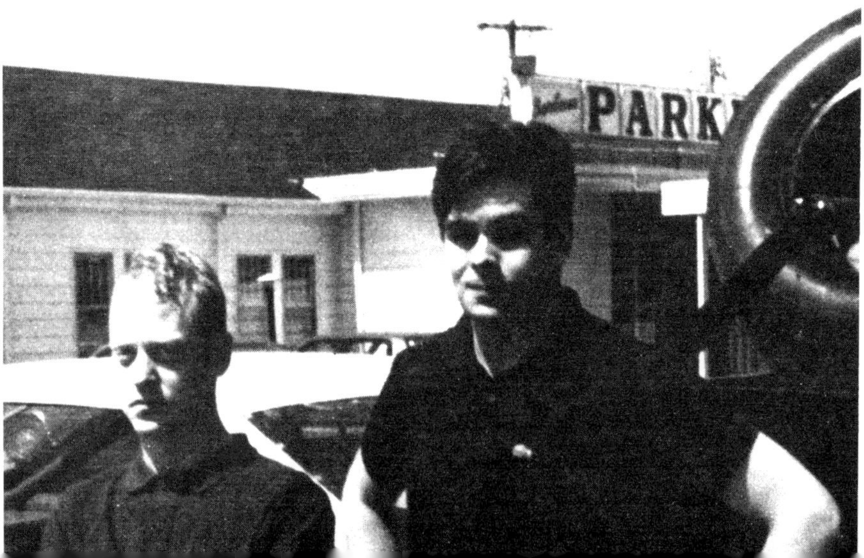
PARK

ANDREW KOPKIND

Slacking Toward Bethlehem

"Withdrawal in disgust is not the same as apathy."
From *Slacker,* a movie by Richard Linklater

Words logically follow things; the ground trembled off and on for eons before somebody shouted "earthquake." But not long ago a word for which there were hardly any corresponding things entered the vocabulary of certain young white Americans. The word was "slacker," and it seemed to bring into existence the phenomenon it was meant to describe. Perhaps because of that reversal of nominal logic, that cognitive flip, "slacker" is still extremely difficult to define. It is increasingly used to describe the generation of the nineties, the early twentysomethings who seem to constitute a youth culture more coherent than any seen since the sixties. But even a cursory tour of the new media will turn up enough slacker references to suggest that a kind of consciousness—less than a movement but more than a mood—is slouching along to be born.

The word emerged from the confines of the subculture as the title of an independent film released in 1991 and still shown in college towns and other hip centers around the country. It is not unusual to find people in their mid-twenties who have seen *Slacker* a dozen or more times, as their ancestors in an earlier community kept going back to Kubrick's *2001: A Space Odyssey*. Richard

KISS MY ASS!
I'M ON VACATION

Linklater, 30, who wrote and directed *Slacker,* the movie, lives in Austin, Texas, which is to Slackerdom what the Vatican is to Christendom. The scores of locals who appear in his film (many playing themselves, more or less) embody the varieties of the slacker experience, the many attitudes that fall into the catchall category. As far as I can tell (slackers by definition don't emote, and the dialogue is sometimes muffled), no one actually uses the word "slacker" in the film, nor is it explicated beyond the title. For the benefit of those who were hopelessly baffled, Linklater interviewed himself in the *Austin Chronicle:*

RL: So, just what is a slacker?

RL: (Acting like he's never heard the question before.) Hmmmm . . . Slackers might look like the left-behinds of society, but they are actually one step ahead, rejecting most of society and the social hierarchy before it rejects them. The dictionary defines slackers as people who evade duties and responsibilities. A more modern notion would be people who are ultimately being responsible to themselves and not wasting their time in a realm of activity that has nothing to do with who they are or what they might ultimately be striving for.

The current usage of "slack" and "slacker" may have originated in a classic underground text called *The Book of the SubGenius,* the bible of a satirical pseudoreligion called "The Church of Bob." J. R. "Bob" Dobbs, the "High Epopt" of the church and probably a fictional character himself, says the book was begun in 1953 and revised in 1979. It is currently published by the Fireside imprint of Simon & Schuster, which should indicate how far slack has penetrated the cultural environment. According to the theology of "Bob," in the beginning there was The Source, Jehovah (a.k.a. Wotan, Yahweh, Ra, etc.); The Teacher, "Bob"; and The Goal, Slack. One of the basic watchwords of the faith is "Give me Slack, or give me food (or kill me)," along with the eternal verity "Fuck 'em if they can't take a joke" and the Austin town motto, "Too much is always better than not enough."

Slack appears throughout *The Book of the SubGenius,* in spiritual flowcharts, in captions of obscure illustrations, and as a supportive element of the theological infrastructure:

the TOUGH PAD
Brillo
STEEL WOOL SOAP PADS
10 PADS

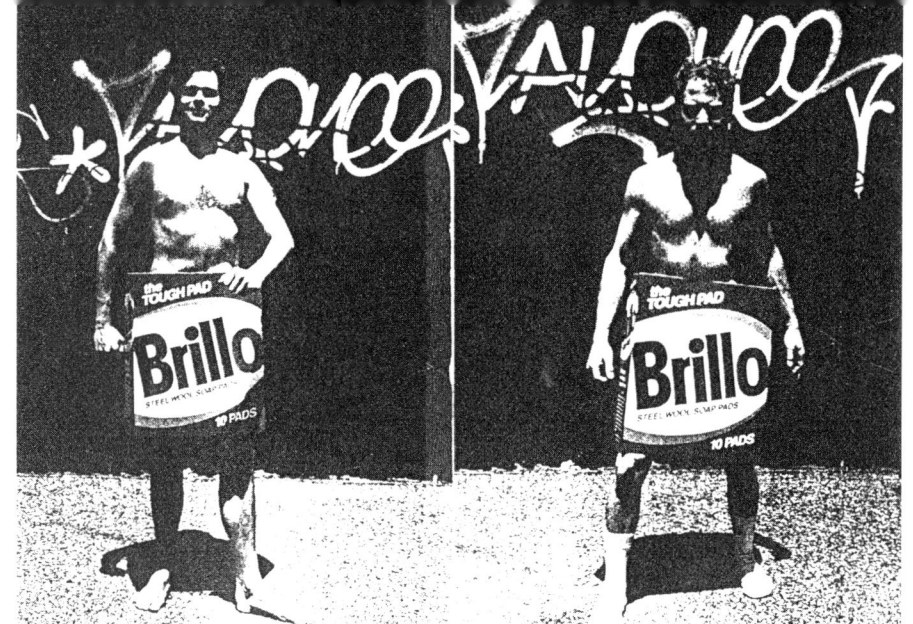

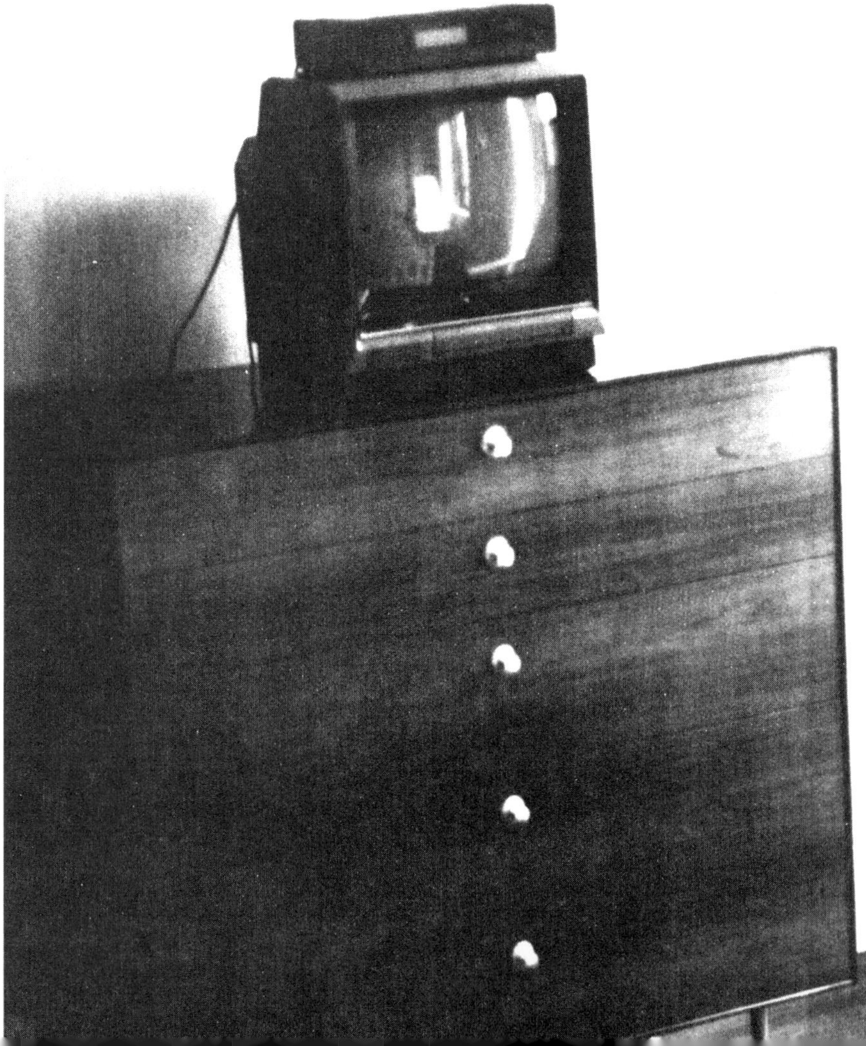

THE INSCRUTABILITY OF SLACK.

The Slack that can be defined is not the true Slack.

Slack, in its cosmic sense, is that which remains when all that is *not* Slack is taken away. But Slack is a trickster. It is unknowable, ineffable, unsearchable, incomprehensible . . . *hidden* in revelation. . . . Sometimes it is in a state of cosmic tension, of AntiSlack.

For those who dare to know the unknowable, "Bob" offers his apostles a path by suggesting film as a way to "Instant Slack." And not just film, but "unrepressedly, unapologetically, PROFOUNDLY BAD" film. "Who among us," he asks, "has not yearned to take $10 and produce the ULTIMATE BADFILM?"

No doubt SubGenius exegetes will read those lines and divine the origins of Linklater's *Slacker*. In a series of tenuously connected vignettes, riffs, and fragments of narrative, Linklater lays out slacker consciousness, the slacker aesthetic, slacker morality, and, above all, slacker attitude better than any manifesto could ever do. (Linklater has said that all the dialogue he gave his characters comes from real conversations heard over many years.) One of the most telling bits occurs when a terminally low-key man, known in the written screenplay as Ultimate Loser, comes upon a group of his friends puzzling over the whereabouts of another friend, who has mysteriously disappeared, leaving only a stack of postcards as clues to his fate:

ULTIMATE LOSER
What's going on?

COMB GAME PLAYER
Oh . . . Paul moved out, took all his stuff . . . left these cards here.

ULTIMATE LOSER
Can I have his room?

COMB GAME PLAYER
Sure . . . I guess so.

                    ULTIMATE LOSER
Cool...

                      CO-OP GUY
Hey, where you headed?

                    ULTIMATE LOSER
Oh, I got some band practice in about five hours so I figured
I'd mosey on out.

    Later, Ultimate Loser meets Pap Smear Pusher, who is trying to sell a test tube with what she claims is Madonna's vaginal wipe. Other slackers come and go: a (pre–Oliver Stone) JFK assassination nut, a man who runs over and kills his mother, a girl just out of drug rehab, a total-media freak surrounded by TV monitors, a hitchhiker coming from his hated stepfather's funeral, an old anarchist professor who makes up stories about his participation in the Spanish Civil War, a psychotic customer at a diner counter, two video interviewers, a man who claims "we've been on the moon since the fifties," and so on. There is no plot, no continuing narrative, no recurring characters. One person meets another, who in turn meets another, who passes another on the street, who in turn sees another driving a car, who narrowly avoids running over another pedestrian, who walks into a diner and watches a psychotic woman at the counter.

    What emerges from such loose connections is an exhibition of pictures from a generation rejecting, as Linklater suggested in his self-interview, pursuits that have nothing to do with what its members want, who they are, or where they are going. In that, Linklater's slackers are close cousins to the characters in Douglas Coupland's best-selling novel, *Generation X,* the other signal media event of the slacker culture.

    Coupland's novel has only slightly more plot than the movie does, but they share more than narrative looseness (the thesaurus gives "slack" as the first synonym for "loose"). There are thematic tropes in common: the danger and wonder of future technologies, the banality of consumption, the thrill of brand names, the difficulty of sex in alienated relationships. Coupland wrote the introduction to *Slacker,* the book, which includes the script, miniprofiles

of all the characters, and several essays, extended notes, and other postmodern flotsam of slacker media culture. The novel is even laid out a little like *The Book of the SubGenius*, with cartoon boxes, illustrations, and pull-quote definitions that have great currency among the readers and audiences of slackerdom:

> Poverty Jet Set: A group of people given to chronic traveling at the expense of long-term job stability or a permanent residence. Tend to have doomed and extremely expensive phone-call relationships with people named Serge or Ilyana. Tend to discuss frequent-flyer programs at parties.

The late philosopher David Sachs once said that it is impossible to talk about consciousness; one always kicks it out of reach just at the moment of capture, as the circus clown boots a hat out of his clutches. It's no easier to describe the slacker sensibility. No wonder slacker art, literature, and film are all fragments and no coherence. One needs cartoon art, lists and indexes, text blocks, sounds and silence, and perhaps computer-generated virtual reality (all of which are featured in slacker product) to get a sense of what's going on:

Beats more than hippies, anarchists more than Marxists, the fifties and the seventies more than the sixties and the eighties. Ozzie and Harriet more than Bill and Hillary, the ecology movement more than the antiwar movement, the First World more than the Third World.

Seventies punk, nineties grunge, Dylan, Spin, *'zines, suburbs, white people, androgyny, divorce, white tees under plaid shirts.*

Temping, hanging out, hiding in plain sight, cable surfing, mall grazing, bartering.

At the end of *Generation X,* Coupland adds a kind of appendix modeled on the *Harper's Index.* He calls it "Numbers," and it is meant to indicate the sadness and madness of modern life: the number of dead lakes in Canada (14,000), the percentage of the U.S. budget spent on education (2) and on the elderly (30), the percentage of income required for down payment on a first home in 1967 (22) and in 1987 (32), the chance that an American has been on TV (1 in 4), the number of murders the average child has seen on television by the age of sixteen (18,000), and three items that illustrate the excruciating hopelessness of many young people's lives:

Percentage of U.S. 18- to 29-year-olds who agree that "there is no point in staying at a job unless you are completely satisfied": 58. Who disagree: 40.

Percentage of U.S. 18- to 29-year-olds who agree that "given the way things are, it will be much harder for people in my generation to live as comfortably as previous generations": 65. Who disagree: 33.

Percentage of U.S. 18- to 29-year-olds who answered "Yes" to the question, "Would you like to have a marriage like the one your parents had?": 44. Who said "No": 55.

Slackers at least have a correct perception of their powerlessness. Unlike the freaks and radicals of the sixties, they have no illusions that "we can change the world." As a matter of fact, they have contempt for those of previous generations who believed they could make a revolution, even a cultural one, and "failed." They don't see, or admit, that a kind of cultural revolution did take place, and that it produced not nirvana (which is also the name of last year's most popular rock group) but—slackers.

The domestic and economic relationships that have created the new consciousness are not likely to improve in the few years left in this century, or in the years of the next, when the young slackers will be middle-agers. The choices for young people will be increasingly constricted. In a few years, a steady job at a mall outlet or a food chain may be all that's left for the majority of college graduates. Life is more and more like a lottery—*is* a lottery—with nothing but the luck of the draw determining whether you can get a recording contract, get your screenplay produced, or get a job with your M.B.A. Slacking is thus a rational response to casino capitalism, the randomization of success, and the utter arbitrariness of power. If no talent is still enough, why bother to hone your skills? If it's impossible to find a good job, why not slack out and enjoy life?

The purpose of "withdrawal in disgust" is not to affect the depleted social institutions, but it remains to be seen if it will nonetheless. Personal decisions have political consequences. Slacking is a solipsistic protest rather than a collective one like the sixties youth culture. It grinds entropy into the system, runs it down, creates paralysis. The democratic deadlock that was so much on pundits' minds last year was a version of that entropy that affects other aspects of the larger culture. Everyone has the sense that "things have stopped moving," that art, literature, social relations, community life are slowing, if only because they are not accelerating. The "big chill" of a dozen years ago was like a late-autumn snap before the big freeze that is now settling in. And you don't have to be a subgenius to see that the conditions for a thaw are nowhere on the horizon.

A generation may seem to be defined by its most immediately engaging members under the media spotlight, but they do not encompass the whole of that generation's experience. In other words, "slacking" means "what slackers do," and little more. Behind the blank affect of what the media packagers call "the MTV generation" is a consciousness shift as profound as that which produced the overdocumented "generation gap" of the 1960s. Indeed, cultural commentators are already gearing up for what *The Atlantic* calls "the new generation gap" that separates the Boomers and the backward-baseball-cap set—a group much less exclusive than the slackers, but not unrelated to them.

For there is a perceptual trait that seems to characterize slackers, neo-punks, your average white suburban high school kid, and many more members of the nineties generation. It is a way of reading the world, of interpreting social relationships, of gauging possibilities, of enduring limitations, of surviving outside the matrix of power. The trait was created, or at least colored, by the banalities of slackers' upbringings, by MTV and Ronald Reagan, by lowered expectations and rising anxiety, by the success and failure of the sixties radicals and the eighties yuppies, by drugs and alcohol and AIDS and racism and rock-and-roll. Consciousness is always mutating, but the change is often mild and familiar, as in the antigenic drift that creates new but tamable flu viruses every year or two. Once in a while, however, there's a real shift, and something quite new, unknown, and threatening comes to life. It seems that hour has come again, or at last.

JAMES HAINING

The Rose Chapel

for Carrie

need after time
so both dark
in no light
except talking

his love for her
to give what
she wants talk
of water

BERNADETTE MAYER

Ice Cube Epigrams

there was an interruption for with & because of
& how come such a wealth of nothingness was like an ice cube

there is no reason to be here
if there are not ice cubes

ice cubes are our exactitude of
philosophy's nothingness we chew them

we touched our faces we knew
we could make ice cubes

      an ice cube
      is neither male nor female

there is a cooler forest
than this city full of ice cubes

            ice cubes exist tomorrow
            blue dawn ridicules the basketball court

the ice cubes are still water
too bad only women make them

            ice cubes—a job of the kitchen
            how do men feel of their availability

ICE CUBE EPIGRAMS

the ice man cometh—
will we drink warm tea?

        july my heart is helpless
        let's buy a bag of ice

the iced glass is a light
it disappears tonight

        i'm going to get more ice cubes
        you can sit in my chair

    i am an ice cube
    i won't pierce your dangerous foot

all i've had to eat is ice cubes
i'm a rich person in new york city

        i am an unfinished ice cube
        i mix my liquid with your strong tea

i'm an ice cube as strong as your hand
airplanes will bring us spices for cooking

        we throw the ice cubes out the window
        our penises and vaginas tense up

    the thrown ice cubes hit the child guards
    reverting back to an identity with the broken glass

        i am frozen water
        eating me is a vacation for poor kids

           we want more ice cubes
           let's not let them not be able to be made

ice cubes have to be here
did our mother neglect us?

                      there must be an end to this summer
                      get me some ice cubes

i am ice that is not a cube
i am a weird squiggly shape that rich people's refrigerators create

               i forgot about that political poem i wrote
               i wanted to read it right away
               like the use of an ice cube

ice-cube air-conditioned poetry-space in new york city
let's read our most recent poems

                    everybody's gone off to the country
                    bet they don't mind drinking their beverages warm

      ice cube politics
      i hope the men will be brief
      because of the life of the cube

i am an ice cube
i do not like being at certain kinds of gatherings
especially when women are excluded

                    i am a female ice cube
                    i observe the strong hands of the truth-tellers

ICE CUBE EPIGRAMS

i am a male ice cube
i notice the trembling hands of the prevaricators

       i am a bisexual ice cube
       i note i see that the people i colden things for
       are willing observers of dawn

i am an ice cube of no proclivity
i colden your water your tea
even the glass itself i have no opinion of

       we are frozen together now
       like bought ones of us often are
       we in revolution will not colden your drinks
       but we will bare our interiors when you put us to
           your foreheads
    & to your aching feet to alleviate from top to bottom
your disbelief in this world's absence of free toys

GEORGES PEREC

Backtracking

For four years, from May 1971 to June 1975, I underwent analysis. It had hardly finished when the desire to say, or more exactly to write down, what had taken place assailed me. Shortly after, Jean Duvignaud proposed to the editors of the magazine *Cause Commune* that they put together an issue on the theme of "the ruse," and I decided then and there that my text would fit most obviously into just such a framework—ill-defined, but bounded by the unstable, the vague, the oblique.

Fifteen months went by, and I made perhaps fifty attempts to get beyond the first lines of a text which, after a few sentences (roughly, those I have just written), bogged down every time in ever more tangled rhetorical devices. I wanted to write, I had to write, I had to restore in writing, through writing, the trace of what had been said (and all those pages begun again, those abandoned drafts, those lines left hanging, are like memories of those shapeless sessions where I had the unnameable feeling of being a machine for grinding out weightless words), but the writing froze solid in precautionary disclaimers and supposedly preliminary questions: Why do I need to write this text? For whom is it really intended? Why choose to write, to publish, to make public, what was perhaps only ever named in the privacy of the analysis? Why decide to hook this drifting effort to the ambiguous theme of "the ruse"? That made a whole list of questions, which I asked with suspicious eagerness—little *a*, little *b*, little *c*, little *d*—as if there just had to be questions, as if without questions there could be no answers. But what I have to say is not an answer, it is an affirmation, something obvious, something that happened, that burst forth. Not something that was buried at the heart of a problem, but something that was there, right next to me, something of me to tell.

A ruse is something that gets around things, but how do you get around a ruse? It's a trick question, an excuse, a pretext serving, each time, to defer the inevitable commencement of writing. Each word I set down was not a milestone but a detour, the stuff of daydreams. For those fifteen months I daydreamed on those meandering words just as, for four years, I had daydreamed on the couch as I gazed at the moldings and cracks on the ceiling.

Then as now it was almost a comfort to tell myself that one day the words would come. One day I would begin to speak, I would begin to write. For years you think that talking means finding, discovering, understanding, understanding at last, being illuminated by the truth. But no: when it takes place, all you know is that it is taking place; it's there, you're talking, you're writing: talking is only talking, simply talking, writing is only writing, making the shapes of letters on a blank piece of paper.

Did I know that that was what I had sought—that obvious thing so long unsaid and always remaining to be said, that sole expectation, that sole tension recovered in an almost intangible stammering?

It took place one day, and I knew that it had. I would like to be able to say I knew at once, but that would not be true. There is no tense to express when it was. It took place, it had taken place, it takes place, it will take place. You knew it already, you know it now. Something simply opened and opens: the mouth to speak, the pen to write: something shifted, something shifts and makes a sign, the wavy line of ink on paper, something with up- and downstrokes.

I assume from the start that this equivalence of speaking and writing is obvious, just as I identify the blank sheet of paper with that other place of hesitations, illusions, and erasures, the ceiling of the analyst's consulting room. I know this is not self-evident, but it is for me, from now on, and it is exactly what was at stake in the analysis. That is what happened, that is what was shaped from session to session over the course of those four years.

Psychoanalysis does not really resemble advertisements for baldness cures: there wasn't a "before" and an "after." There was a present of the analysis, a "here and now" that began, lasted, ended. I could just as well write "that took four years to begin" or "that ended over four years." There was neither beginning nor end: long before the first session the analysis had already begun, if only in the slow decision to undertake analysis and in the choice of an analyst; long after the last session the analysis goes on, if only in this solitary duplication which mimics its persistence and plodding. The tense of the analysis was a stuckness in time, a ballooning of time: for four years there was an everydayness to the analysis, a routine: little marks in a datebook, work strung along the density of the sessions, their regular recurrence, their rhythm.

In the first place the analysis was just that: a particular way of separating days—days with and days without—and on the days with, something resembling a fold, a retreat, a warp: in the layering of the hours, a suspended, alien moment; in the day's flow, a kind of halt, a pause.

There was something abstract in this arbitrary pause, something that was both reassuring and frightening, an immovable and timeless time, an immobile time in an improbable space. Yes, of course, I was in Paris, in a *quartier* I knew well, in a street where I had actually once lived, a few yards from my favorite bar and from several familiar restaurants, and I could have amused myself by working out my longitude, latitude, altitude, and orientation (my head west-northwest, my feet east-southeast). But the ritual protocol of the sessions extracted space and time from these coordinates: I arrived, I rang, a girl let me in. I waited a few minutes in a room set aside for this purpose; I could hear the analyst showing the preceding client to the door; a few moments later, the analyst opened the waiting room door. He never crossed the threshold. I passed in front of him and entered his consulting room. He followed me, closed the doors (there were two of them, creating a tiny entrance hall, something like an airlock, which further emphasized the enclosure of the space), and sat down in his armchair while I stretched out on the couch.

I stress these banal details because they were repeated, two or three times a week, throughout those four years, just as the end-of-session ritual was repeated: the doorbell rung by the following client, the analyst mumbling something like "Good" without the word ever implying any kind of appreciation of the material stirred up during the session, then standing up, me standing up also and, when appropriate, paying him his fee (I didn't pay at every session, but fortnightly), him opening the doors of his consulting room, showing me to the main door, and closing it behind me after a ritual leave-taking that most often consisted of confirming the day of the next session ("Until Monday" or "Until Tuesday," for example).

At the next session, the same movements, the same gestures, were repeated exactly, identically. The few times when it happened that they were not, and however minute the modification may have been to one of those elements of ritual, it had a meaning, even if I do not know what it was; it signified something, perhaps only that I was in analysis, and that the analysis was that and not something else. It matters little, under the circumstances, whether these modifications came from the analyst, from me, or by chance. These tiny deviations, whether they made the analysis spill over into the convention in which it was wrapped (as, for example, when on very rare occasions I took the initiative to leave and opened the doors myself) or, on the contrary, robbed the analysis of a piece of time that belonged to it (such as when, in the absence of his secretary, the analyst had to answer the telephone himself or let in the next client or deal with a Salvation Army collector at the door), all pointed out the function that these rituals had for me: to put a frame of space and time around that unending discourse that through the course of sessions, of months, of years, I was going to try to make my own, to take charge of, in which I would seek to recognize myself and to name myself.

The regularity of these entry and exit rituals thus became for me a first rule (not of psychoanalysis in general, but of the only experience I could have of it and of the memories that remain to me of that experience): immutable by agreement, repeated calmly, these rituals were a serenely polite way of marking the boundaries of this closed space where, beyond the city's hubbub, out of time, out of this world, something would be said that might come from me, be mine, be for me. They seemed to guarantee the benevolent neutrality of that unmoving ear to which I was going to try to say something; they were so to speak the bounds—polite, civilized, slightly austere, slightly cold, a touch stilted—within which the muffled, stopped violence of the analytic dialogue would burst out.

For four years, stretched out on the couch, my head on a white handkerchief which, before the arrival of the next client, the analyst would throw casually onto a little Empire filing cabinet already strewn with the crumpled handkerchiefs of preceding clients, my hands crossed behind my head or on my stomach, my right leg stretched out and my left leg slightly bent, I plunged into that time without history, that nonplace that was going to become the place of my history, of my speaking still to come. I could see three walls, three or four pieces of furniture, two or three prints, a few books. The floor was carpeted, there were moldings on the ceiling and fabric on the walls: a precise and tidy decor, seemingly neutral, changing little from one session to another, from one year to another—a dead, calm place.

There was not much noise. A piano or a radio, sometimes, rather far off, someone, somewhere, using a vacuum cleaner, or, on fine days when the analyst left the window open (he often aired the room between sessions), birdsong from a nearby garden. The telephone, I've already said, almost never rang. The analyst himself made very little noise. Sometimes I could hear his breathing, or a sigh, or a cough, or stomach rumbles, or the striking of a match.

So I had to speak. That's what I was there for. That was the rule of the game. I was shut into this other space with this other person: the other was sitting in an armchair behind me, he could see me, he could speak or not speak, and generally chose not to speak; whereas I was stretched out on the couch in front of him, I could not see him, I had to speak, my speech had to fill this empty place.

But speaking was easy anyway. I needed to talk, and I had a whole repository of stories, problems, questions, associations, fantasies, puns, memories, hypotheses, explanations, theories, landmarks, hideouts.

I skipped easily along the only-too-well-marked-out paths of my mazes. Everything had meaning, it was all connected, obvious, could be unraveled at will: signs waltzed by, parading their amiable anxieties. But beneath the ephemeral flashes of verbal collisions and the controlled titillations of the Beginner's Book of Oedipus, my voice encountered only its own emptiness: neither the faint echo of my own past nor the clouded turbulence of my affrontable enemies, but the hackneyed catchwords of mummy and daddy, pee-pee and wallop; neither my real emotions, nor my fears, nor my desire, nor my body, but readymade answers, anonymous jumble, the thrills of an amusement park railway.

The wordy raptures of these little pansemic vertigoes faded fast; it took only a few seconds, a few seconds of silence during which I waited for the analyst's acquiescence, which was never given, and I would then fall back into a bitter moroseness, further than ever from my speech, from my voice.

The other, behind me, said nothing. At every session I waited for him to speak. I was sure that he was keeping something from me, that he knew far more about it than he was prepared to admit, that he had something in his mind all the same, that he *knew* something. As if the words that went through my head flew straight into his head and settled deep inside it forever, building up over the sessions a great lump of silence as dense as my speech was hollow, as full as my speech was empty.

From then on mistrust set in and enveloped my words as well as his silence: it became a tiresome play of mirrors where images endlessly reflected their Moebius garlands, dreams too beautiful to have been dreamed. Where was truth? Where was untruth? When I tried to be silent, to be no longer stuck in this ridiculous repetition, in these illusions of emerging speech, silence immediately became unbearable. When I tried to speak, to say something of me, to confront that clown inside me who juggled so cleverly with my story, that magician who knew so well how to mystify himself, I immediately felt as if I were starting again on the same puzzle, as if, by going through all the possible combinations of pieces one by one, I might one day find the image I was after.

At the same time something like a crash in my memory set in. I began to be afraid of forgetting, as though unless I made a note of everything I would be unable to hold on to any part of fleeting life. Every evening, scrupulously, with maniacal conscientiousness, I kept a kind of diary. It was the complete opposite of a "personal" diary; I entered in it only "objective" things that had happened to me: time of waking, timetable, journeys, purchases, progress (measured in lines or pages), people met or just seen, details of the evening meal I had eaten in this or that restaurant, books read, records listened to, films seen, etc.

As I panicked at the prospect of losing my traces, I began frenziedly to collect and to sort things. I kept everything: letters and their envelopes, cinema ticket stubs, plane tickets, bills, check stubs, handouts, receipts, catalogues, summonses, weeklies, used felt-tip pens, empty lighters, and even receipts for gas and electricity payments for an apartment I hadn't lived in for over six years, and sometimes I would spend whole days sorting and filing, thinking up a system that would fill up every year, every month, every day of my life.

I had been doing the same thing with my dreams for some time already. Long before the beginning of the analysis I had begun to wake myself up in the night to jot them down in black notebooks that never left me. I very soon became so adept that dreams offered themselves to me fully written, including their titles. Whatever my present feelings about these dry and secret utterances in which the reflections of my own story seem to reach me only through innumerable prisms, I finally conceded that these dreams had not been lived to become dreams, but dreamed to become texts, that they were not the "royal road" I thought they would be, but winding paths taking me ever further from a recognition of myself.

Made cautious perhaps by the ruses of my dreams, I transcribed nothing, or almost nothing, of the analysis itself. A sign in my datebook—the analyst's initial—indicated the day and time of the session. In my diary, I wrote just "session," followed sometimes by an adjective, usually pessimistic ("gloomy," "dull," "drawn-out," "not much fun," "totally boring," "crappy," "rather stupid," "rather shitty," "depressing," "ridiculous," "harmless," "nostalgic," "feeble and forgettable," etc.).

Very occasionally I marked the session, by something the analyst had said that day, by an image, by a feeling (for instance, "cramp"), but most of these notations, whether positive or negative, have now lost their meaning, and all the sessions—with a few exceptions, when the words that would bring the analysis to its term rose to the surface—are merged in the memory of that expectant hovering, of my confused glance seeking ceaselessly in the plasterwork of the ceiling the outlines of animals, human heads, signs.

Of the actual process that allowed me to escape from these repetitive and burdensome acrobatics and gave me access to my story and to my voice, I can say only that it was infinitely slow: it was the process of the analysis itself, but I only knew that afterward. First that hard shell of writing behind which I was concealing my hunger for writing had to give way, the high wall of prefabricated memories had to crumble, my sanctuaries of ratiocination had to be reduced to dust. I had to go back on my tracks, to travel once more the path I had trod and of which I had lost the thread.

I have nothing to say about that underground place. I know that it took place and that henceforth its trace is inscribed in me and in the texts I write. It lasted as long as the time it took for my story to come together: a story that was given to me, one day, with surprise, with wonder, with violence, like a memory restored to its own space, like a gesture, a warmth regained. That day the analyst heard what I had to say to him, what for four years he had listened to without hearing for the simple reason that I hadn't been telling him—that I hadn't been telling it to myself.

Translated by David Bellos

Translator's Note

"Backtracking" was written and published in 1977 while Perec's novel *Life: A User's Manual* was in progress. Its French title, "Les Lieux d'une ruse," is particularly awkward to translate: it means both "The Site of a Ruse" and "The Rhetoric of Deception," since Perec often used the word *lieu* ("place") in its older rhetorical sense (present in English in the word *commonplace*, for example). Perec's style in this article (unlike any other piece of his writing) is grave, contorted, almost cumbersome—as if to require the reader to repeat some of the author's own "hard work" in analysis.

EDVARD KOCBEK

Occurrence

The same thing keeps recurring:
a twitching that I cannot subdue.
From time to time a rhythmical crackling,
as of wood settling throughout the house.
At night and by day an easing of tension,
first in the furniture, then in the floor,
in the wall somewhere, the light fixture, my books.
Each time someplace new, each time inevitable.
As though building toward an earthquake or
as though a treacherous power were mounting
and the house might collapse, or somebody
immured in the wall would knock and
step through it any minute. I swallow
with difficulty, ensnared in the creaking.
I sense it acutely and I know: the warm silence
of things, the horrible aloneness of primeval,
wearisome matter. Even now the ocean washes over
England. Even now glowing magma settles
beneath our feet. In the dark I decipher the unknown writing
on the walls. In the dark I see huge eyes,
and in dreams a horrible land of whirlwinds.

A Plea

I have been working on the following plea
and would like it to reach the right hands:
Adam, man of earth, named all
things and creatures, says the Bible.
But science asserts that in its own unique
way each of two thousand languages has fixed
all objects and commands its native realm.
Jews do not dare to speak God's name,
the Greeks held lapses in speech
to be a violation of the soul, not just mistakes,
we Slovenes have an articulate bridge from
the singular to the plural—the dual.
Yet man keeps changing
into a lost object
estranged from the soul of the world.
Thucydides ascribed the spread of plague
in Athens to the semantic shift of words.
Confucius would have taken power in society
if he first could have tested the rightness
of the names of all things and phenomena.
Marx shifted the authentication of meaning
onto work and the building of the world.
Christ directed the word toward love,
and Heidegger toward the nothing which is more than nothing.
I constantly reread the story of Babel.
The world's plunging through universal darkness
is closely linked to mistakes in language,
catastrophes are an eruption of misplaced trust,

A PLEA

because a robber begins to blunder through the forest
when he loses touch with a particular tree.
My plea has to do with the tree.
When I say that I see a forest, there is nothing left
in common between me, who sees the forest,
and the tree, which is not me.
Not to mention the rest: the rest is still worse.
This has been written in the forest, among robbers.
I entreat the soul of the world to awake.

Translated by Michael Biggins

GERALD BURNS

Atalanta in Cleveland

would be nice, backlit set like what you see through the pane in a
translucent Easter egg, instead of cut paper tinted everything blown glass,
with verdure of spun glass. We consider appropriate the tinted printed bunnies
with baskets on their paws, tiggy cottages, that rabbits should deliver, even
produce, eggs. It's mixed, a muddle held together (apparently) by a metaphor.
In Swinburne's *Atalanta* the boar gores the godlike young man, who
falls bleeding. The fall makes no sound, is (you'd say) noiseless, and
his blood really is clear, ichor like when you squash one of the lighter-
bodied streambound bugs, nymphs indeed (their jaws as I said like steamshovels),
writing on some rigid surface, rock or branch, in ink near their color.
You could, if you could get through the glass (celluloid), if it weren't so *small*
and of a perspective like ours but the scale reduced, like buildings tramped
by a reptile, insert, intrude, insinuate ourselves, like Satan in Eden spit
ourselves within, become or find ourselves inside the egg, sky one uniform
pale, an arch of whity-gray, cement cyclorama like the one O'Neill's players
built in Washington Square to be lit like air, you would be there among
the rabbits, Mrs. Bunny and her children, wide dresses, pinafores all flat
cutouts, the cottages unenterable, no more rooms behind than the shrubbery,
but again I'd like this altered, from the commercial one with mock-icing
frame to the porthole in the end to the one with all inside of blown glass,
its baskets triumphs like the concrete ones on lawns, that the handles
endure, stay up, in such a substance. Imagine (lowest verb) your wandering there,
among these, fairy renderings of trees, dogs, objects, cottages flat as translucent
lollypops, the ones you'd buy veined, oversize, to stick in the mouth like a
     phonograph
record and lick for hours, our pleasure in any transparent thing aboriginal, itself
     transparent,
to be *in* that, a world of it, the mailbox (now three-dimensional) palest

french-blue tint, with inside settled like eggs, letters in a heap, clear lemon, pink
that as you peer through maintain themselves, the Xes for crossed flaps on some,
and on the upper lefts (to right them, sort their orientation) purple stamps, just
     the color
too thin to see as added other than as tint, the word going back to tinct, as in glaze
or overlay you see perfused. That may be the fascination, that surface events
are *stated*, not just posited, to invade these depths. Indeed, thickness is mostly
known by plotting surface character *around* the rim, past seeing, where the rough
treetrunk becomes, perspectively, smooth as a winebottle or Gibson Girl's cheek on
the side away from one, faint pink on bunny blown-glass basket rose repeated
oddly on some highlight in her shawl's faint blue, the rabbit herself clear to
indicate white fur's complicity with color as applied, as if by the printer
to Sunday funnies' line. "Imagine" being in this, as to Swinburne his
Greek, loved Greek must have been those egg-like characters (so few capitals,
so few proper names!) on clear pages out of Oxford. I lately saw
Housman's classic text in a library book sale, for sale for pennies
and didn't buy it for lack of the language and imagining its people and terrain
through characters, a frieze of type (as Assyrian letters pour or swarm over
a stone frieze) as white as their statues, washed free of color, or how it used
to take them as magical that a thin bowl lip in alabaster diffused light
through. We saw matched deco lamps in an antique shop, pale frosted green
verticals, like natural tourmaline crystals domesticated with metal top knob,
a metal piffle in the middle, on square greek key-cut footed base of same
lime-sherbet in gin glass that lit, the cords to them twisty-gray silver ropes
to be distanced, distant, from the lamps that, even unlit, kept the light.
Greek for the old ones must have been like that, shape and color in no
necessary relation but apt, as the dancer, breast free and gleaming in
blackest bronze, robes swirling about her, might be seen by them as a
philosophic pleasure *as* supporting by one extended bacchic arm, its muscles
relaxed as Donatello, no Atlas effect intended, some frosted globe by balustrade
that, as you came in of an evening, dripping, flipped a switch, lit.

DAVID SEARCY

from *Ordinary Horror*

1

Here's a horror story for you. An old fellow, a widower about seventy years old, lives alone in an aging tract house in one of those extended tract house neighborhoods that, given twenty or thirty years to mellow, lose none of their bleakness but gain some comfort from the fact of survival—the fact of such ordinariness being able to survive, coming to seem more or less permanent, which gives the people who live there a kind of necessity or inevitability, whether they know it or not.

This old man loves to grow roses in his backyard. And whether he knows it or not, he loves their springing from such ordinariness. He even has them blocked off, gridded into organized beds like a neighborhood of roses, so that when he looks out the sliding glass door of his little den at them blooming, they're even more miraculous, as if no amount of constraint or definition can keep them back, and the arrangement of his garden, designed of course to emphasize this, has symbolic implications as well.

He likes a cup of coffee in the morning on the patio among the rose beds probably better than anything—better than gardening, in fact, because his inactivity is proof the roses are stable for the moment, protected and receptive to the notion, however faint, that protection is reciprocal. Nevertheless there's a little anxiety most of the time, and he probably understands he's set himself up for it, having invested so much so visibly. It's the character of the neighborhood for things to be visible in any case; so many similar houses so close together make anything not belonging to the architecture stand out. Especially, one imagines, when viewed from above. There's a feeling of overexposure to sky or space that has to derive from the uniformly limited elevation of everything—low-pitched and flat-roofed single-story houses and too few or the wrong sort of trees to provide a canopy. Domestic space stops about twenty feet up, which makes afternoon light seem too abrupt, striking everything at once, and dawn and nightfall seem more sudden and even somehow alarming on cloudless days in the summer when there's hardly any transition.

Lately the old man, whose name is Mr. Delabano, is more than usually concerned about his garden because of the appearance of little piles of sandy soil here and there in the yard and on the grass paths between the beds. He thinks at first it might be squirrels, but it's too early in the year for that, and this is too destructive anyway. Nor does it really look like excavation: the piles of earth seem to have been pushed up from below. So he decides it must be moles or gophers and does his best to control the damage, hoping that whatever it is might just be passing through and he won't have to confront the problem directly with poisons or the terrifying spear-traps he has seen advertised somewhere for this sort of infestation. He's determined, as long as it doesn't get out of hand, to wait before seeking advice. He's like someone with a suspicious physical symptom, afraid to find anything out; but he dwells on it anyway, especially at night, when he imagines the damage occurs.

Every night he thinks: In the morning there'll be fewer new mounds than before; he'll pack them down, replace the grass, and maybe that will be that; he won't have to consult anybody or speak to his neighbors about it or buy chemicals or dispose of dead creatures or do anything at all, just let nature take its course. The last thing he wants is to hire someone. Who knows what they might do, like firemen in the house destroying more than they save. Just have the patience to let things alone for a bit. These things are bound to come and go.

But naturally it gets worse. He begins taking his coffee in the kitchen, looking out the little window above the sink and wondering if his yard is really more heavily infested than his neighbors', or if it's only that his repairs are more conspicuous. He wonders if maybe a cat or a dog might help. Aren't terriers supposed to chase rodents? Then, leafing through the Sunday newspaper supplement, he experiences one of those moments of perfect coincidence or grace. A big display ad on the inside back page in very large print reads

> How to Chase Gophers from your Yard and Garden
> Get rid of burrowing rodents without traps or poisons

beneath which is a strange heraldic-looking cartoon of three gophers or whatever in the process of being cast out, suspended in midtrajectory, each emitting a cartoon drizzle of anxiety droplets, and four spiky plants (one on each side of each rodent) that look like schematized bromeliads of some kind. Below that are several paragraphs of fine print and an order form. It's the plants that do it—exotic, South American, never-before-available and now only briefly in limited supplies. Nonflowering and more effective than spurges. Root systems antithetical to garden varmints but harmless to pets and everything else. Thirty-nine dollars and ninety-five cents. How wonderful, he thinks, just a post office box. Gopherbane, Grand Rapids, Michigan. Nothing to do but send in the form.

• • •

In a corner of Mr. Delabano's garden right next to the patio, in its own raised bed with a white wooden trellis where the light strikes first in the morning, is an "antique" rose that he and his wife discovered clinging to the remains of an old fence rail on a trip through Virginia a couple of years before she died. He's certain it's not wild, but he has no interest in research, preferring to keep to himself the thought that it might be unique, the only example of some unspectacular nineteenth-century cultivar, not far removed from the wild but improved nonetheless, an artifact of sorts like a little flame about to wink out when they found it. Waiting for UPS or the postman to ring, he thinks about that rose. Listening to the winds that sometimes come up at nightfall so violently in the summer, sweeping across the plateau of rooftops and mimosa trees and buzzing the weather stripping like a bassoon reed, he thinks about that simple thing.

In the mornings he attends to it more carefully than to the

others, and when little piles of dirt erupt within the rose beds themselves, he drives lengths of a concrete reinforcing rod at two-inch intervals entirely into the ground around it. This takes him the better part of a week, and although it exhausts and calms him for a while, it's obviously an escalation of the disruptive sort he'd hoped to avoid when he responded to the newspaper ad at the beginning of summer. Now he feels compromised, tries to think of this as a temporary measure, although he can't really see himself ever pulling up the spikes. Certainly they're better than poisons. He doesn't even like to use sprays. Most of his roses were chosen for their hardiness and resistance to disease, and even though this requires rejecting some of the showier varieties, he feels compensated by a kind of vitality that permits him to imagine his roses outliving him, carrying along something of his affections like the antique rose which he imagines somehow still retains, in a way not clear but powerful to him, the possibility of the people in whose garden it grew.

Whatever particular longings or regrets drive such thoughts are absorbed in his regard for the roses. It's the sentimental absorbency of roses that's most valuable to him, in fact. It relieves him of any lingering sorrows, draws them off and releases them to the air. This is an image that actually occurs to him sometimes in a dreamy sort of way: an almost mechanical, even industrial, relation between himself and the roses—little chimneys of the spirit concentrating and releasing something essential to him and (by vague and mysterious extension) to the whole neighborhood, which he feels is such a superficial imposition on the prairie, the great flatness above which his roses bloom like a signal and whose ancient surface, he suspects, still subtly inflects the network of little streets and alleys. On the whole this seems to be a satisfactory cosmology. It invigorates the bleakness; gives a glow to the pale brick, the white-trimmed green asbestos siding and thin white curtains in the late afternoon. But it's delicate. It can't support serious turbulence. It has to be maintained and balanced against ordinary necessities; so he thinks of the spikes as a kind of prosthesis, rusting away as balance is restored, pinning things in place until then.

Cleaning up after supper, standing by the kitchen sink and looking out the window, he can't detect any real damage to the roses. One or two might have fewer blooms than he'd like but that's so variable. He looks around for the newspaper ad. He's had nearly two months to memorize it, but he likes to keep it and look at it now and then for reassurance. He looks under the phone book where it's been; he looks in the drawers of the telephone table and everywhere else it could possibly be, but he can't find it. He looks in the back of yesterday's Sunday supplement, but now there's a different ad. In fact, he can't recall its having appeared in the paper at all since he placed his order. Maybe it ran only once, or maybe he just never noticed it before and now it's stopped—supplies used up or the company out of business. What was the name? He's lost it. He should have express-mailed his order. What if he missed the tail end of the offer?

That night the winds are worse than usual, keeping him awake past midnight listening to the weather stripping and thinking he should have put a trash bag over the antique rose to keep it from getting whipped against the trellis. For a while he lies there trying to remember exactly what the cartoon plants looked like in the ad—how many spikes each had and whether these emerged symmetrically or alternated along the stem.

The next morning he decides to try the local branch library, but he's too early and has to drive around awhile until it opens. Then, unwilling to deal with the computerized card catalogue and disappointed with the depth of the old newspaper file, he wanders more or less at random among the stacks, taking much longer than he would like, gathering at last a not very satisfactory general gardening book with a chapter on pests and something from the medical section called *Amazonian Biotoxins: Their Perils and Promise*, which attracts him because the pharmacological society emblem on its cover features a stylized plant that looks a little like what he remembers from the lost advertisement.

By now it's past eleven and he's afraid he's missed the mail. He's afraid he might get home and find a yellow note on his door telling where to claim his package the following day after ten hours of miserable uncertainty. But there isn't a note; there's a package. Right by the front door. It's a two-foot cube, plain brown paper and no return address. What else could it be? He places it in the center of the kitchen table, then puts on his yard clothes and goes out to repair the damage from the night before; it's not quite as bad as he feared. Then he's back in the kitchen, washed up and ready for the package. Could it have been in the mail all this time, misrouted or something? How long can plants survive, wrapped up like that in the summer? He tries to make out the postmark, but it's smeared. It looks like July maybe—that's only last month—but it might be June.

Holding a paring knife just back of the tip, he scores through the paper and then through the masking tape along the top seam of the cardboard box, folds it back, and is struck by the smell. It can't be spoiled. He can't believe it. He pulls out the wads of foreign language newspaper and withdraws a little foil-wrapped, wire-reinforced wooden crate inside which, nestled in a bed of what looks like moist rubber bands, are the plants: four of them, much smaller than he expected, but alive as far as he can tell. The smell seems to come from the rubber bands. They're sticky, like old newspaper rubber bands that have begun to decompose, and they smell terrible, but he can't say like what. They must be a sort of mulch or peat moss, he thinks. There are no instructions anywhere, absolutely nothing except the little crate and its contents. He eases one of the plants out of its nest, picking off the rubber bands. It's only about four inches long, with a root system nearly the same size, and it doesn't really look much like the pictures in the ad. It's not really spiky; the leaves are more spoon-shaped, each with a fringe of short nettle-like spines and covered with fuzz like an African violet. A flickering of the light like a power surge brings his attention back to the room, which seems gradually to have become quite dark for midday. Through the glass door he can see heavy clouds moving in; another flicker of lightning and a long roll of thunder. He'll have to hurry to get them in the ground, but there's root stimulator already mixed and an open bag of peat. He'll throw in some of the rubber band stuff as well—make them feel at home perhaps, and it can't hurt.

The rain starts almost immediately, however, and by the time he's finished he's gotten soaked, and his shoulder hurts, but he's in a better frame of mind. He stands by the sink, looking at the garden in the rain. There's one by the antique rose just outside the defenses and the others are like traffic lights at intersections of the paths between the beds. Tomorrow he'll place rings of aluminum edging around all four.

• • •

ORDINARY HORROR

He sleeps late the following morning, awakened about ten by cicadas chattering so loud he thinks there must be a new crop. Light seems to rush in through the curtains as if the air had thinned, the glare and the noise combining to make him feel (not unpleasantly) precarious, barely contained, his house paper-thin as he imagines Japanese houses to be. He lies there for a long time listening and admiring the light. He remembers finding cicada husks—*nymphs*, whatever they were called—translucent like wax paper, attached to trees and the sides of the house, empty and open along the top where the new forms had emerged. Maybe these loud ones were the seven-year kind. Or was it seventeen? He'd heard of seventeen year locusts, he thought, and maybe some that stayed in the ground even longer. What possible use could that be? He can hear cars go by every now and then, but other than that there's no neighborhood noise; everyone's left for work or day camp, everything's fallen silent but the cicadas chattering in waves. It's hard to think of the last time he stayed in bed so late. He can remember being sick as a child and the strangeness of the vacuum on a weekday midmorning when all the day's business had left him behind. How everything glows now; how the room almost blooms with light.

Outside, there's some sweeping up to do after the rainstorm, but things are in pretty good shape. The new plants look all right and there aren't any fresh molehills, if that's what they are, although the rain could have something to do with that. He can tell it's going to be hot, and though it's nearly eleven, he takes his coffee out on the patio, faintly aware that as a celebratory move it might be premature. Still, the day seems promising, and there are two buds on the old rose about to open.

He makes the rounds, shaking the rain off the rosebushes, and returns to the old rose, shakes it gently, then teases open the small apricot-colored buds with his fingertips, blowing into the blossoms to help them unfold. There's nothing like it, he thinks. None he knows of smells quite like it; all that's left to carry the scent of someone's garden, some household, a family—who knows, a hundred years ago—as if they still existed.

The cicadas are overwhelming. Ordinarily he likes their gentle buzzing in the summer, coming and going more or less with the blooming season. He plucks an empty husk from the antique rose and, looking around, notices quite a few others. Just about every available vertical surface seems to have acquired at least one or two cicada husks—the birdbath, the rubber wheels of his garden cart, and the brick of the house just above the foundation, where there is a very good collection. Surely one can't actually have a plague of cicadas. They weren't really locusts. He didn't think they fed after emerging, or even had mouths for that matter. All they do is buzz. He leans back in the recliner. It's hypnotic after a while—the oscillating buzz, the heat, and the clear sky—like the ocean or the TV after sign-off. He can hear the summer school carpoolers, the first wave of the day, the youngest ones returning—barely audible beyond the cicada noise: doors slamming down the street, little yelps and squeals. It's amazing, he thinks, how sound travels through the neighborhood. With everything so flat and open it seems it should all reflect off the concrete and diffuse straight up, but, especially in the summer, it's as if there were a heavier layer, a high-pressure zone or something, hovering just above, keeping sound from escaping and sending it along like whispering through a pipe.

He rouses himself after a moment and gathers his tin-snips and a roll of corrugated aluminum edging for the borders around the plants—mostly just to mark them, distinguish them from weeds. He leaves about an inch and a half showing above the ground; so much the better if it catches a little water.

It's uncomfortably hot now and the cicadas have become oppressive. He returns to the kitchen, where the noise is muted and he can still see the little plants—maybe already a shade greener than yesterday—protected and waving slightly in the breeze.

• • •

Mr. Delabano is used to the sounds of the blackbirds and starlings that have lately begun passing above his house at about the same time every morning. Now and then, if they come by directly overhead, he goes outside to watch as they stream across in a fairly continuous ribbon for maybe a minute or so, crackling and whistling like radio static. So, the next morning, it's only after this same noise continues for quite a while longer and with much greater volume than usual that he puts down his electric shaver and listens to it. His bathroom has one of those frosted-glass privacy windows, so he can't actually see what's going on outside, but something peculiar is. Some sort of commotion, most of it birds but something else as well—a chattering and batting against the house like hail or the first big drops of a heavy rain. What in the world? Something hits the frosted window, then something else—he can't make it out. But there's a great flurry of wings—furious, darting shadows projected onto the translucent glass. The racket is pretty alarming; he ties his robe, retrieves his glasses from the top of the TV, slides open the glass door to the patio, and is immediately struck sharply in the forehead by a small flying object and involved in such a terrific flapping and buzzing swirl of conflict that he loses his balance and falls back against the doorframe, banging his ear and losing his glasses in the monkey grass. Now it's like trying to see through frosted glass again. Blackbirds are everywhere, jeering and whistling, and cicadas rattle wildly about. It's some sort of feeding frenzy. He recovers his glasses and edges around toward the fence, keeping close to the house. He's startled by someone yelling practically right behind him: "You must have something they like."

Mr. Delabano jerks around; it's his neighbor, the one who likes to barbecue outdoors.

"You've got something they like over there." He's standing just the other side of the fence with his hands in his pockets, smiling and watching the terrible goings-on with delight.

"It's the cicadas," says Mr. Delabano, aware now of the extent to which the invasion appears to be restricted to his own backyard.

"You must be raising them, I guess."

"Oh no," says Mr. Delabano turning away, not understanding what is meant at first, then recognizing that sort of teasing wit that always makes him uneasy and uncertain how to respond.

"That's the Grackle Express."

"What?" says Mr. Delabano, feeling trapped against the fence, unwilling quite yet to penetrate the holocaust again.

"The Grackle Express. The whole thing, as far as I can tell. I've been watching them for a couple of weeks; every morning probably thousands of them, right on time, but it's the first time it ever stopped. It was really pretty amazing. The whole thing just kind of folded back and swooped right down. Really spectacular. What happened to your ear?"

Mr. Delabano takes his hand from the side of his head and looks at the blood, but doesn't say anything.

"The birds get you? Boy, that's Alfred Hitchcock stuff, isn't it." To Mr. Delabano's horror, the younger man jumps the fence to examine the injury. The sudden movement and the clatter of the cyclone fence seem to disturb the birds, and a general departure begins; like an unfurling flag they lift up in a single great undulation, then, swirling around, roll out toward the northwest, leaving behind a few stragglers and a scattering of damaged cicadas intermittently buzzing and flopping around.

"Now that's kind of spooky, isn't it?" says the neighbor after a moment of silence. And it does seem strange—such complicated mayhem having gathered so much energy just to stop like that, like an event run backwards.

"I don't know what it is," mutters Mr. Delabano, noticing his collar is wet and allowing himself to be accompanied back into the house.

• • •

"Did you ever make buzz-bombs or whatever they were called when you were in school?" asks Mr. Delabano's neighbor, putting away the medical supplies.

"I don't know," says Mr. Delabano with a towel around his neck and a complicated-looking bandage covering the lower part of his right ear.

"Oh, it was sort of a practical joke," he continues, gathering up the band-aid wrappers. "Kids used to make these things—I don't remember how they did it—but they'd be addressed to someone, looked just like a regular note all folded up, the kind kids passed around all the time in class, but these were sort of like letter bombs. Somebody would get one passed to him, and right in the middle of class he'd open it up and the thing would just rattle and buzz as loud as anything; sounded just like those cicadas out there, but even louder, so the guy who gets it gets in trouble. Some way they had a wound-up rubber band inside with a little paper spinner, so when you opened it it rattled like hell, and you never could find out who sent it."

"No, I never got one of those," says Mr. Delabano, who has no idea what to make of this but urgently wants to inspect his garden and would prefer to do it alone. But his neighbor just stands there, his hands back in his pockets, silent now and gazing into the backyard through the open glass door. A light breeze carries a faint spicy, musky scent into the room.

"Boy," says the neighbor softly after a minute, "my wife sure loves your roses."

It's mostly the old rose—more detectable at this range than others. A powerful fragrance, Mr. Delabano assumes, was one of its primitive characteristics.

"Hey, I'm going to be late." His neighbor turns suddenly. "Listen, if you need anything, if you think you want a ride to the doctor or anything, let me know. I'm Mike Getz. This is crazy, you know, we've lived next door for a year and now I'm introducing myself."

Mr. Delabano takes his hand. "Frank Delabano," he says.

"Yeah," says Mike Getz, "we've admired your mailbox; my wife wants one of those too. So maybe I can get you to come over for a hamburger some weekend—tell my wife how to grow roses. You aren't dizzy, are you?"

"Oh no, I'm fine," says Mr. Delabano, trying to look recovered.

"Well I'm really sorry about your ear. Anyway, let me know, okay, if there's anything." And then he's gone. Out the back door and over the fence.

Mr. Delabano doesn't move for a while. He sits at the kitchen table waiting for events to die away a little, feeling the breeze through the open door. In a minute he'll get up and go look at his ear in the bathroom mirror, then he'll check the roses.

2

The last days of August settle into a pattern of storms and drizzle, which gives Mr. Delabano a kind of cover, keeping him indoors most of the time and making it easy to avoid social contact. It's not the best weather for roses, but it's comforting to him, filling the outside world with predictable phenomena and washing away signs of disruption.

For a day or so following the grackle invasion he's startled by an occasional death rattle in the house—once in the middle of the night, a furious buzzing and thrashing about right under his bed that unnerves him strangely, sets his heart racing all night as if something were concentrated in the incident, even in the silliness of it. A thorough sweep of the house turns up quite a number of cicadas, a few of which reactivate when disturbed. They seem to be off or on, nothing in-between; like an old wind-up toy that, apparently run down, pops loose another coil in the spring and whirls into action again. He tries to imagine the sort of noise the paper grocery sack containing them would make if they all switched on late at night in a chain reaction. This thought is so unpleasant he takes the sack out to the alley in the rain, pausing on the way back to check the roses. But it's the new plants that interest him. Kneeling under the umbrella, he decides they've definitely grown, maybe an inch; it's not just the soil settling at the roots. And really a deeper green as well. There's no doubt. He realizes he hasn't any idea how large they're supposed to get. He had thought perhaps a foot or so, but what if they really take off? Huge, exotic, waving fronds overwhelming the roses. Surely not. How could they sell something like that? In any case there haven't been any new mounds. Not a one. There would be some patching up to do when things dried out—places where soggy ground had slumped above the tunnels. But no new activity at all.

He scoops up a little dirt and packs it around the base of a plant to replace what's washed away, and encounters something that feels a bit like insulated electrical wiring. "My goodness," he says to himself, excavating and uncovering a substantial tangle of the stuff. "Goodness," he whispers again. It's the root system. They're growing more down than up. Like a carrot. Of course it's the roots that do the trick—"antithetical to garden varmints." Still, it's phenomenal. They must love the rain. He packs the soil back down around the roots, then stands up to survey the garden. Roses and roses with names like racehorses. Maybe something huge and primitive wouldn't be so bad. No gophers for a hundred miles.

He gazes down the line of backyard fences. It's still pretty early—nothing going on in the neighborhood. Just steady rain. All the kids would be inside watching Saturday morning cartoons. He's glad there's no one to see him standing among the roses with his black umbrella; he probably looks silly, somewhat funereal. How sad Mike Getz's red smoker and his barbecue grill look in the rain. How sad all the yards look—all the swingsets and wet grass. The whole neighborhood seems like an old campsite. As if no one had really expected to stay so long but simply got used to it, forgot to move on, or forgot the reason for doing so, and the houses, never built to withstand so much time and weather, finally resemble those World's Fair pavilions preserved for civic or sentimental reasons beyond their intended life, settled into a condition of continuous rejuvenation and repair. He remembers a very old inn in Virginia where he and his wife stayed for a night one summer—the summer they collected the rose. Parts of it were supposed to be seventeenth-century, and in the dining room there was a hole in the wall, about two feet square, that had been framed in glass, with a little plaque next to it explaining how they had dug into the wall looking for a water line or something, but what they'd found—and what made them decide to leave it alone—was a stratified sequence, a foot and a half thick, of older and older construction and reinforcement going all the way back to what seemed to be mud and wattle at the very center. It had to be the earliest structure on which the hotel was based—maybe not much more than a hut or a barn—and everything had just been built on top of it year after year, getting bigger and shinier like a pearl.

Off to the north he can see a stream of blackbirds—the Grackle Express, Mike Getz had called it. Maybe they've altered their route, which was fine with him. He touches his ear. He needs a fresh bandage if he can figure how to undo this one. Purely out of habit he gives the old rose a shake as he walks back into the house.

It's difficult to see in the mirror exactly what his neighbor has done. It's an elaborate construction of gauze and band-aid ends— he hadn't any medical tape—probably quite expert, but it's hard to know where to start. So he starts at the top with his right hand, holding his ear with his left. Then he stops, concerned about the odor. It can't have gotten infected so quickly. It's not that sore, and it wasn't a bird anyway, just the doorframe. But what is that? He pulls the bandage off quickly, and sure enough, the wound's not too bad: the bruise is impressive, but the cut is beginning to heal. The odor, however, is puzzling and disturbing—not decay exactly, but carrying some very unpleasant association like that, or like the smell of alcohol, which as a child he hated more than anything because it reminded him so vividly of the doctor's office that all it took was a whiff and he could feel the needle or the lance. But what does this smell like? And where is it coming from? Is it him? He sniffs around the bathroom. It's in there someplace. It reminds him of something. The plants. Or the mulch, the rubber-band stuff. Something like that, definitely. He looks at his hands. His left is soiled from scraping around in the garden. He brings it to his nose and it's really unpleasant, as bad as the doctor's office. Just the left hand though. He remembers digging around the roots of the plant. For a second he just stands still, trying to isolate the association. It's not just the smell of the rubber-band mulch; there's a component of that, but the main thing—what is it?—is something else altogether, actually uncomfortable, like when the cicada went off under his bed. He turns on the hot water and washes his hands, then washes again and a third time with Comet cleanser, which seems to do the job pretty well. Powerful stuff, whatever it is; he looks at the pale reddish stains that won't wash off the fingers of his left hand.

He finds it hard to get into his daily routine, somehow. He tends to pause in the middle of things, forget what he's doing, finding himself at one point with a lapful of dirty clothes, sitting on the edge of his unmade bed and gazing at the curtains, lost in the gray light and letting his thoughts dissolve, go nearly blank as if waiting for something to appear. Something should, it seems to him. Any minute. The unpleasantness, or at least the sharpness of it, has evaporated. He's left with mostly a sense of depth or distance, something descended toward, approached and withheld, and the odd suspension that follows. It's not unlike the sort of evocative but mysterious odor anyone may encounter from time to time, in the way it sets one's thoughts rummaging, working down through the possibilities toward something as faint as an old girlfriend, a whiff of elementary school. Disinfectant and manila paper. Except for the feeling of inaccessible depth, it's like that, but he can't reach the right level. Something before grade school. Even before the tastes and smells of things that don't belong in one's mouth, like pennies or bitter dark brown furniture varnish. Even more primitive than that, and even stranger.

The rain continues all day and into the evening—white noise like that of the cicadas, making a sort of blank screen against which random musings seem illuminated that might otherwise pass, nearly unnoticed, into the background. He's gradually lost all sense of the disturbing odor; having reflected on it too long and too closely, he's desensitized, unable to summon even a reliable report of his own reactions; it's a rumor. And, as such, dismissible.

3

The start of the regular school year marks a favorite time for Mr. Delabano. The approach of fall, the strollers and cyclists who appear as the evenings get cooler, a sudden rise in the overall bustle, the to and fro of neighborhood activity breaking around him, coming and going like a tide. At no other time does he feel so embraced and isolated, the best of both: so invisible in the garden, less likely to be greeted or noticed, yet necessary somehow, a consequence of what surrounds him. But for some reason this year it seems more subdued, reluctant to quicken. Maybe the population is aging, or maybe everything is just waiting for the first cold snap—the first call to autumn that, in the best years, when it's sudden and clear, can really stop one for a moment, spin one's mood around like a weathervane and hold it in an odd direction, an oblique combination of exuberance and longing. So far, though, it's a bit flat. Summer tailing off to nothing in particular; a general deflation detectable especially in the gaps, the spaces between movements.

By now he's fairly confident of having escaped Mike Getz's threatened invitation. Sunny weather brings him outside with an increasing certainty that the critical period has passed, an exchange of waves across the fence having provoked no further approach. The trouble is he'd have no way to refuse. He'd have to go, stand around in the kitchen and the backyard, speak to the wife and meet the children. That would be difficult. It's not that he doesn't like children. In fact he really loves them, in a way, at a distance—distant voices, bright, loud little blips up and down the street marking the centers of people's lives, monitoring their happiness or alarm. At some level he's suspicious of children—not as personalities but as potential inconsistencies were he to admit them completely. He suspects that children at close range are incompatible with roses. And today the roses need weeding. The ground has had time to dry out, and it's a nice day. Following the rains, a pretty good selection of grassy and leafy odds and ends have begun to poke up through the pine bark, and although it's tedious, he finds it soothing to work from bed to bed; his shoulder feels fine and his ear no longer bothers him. Best of all: no molehills, hardly even a trace—the pits are filled and he's patched in some sod. How quiet it is this time of morning, the ebb of daily events. The cicadas have largely vanished—just a ghost of their former presence barely audible from somewhere, part of the background. No traffic to speak of, no wind. Not a cloud in the sky. He works his way toward one of the new plants. He thinks he'll tidy up their little beds too, but reconsiders. They're okay, he decides; it's best not to fiddle with them if they look okay. And they do. Healthy as they can be—a very deep green now, almost blue-green, and somehow plumped up, as if storing moisture. They're about a foot tall and, until recently, seemed to have stabilized at that height, somewhat to his relief. However, each plant has produced a little spike or tendril at the top and he's been anticipating another growth spurt, expecting it to unfold into a new leaf or leaf-bearing segment. Looking at it today, though, it's obviously a different sort of structure. The tiny knob at the end appears to have doubled in size since yesterday and deepened in color as well. It looks like a little bud now at the tip of the spike, definitely blue and convoluted like a complex knot—what's it called?—a Turk's head.

Something intrudes into his peripheral field of vision, and he has to stop himself from turning around. Someone's standing at the fence. It must be Mike Getz, but he doesn't want to look. Maybe he'll go away; just stay busy, pull some more weeds, and he'll wander off. Why isn't he at work? Maybe it's possible to reach the toolshed; it's in the right direction. If he can just get up quickly and head for it with sufficient purpose and urgency, he can escape among the pots and peat bags.

"Hey, Frank."

Dammit. Just pretend not to hear; old men are hard of hearing—just scoot over to the next bed and keep weeding.

"Mr. Delabano," his neighbor calls again, and there's no help for it. Mr. Delabano rises, wipes his hands on his trousers, and approaches the fence. Mike Getz looks dressed for work—blue blazer with some kind of ID card affixed to the lapel—and he's holding a dog leash.

"How's your ear?"

"Oh, fine," says Mr. Delabano. "Completely healed, I think."

"That's great. Say, I've got a problem. This is silly, I know, but my youngest one is having a fit; we can't find the dog—Mitzi, she's real important to Janie, and she just took off last night I guess, dug under the fence, and we both have to be gone all day, so we thought since you'd be here maybe you could sort of keep an eye out."

"Sure."

"In case she comes back—you know what she looks like, little curly black mutt."

"Oh, yes."

"We sure would appreciate it. That side gate's open; if she turns up you could just put her back in. I've got the hole plugged."

• • •

It occurs to Mr. Delabano later that morning, sipping his coffee and contemplating the dog leash on the kitchen table, that he's in a moral dilemma. Recovering the dog would probably get him invited to a cookout. Failure, on the other hand, might leave everyone too distracted to think of such things. Maybe the dog got run over.

He moves to the living room and opens the curtains to the picture window. No dog. That's that. It remains only to return the leash with minimum engagement. But he continues to look. Up and down the street nothing's moving. No people. No cars. Even the trees are perfectly still. He can remember seeing the little girl and the dog playing together. Much yapping and dashing about. He turns to get the leash, pausing to survey the room for a moment, unaccustomed to this light. It's kept as his wife kept it. The sort of formal little front room no one's really intended to occupy unless there's an occasion. Floral-print upholstered furniture set at precise angles, porcelain knickknacks here and there, and a real oil painting above the couch: Texas hill country, a dirt road receding through rolling bluebonnets.

Standing outside on the front walk with the leash in his hand, he feels ridiculous and exposed. He's going hunting for a little black dog. A missing puppy. He's got about an hour before the preschoolers begin to repopulate the neighborhood. So many children, he thinks. It's hard to make a case for an aging population; the neighborhood's like a playground sometimes—several swingsets in several backyards going at once, squeaking in sequence like echoes, like a flight of geese or loons. Why, he suddenly wonders, should Mike Getz's wife want a mailbox like his: tulip silhouettes and the name and address in stamped aluminum? It's like a historical marker out there by the street. You'd have to live here for twenty years to need a mailbox like that. Perhaps longer. Have watched the last houses go up, the last open field divide into lots. There must have been wildflowers then, even bluebonnets. Maybe a few. He can't recall.

He looks up and down the street again. It's so flat and open and quiet, it's hard to imagine anything hiding, anything really out of place. There's no little dog out there, he's sure. If it had really been run over, Mike Getz would have found it. He's not going to find anything. There's not even a squirrel. He hangs the leash on his neighbor's front door and hopes it's enough. Then he stops again on the walk, taking a last official look around for a minute, listening for something—dogs barking, he supposes, just a chance. It really is abnormally quiet. Quieter than summer, these vacancies in the daily traffic. More quiet than he can remember; in the country at least there are insects and birds. Maybe he's actually getting hard of hearing. He can hear his footsteps, though. He can hear himself breathe. But don't people sometimes become deaf to certain frequencies? He listens for the cicadas, the survivors out there somewhere, tries to distinguish them once more from the subliminal hush of the general background, but there's nothing, no insects, no birds. This must be what they mean when they talk about earthquakes, how quiet it can get. He's heard stories about how animals, even insects, respond to a big earthquake—to something—before it happens, before people can feel it. Some kind of tension they're supposed to smell or sense in some way. And just for a second he feels slightly chilled, uneasy for no reason he can think of. He hopes he's not getting sick, a touch of fever. Maybe he ought to lie down for a while. He's certain the dog is gone for good. Somehow there isn't any doubt. He can imagine it still running, miles away by now, hightailing it down the middle of the street.

• • •

Every day for a while he expects to hear from Mike Getz. But there's no phone call, no greeting across the fence. In fact there's hardly a sign of anyone next door. It was probably impolite just to leave the leash hanging on the knocker like that. He thinks how sad and abrupt it might have been for the little girl to come home and find it there, and he hopes things hadn't worked out that way.

But he doesn't dwell on it. He's become preoccupied with developments in the garden. The little tendrils issuing from the tops of the new plants have thickened considerably and now extend another foot above the leafy portions. What's really interesting, though, are the knobs or buds—whatever they are—at the tips. They're the size of golfballs, deep blue and still growing. The entire arrangement is quite remarkable—more like exotic garden ornaments than real plants. The leaves, once spoon-shaped, have inflated, and the fuzzy covering is more pronounced, so that in a certain light there's a kind of halo around them. The fringe of spines, on the other hand, has disappeared entirely.

He wonders what sort of season they have, and how it's going to look after the roses drop their leaves and these are left on display. What neighborly inquiries that will invite. Most of all he wonders about the big knot-shaped structures on top. If they really might contain flowers. Every day they're a little larger and, he's fairly certain, bluer. It's likely to be impressive, whatever it is, and although he's enchanted by the possibilities, there's some concern as well about the effects—how much attention it will attract, if there will be a fragrance.

• • •

By the weekend he thinks he can detect some separation among the ridges and convolutions of the buds. A slight pulling apart; apparently all four plants are on exactly the same schedule. They're going to be flowers, he's sure, and he's hardly able to concentrate on anything else, tending to wander back and forth between the kitchen and the garden all day. Gazing out the window.

When the wind picks up at night, he worries about the possibility that the stalks will snap—he has no idea how resilient they are, what kind of conditions prevail where they come from. But he hesitates to interfere, install supporting stakes or anything, for fear of disrupting something. He feels he should keep his distance, let things happen.

In his bed he thinks about them, what they must be like in the wild—fields of them perhaps, quiet fields receding to the horizon. And in the morning he awakes with a disturbing conviction that there's something wrong: they're not supposed to bloom. They're nonflowering, he remembers that from the ad. He's certain it was one of the main points, as if it were a desirable quality. Nonflowering is what it said. "More effective than spurges"—whatever those were—"and nonflowering." As if to suggest one wouldn't want them to. So what are they doing? If not flowering, then what? He lies very still; there's something else. "Gopherbane," he says aloud after a minute, sitting up suddenly. "Grand Rapids, Michigan." He'd forgotten that completely. Entirely forgotten. What time is it in Michigan? It doesn't matter; it's Sunday. Just get a number, find out if there is one.

Standing barefoot in the kitchen, thumbing through the phone book, he can't seem to find what he wants. He tries information, which refers him to the regular operator, who gives him the area code and a long-distance information number, and then he's got directory assistance in Michigan looking for a listing, unable to come up with anything and asking for the spelling again, but by this time Mr. Delabano isn't paying attention. He's looking out the window into the garden, holding the phone but unaware of it until it starts buzzing at him. He hangs it up slowly, still looking out the window. "Oh, lord," he says softly. "Oh, my goodness." He steps out onto the patio and pulls his robe around him. It must have been a front last night. He can't stop shivering, the concrete's so cold. It's like a dream. They've bloomed. Huge blue roses. Completely open and so much like roses, the nearest one, the one by the old rose, already in bright sunlight and glowing blue—not powdery blue but deep, like the kind of glass some medicines come in and almost transparent like that. He moves a little closer. The musky scent of the antique rose—the last blossoms of the season probably—and that's all. Still he keeps that distance, looking at all of them. It's like a moment from childhood—a seminal encounter with some intense and basic thing, memorable forever afterward; fascination so deep and simple it doesn't even communicate with the higher faculties, maybe only a stage removed from the impulse toward the mouth. He can almost taste the blue. They're not really like roses so much as rose schematics. Like Tudor roses. Stiff and symmetrical. Monumental. Representing roses or something essential to them. For a second he remembers the smell—the chilly, unfathomable discomfort—then it's gone. His feet are so cold he's really starting to shake, but he stands there for just a moment longer listening, wanting reassurance, reconciliation with the ordinary facts. Down the block there's a honk and a door slamming, and much further off someone is calling a dog, it sounds like, whistling for it, over and over, until Mr. Delabano's feet are too cold and he retreats into the kitchen.

• • •

Monday is Mr. Delabano's day to get groceries. He doesn't really need to stock up every week, but he imagines it's good for him to get out at least that often—and probably good for the old station wagon as well. Lately he favors a new shopping center at the edge of town—it looks like the edge of the world and that's one reason he likes it. It has anticipated development and preceded it into the uncharted regions to the north, the flat prairie remnants otherwise penetrated in that direction only by highways and a few farm roads and where there will be apartments and expensive-looking prefabricated neighborhoods in a couple of years. But now it's still possible to feel as if one has come to the verge of something. An outpost of sorts. It interests him the way a roadcut or maybe even a subduction zone might interest a geologist, to be able to see the laminations of which the everyday world is composed. Sense the process.

More than groceries, what he wants to get is film and a neck strap for his camera, which, to avoid mistakes, he's brought along, even though he's afraid its antiquity might excite some comment.

It's the camera he carried on trips with his wife, and he wants to use it now to take pictures of the blue flowers.

• • •

Driving home, he takes a meandering route down small streets, his window open, enjoying the cool air—almost cool enough to constitute the first snap of fall, almost suggesting the smell of smoke, but not quite. He tries to imagine these houses growing old and abandoned and strange, but it's impossible. They're part of the collective, the streets and walks and other houses. They're intended to face each other, not emptiness. If everyone simply left one day, how long would it be before you noticed something wrong? If it were late fall and the grass weren't growing, it might be a while. All those colorful toys would still be in the yards—brilliant plastic tricycles and such. And even deteriorated it wouldn't look right; it could never look quaint or interesting, like a ghost town or one of those mysteriously abandoned Incan or Mayan cities in South America or wherever, any more than an old tent could look quaint or interesting or even strange. These houses are so plain. They don't aspire to much, so there's not much possibility of failure. Anything quaint has to have failed in some way, he suspects. Maybe, after all, the shopping center isn't so far removed from the prairie. Think of Rome. Goodness, the possibilities. Like living on a fault line. Here, though, collapse seems hardly possible—perhaps a gradual subsidence, but that's all. That's the serenity of it. The flatness; the ordinariness and even the safety in a way. Not to be threatened with quaintness, to have no intermediate stages between the present and whatever the final one is—dissolution, the prairie. Younger people always seem to be moving in and out of this condition, which is fine with him; it keeps the neighborhood young and, as long as one avoids attachments, stable in a peculiar way, continuously rejuvenated. They move in, produce children, or having produced them, stay awhile and leave. Presumably for something grander, a more complicated situation—and, perhaps, away from the sense of exposure that comes with ordinariness, the flatness of it. The emptiness overhead which, he can understand, might become oppressive to younger people whose gaze is less constrained and habitual, who are more likely to crane their necks to follow footballs or tossed children or, just hanging around outside at night, to pay attention to the suddenness of the vertical transition between home and space.

He's approaching his own neighborhood now, the intersection where he has always felt a stop sign is needed and where he always stops on principle, sometimes irritating people in cars behind him. There's no one behind him now, though, so he waits there long enough to scan the lawn-service and lost-pet notices stapled to the telephone pole. He's never seen so many. Fall clean-up, general yard work. Lost boxer dog, reward (with ornamental dollar signs). Lost white male cat, "Rocky." Firewood. Lost schnauzer. Lost dog. Lost dog. There's a honk behind him, and he has to move on, slowing down again and pulling over a little as the other car zooms by. "Rocky," he says to himself, wondering about a cat that would really answer to that. Probably it wouldn't. It was such a carefully printed sign, though; there must be others around. The "Rocky" in quotes was a kind of desperation, it seemed. It had always been hard for him to understand that sort of devotion to a creature that seemed so ephemeral. Weren't house cats supposed to be accidents in a sense? Hadn't he read that? Not your ordinary natural selection exactly, nor, at first, intentionally bred, but a prehistoric accident—some wild ancestor having taken to following human (or semihuman) camps around and then catching a virus that altered the genetic makeup toward something adoptable: that's why house cats and people share vulnerability to certain diseases. And that's why the bear has a short tail, he thinks. Oh dear, what's that? He twists around to look behind him, then in the rear-view mirror as he slows down and stops in the middle of the street. He can see it back there in the mirror. It looks like an animal, a dog maybe. What if it's that dog, the little girl's dog? Mitzi, he remembers. Oh hell, what if it is. Got run over after all. He backs up slowly, easing over to the side, watching in the mirror. He still can't tell what it is. Maybe it is just trash. It's been a week since the dog ran off. He parks by the curb and turns off the engine and sits there for a minute, surprised by the silence. It wasn't like this in the parking lot. Maybe it's having the window rolled down—the wind and the engine noise, and then the contrast, suddenly stopping like this. He gets out and looks around, feeling self-conscious again, but everything's quiet. No one outside. He walks back toward the object. It's not a piece of tire or clothing, although he keeps trying to resolve it into something like that even as he comes quite close. It is an animal. But it's not a dog or cat. It's more like a raccoon or something. Lord, what is it? It's dead but not badly damaged. What could it be? It's not a raccoon—no little mask and the snout's too broad. He feels he ought to know what it is—just lying there like any commonplace dead animal, nothing really extraordinary about it, but unidentifiable in a way that's frustrating, like not being able to name something simple like a color. Everything's so quiet. He looks around again, then walks back to the car and returns with the camera. He realizes this is probably going too far, that right here he's passed into the realm of the truly eccentric, but he wants a picture nonetheless. He glances around once more, then frames the animal in the viewfinder and snaps the picture. He moves back a bit, looking at it more from the front. He should be embarrassed, right out in the street taking pictures of a dead animal. He kneels to get a better shot. From this angle he can see the animal's black nose and its mouth barely open, a thin line of teeth and, behind this, the bulk of it—a little hill of fur, dark brown, almost black over the head, its feet pulled under except for one front paw, the claws very long and blunt. It's one of those cool, sunny but very hazy days—no clouds really, but uniform haze, enough to scatter the light, make everything bright and almost shadowless. Ideal for taking pictures. He snaps one more. He can't seem to withdraw from this. What would he say if someone approached? Road Victim Inspection. What would he really say, though? Old man in street taking pictures of dead animal. He stands up, replacing the lens cap. He looks around again. But the quiet seems to isolate him. All the houses look unoccupied, dormant—Monday morning, everyone at work or school. There's no one to notice him. It occurs to him that he lives mostly in these little spaces, comes out like a mouse sniffing the quiet, testing the absence. Goodness, he thinks, it's not that bad. Look at all those houses. All so straight and simple with a street down the middle. Why would any wild animal want to come here? It's not as if there were no place else to go. What would such a neighborhood even look like to an animal like that?—it must look uninhabitable, a place designed to leave wild animals dead by the curb, channel them into the street like a chute and leave them. He wonders if it was coming or going. Surely it wasn't going. One would have noticed such things living in one's neighborhood. It can't be a badger, can it? Badgers have stripes. And wolverines live up north, don't they? Mostly Canada and Alaska. A generic dead animal then. Proto-animal. Ex post facto animal. He thinks of all the lost pet notices. A mysterious exchange program. He looks down the street. There's a car approaching and he'd better go.

4

Next door to Mr. Delabano, on the side opposite Mike Getz, live two sisters in their mid- to late sixties—widows or spinsters, he has no idea—who tend to keep to themselves, seldom venturing further into their backyard than the big screened back porch where, in the best light on warm days, he can sometimes make them out as shadowy figures sitting together and watching TV, occasionally on into the evening, looking more and more ghostly through the screen in the glow. In his opinion they look a bit ghostly even in broad daylight under the best conditions, although such glimpses are fairly rare. Mr. Delabano judges them to be a different species from himself—not truly reclusive, which he imagines requires reflection and intent. Rather he suspects they are loonies. Fluttering about each other, adrift in some dim fantasy that entirely insulates them. So it's a little surprising to look out the kitchen window while making his morning coffee and spot one of them standing at the fence, glancing back and forth between the blue flowers and his patio door as if hoping for him to emerge like a curator or a salesclerk. He assumes it's the blue flowers. They've never shown any interest in the roses, which, this late, are not at their best anyway. It's the blue flowers. He pours a cup of coffee and moves away slightly from the window, watching her—a thin yellow housecoat, both hands on the fence rail, gazing at the huge blossoms; the housecoat and her loose gray hair lifting a little in the breeze. Except when she pauses to glance toward his back door, her mouth moves constantly. She's talking to herself, he thinks. There's no sign of anyone else. What in the world could she be saying? The breeze is toward the west, bending the tall stalks in her direction, so that it looks as if a very strange sort of communication is taking place. Loony to beat the band, he decides, leaning against the stove and sipping his coffee. He's almost tempted to go outside just to see what it's all about. Now she's stopped talking; she's stepped back from the fence, standing there with her hands clasped in front of her, still looking at the blue flowers. What an expression. She's beaming—the sort of smile one might bestow upon a virtuous child.

His clothes dryer is dinging at him. It won't stop until he attends to it, which only takes a couple of minutes, but when he gets back she's gone. He waits a little while to be sure, then he goes outside to look at the blue flowers.

They look a little bigger than when they first bloomed, but he thinks that's mostly because they've stiffened, solidified somehow, the petals straighter, less delicate and less like a rose. The color and the glassiness, though, are more pronounced, and especially at the centers, the blue has darkened or actually reddened—a very deep red where it funnels in toward the central structures, the stamens or pistils, whatever they are. It's curious how it grades to red without passing through purple; the eye tends to follow it as blue, denser and denser, into the center without immediately realizing the color shift, as if a cue were missing. He remembers some plant book's contradictory description of the foliage of a certain tree (a type of Japanese maple, maybe, at a certain time of year) as greenish red. He had wondered about that at the time, but later saw a tree of the sort described, and perhaps fooled himself into believing he understood what was meant, although reflecting on this, he doubted it—it was probably just gray or brown invested with the suggestion, with the memory or expectation of green or red.

There's a slight fragrance now. Nothing disturbing but not very floral either. It reminds him of cherry laurel or photinia—the clusters of tiny white flowers that appear in the spring with such a dry, penetrating smell that carries no sense at all of flowers or finished product but rather of something less refined and more essential escaping though little blossoms inadequate to transform it. A smell that seems to give more direct access to the forces involved—a little like the smell of an overloaded electric motor, suggesting heat, insulation about to burn—and for some reason

ORDINARY HORROR

the bees love it. A whiff of it tends to make you look around for bees, and maybe that's why it seems so penetrating that you sense it at the back of your neck.

There are no bees here, though. No insects at all as far as he can tell. He bends down close to the flower—very faint, but there it is, like that dry springtime smell of tiny white flowers, inappropriate for something so heavy and coherent, especially this time of year. Maybe it will improve. He looks across to the sisters' yard, toward the screened porch, trying to detect them. But it's too early; the porch is all shadows and he doesn't think they've rolled out the TV yet. It's fairly loud when they do that—wheel the TV on its little trolley out on the screened porch, usually in the mornings, noisy plastic wheels, it sounds like, rattling across the threshold and onto the concrete. He wonders why things are so quiet on the other side. He hasn't heard anything from Mike Getz lately. No cookouts or weekend gatherings in the backyard. No yappy little dog either, of course. Maybe they're out of town. He can hear the Thursday-morning garbage truck banging and whining its way up the alley. Now he can see it. Bright orange like a rescue vehicle. He returns to the kitchen to wait for it to pass. Sometimes the men like to talk, and he can't imagine what he'd be able to say if they made some remark about the flowers. It's uncharitable, he knows, but he's a little mistrustful of the good-natured garbagemen. Like a merry undertaker: it doesn't seem quite right. Undignified maybe. Disrespectful. He wonders why they want such brightly colored garbage trucks. It seems to him they'd prefer inconspicuous ones. He thinks of an old Andy Griffith movie in which Andy played a bumpkin buck private who, for some hilarious transgression, is given latrine duty, which he mistakes for an honorable and challenging assignment, rigging all the toilet lids with a system of cables connected to a foot pedal whereby he can pop open a whole row of them at once for inspection like a presentation of arms. The humor seemed to reside in the effortlessness with which notions of honor and worth can be appropriated, how malleable they are. He remembers it was a funny scene—the inspecting sergeant saluted by ranks of Prussian toilet seats—but it made him uncomfortable. Not the suggestion of the arbitrariness of military behavior, which is fair game, but the apparent depth of the buck private's gratification, the idiotic assumption of glory. It's really uncharitable, though. Probably un-American as well, to feel that way. In any case, it's not exactly the same as with the jovial garbagemen, who make him uncomfortable, he suspects, because their manner suggests they know something he doesn't, although it's possible the other might reduce to that also. The truck is at Mike Getz's house. It looks like the cans are full, so presumably he's home. Here it comes slowly past his house now. His cans are still upside down, so it continues on with the crusher whining, one man driving and two on the back. Not a glance toward his backyard. It must be a new truck. It's a brilliant orange. Passing behind the blue flowers, it looks radiant: it's like a huge whale shark he once saw on a television documentary, swimming past the submersible's viewport so slowly and so close it seemed to take several minutes, dragging one's thoughts down with it toward unimaginable depths and leaving the little submarine feeling precious and accidental. The blue flowers seem like that at this moment: inexpressibly compressed and precious as the garbage truck moves past. He can hear it for what seems like a very long time, whining on down the alley to wherever it goes. Then he hears the clatter of the TV trolley next door rolling out onto the porch—a sign that it's going to be a nice day.

• • •

Mr. Delabano doesn't watch much TV. His wife used to watch it, and liked to go to the movies as well, but without her he hasn't any interest. Tonight, though, he wants distraction. All day he's felt a little uneasy—nothing he can put his finger on, just sort of anxious for no particular reason, and what he'd love to find on TV, he's decided, is one of those nature documentaries like the one with the huge whale shark. He's got cable (his wife insisted), so there are quite a number of possibilities. Surely one of them will have some kind of nature program; he used to flip past them all the time. Something far away. Really exotic.

He puts a frozen dinner in the microwave and turns on the TV. The remote control stopped working long ago, so he kneels in front of the screen, flipping channel by channel down from the top; first the weather, news, and public service channels, then into

ORDINARY HORROR

the lower 30s and 20s (usually old movies and children's programming) followed by a couple of Spanish-language channels and the mysterious channels 20 through 17 (usually jammed or blanked out), and on down to the single digits and the networks. He backs up. There was something. A patch of desert with foreign-sounding music. Where is it? He can't seem to get back to it. Then he has it again, but only for a couple of seconds before it goes blank. It's channel 17. Something restricted. He checks the TV section in the newspaper, but there's nothing worthwhile. Channel 17 isn't even listed. So he eats his TV dinner in silence, standing at the kitchen counter and looking out into the darkness. He wonders what that was on channel 17. Desert and foreign music sound like just the ticket. He finishes up and returns to the television, flipping channels from the top again till he gets to 17. How strange. There's a voiceover now in a foreign language and a shot of a group of large animals of some kind on a ridge very far away, beyond which rises an incredible mountain range, snow-covered and rosy orange with the most wonderful light—all this in about two seconds—and then it goes blank, not staticky, noisy blank, but dark and quiet like his kitchen window. He turns off the TV. Maybe that will do. Maybe just that glimpse can carry him to sleep. He puts his dishes in the sink and gazes out the window for a moment, then turns out the light.

• • •

Something bothers him in the night. It's like mosquitoes, something nagging at him, pulling him out of shallow dreams to listen for it, but there's nothing at first. Then later he hears it. He wakes up and it's still there; he thinks it's a cat. It's coming from Mike Getz's house—Mr. Delabano's bedroom is probably not twenty feet away. Cats can sound like anything. There it is again, breathless and thin, a sort of oscillating wail; a pause and then again. Oh dear, it's a child; surely not, that's what cats always sound like, a child or a woman, and it's so startling when one does that—invests, by mistake, a human being with the weird passion of even such a small animal. Then you realize it's a cat and it's okay. Perfectly all right for that sort of thing to continue as long as it's a cat. But he's still listening, and when it begins again it's a little louder, really desperate. It isn't a cat. There's what sounds like a door slamming inside the house next door, and then the other sound fades and then it's gone. It has to be the little girl, he thinks. Such a sound; what could be the matter? Maybe it's only because it's the middle of the night, but he doesn't think he's ever heard a sound like that. He stays awake for quite a while, sitting up in bed unable to stop listening, receiving every little noise as information. Toward morning he drifts off for maybe two or three hours, but that's about it, and he's up at the usual time, peering through the curtains at the overcast sky, feeling the chill of the glass against his cheek. Another front, it looks like; maybe fall is really here.

• • •

Outside, standing in the driveway and holding the paper in its plastic wrap, he wonders if this could be fall. Probably he should watch the weather report at night. It's actually rather cold and there's a hint of smoke. The first smell of smoke really counts as far as he's concerned. And it's always instantaneous, somehow; as soon as the temperature drops below a certain threshold there's smoke, as if someone were always ready, logs in the fireplace and set to go. Now let there be briskness, he incants to himself; let there be cyclists and noisy children. He waits for the mood to communicate itself, waits to be melancholy and invigorated at once, but it won't come. Maybe he's finally too old. His thoughts keep returning to the sounds last night and the little girl. It's just cold air and that's all—no content.

Walking back in, he has an urge to open up the front of the house. He draws all the double drapes in the tiny formal dining room—the heavy damask outer curtains (with some difficulty) and the gauzy inner ones. He does the same in the living room, uncovering the full width of the picture window, then sits down facing it, sinking a little into the floral print couch, still in his robe and holding the newspaper. "Let's go," he thinks. He wants something accidental, exuberant perhaps or disruptive—not much. There's a carload of kids on the way to school, but that's not it. He wants the world to pass by the viewport with some energy. Things should be happening all the time out there—little, noisy, random things, the excess one expects and gets used to. But it's not there, or it hasn't been, or maybe he's really too old. Not detecting it: lost his ability to sense it or to respond. It's become too subtle for him. Like losing one's ability to taste—he's heard of that: old people to whom everything tastes like pabulum. That's what he feels like, looking out the picture window sensing only the most requisite and general things: the fact of houses and the fact of street. It might as well be prairie. Maybe this is the way it happens when one gets old without an illness to provide a format. Sooner or later the particulars go away. You're left with generalities. Everything eventually gets more and more generalized, including yourself, and then that's it. Look how big that picture window is. That was something when he and his wife installed it. It was something new. Very fashionable and expansive. They spent a lot of time in the living room, admiring the view, passing by the window on the way to some other room, standing by the picture window—it really let in a little too much in a way, and so after a while there were curtains. Now it seems to let in very little. Like an ear trumpet, hardly any use at all. He has an image suddenly of the distant animals in silhouette against the radiant pink range of mountains. Where could that have been? The Himalayas? Afghanistan, Nepal, someplace like that. It's hard to imagine it, someplace that far away. Somehow it's not comforting. Not restful. He gets up and looks at the bluebonnet picture above the couch. He decides he doesn't like it either, the empty horizon, everything going over the edge.

    He starts the coffee maker, then goes into the bedroom, opens the curtains, and looks out the window facing the side of Mike Getz's house—a plain wall of red brick with a single window and a low boxwood hedge. It looks so dark in there. It must be the younger girl's room, or maybe both girls use it, but he's sure it was the younger one he heard last night. Such a small, simple house. What could go wrong in there? There shouldn't be room enough for anything to go seriously wrong. It shouldn't be large enough to contain the sort of threatening darkness he imagines as he looks at the window and thinks of last night. He strips the bed and carries the sheets to the little alcove behind the kitchen where the washer and dryer are. Then he pours some coffee and takes the paper over to the recliner that faces the glass door to the patio. It really is official now, he thinks. It has to be fall; the vinyl of the recliner is so cold on the backs of his legs that he has to force himself not to move for a minute until it warms up. He pulls his robe under him a little more and settles back. He can see the garden quite well from here—a few roses, but mostly the blue flowers. He can see all four. On such a gray day they seem unnaturally brilliant and concentrated. He takes off his glasses and he can still see them: dense blurs like blue lights.

He reads without his glasses, which are only for distance. He has to hold the paper pretty close, but it's better than bifocals, which give him headaches, and he refuses to deal with a separate pair. Above the newspaper he can see the blue blurs. It's an interesting effect. Everything tends to wash toward gray except the flowers. He flips through the paper and folds it back. Every now and then he glances up again at the blur of the garden. All gray except the flowers and a streak of pale yellow—the four blurred circles of blue and the yellow off to one side. He puts on his glasses, and for a minute he's still not sure what the yellow is. And then it resolves, and for some reason he's startled. She's standing a little away from the fence, perfectly still this time, none of the quirky behavior she displayed before, just standing there in the same thin housecoat apparently looking at the blue flowers. She must be freezing. Where's the other one? he wonders—the one he thinks of as the older one? He lays the paper in his lap and rests his coffee mug on it. If this one were a child, he'd expect someone to call her in or bring her a coat. What in the world is it? Such attention. There's something it reminds him of—the wire fence and the motionless figure. Transfixed. At the zoo he's seen that. He remembers noticing once or twice when a child seemed to have fastened on some caged animal—a very young child almost in a trance, ecstatic, it seemed to him, engaging some creature, entering in some deep childish way the real possibility of it, ice cream dripping, until jerked along by an older member of the family. He remembers a screaming baboon, a male mandrill. Whether the screaming was a response to the child's attention or the other way around, he had no idea, but the little boy seemed altogether beyond fear, completely captured by the moment, the big baboon right up at the front of its cage, its terrible blue-and-red face wide open with inch-long canine teeth, barking and screaming, impelled by who knows what. It was early spring but cold. Even a few snow flurries. He had come from the hospital still dazzled by the whiteness of that place—his wife's room, whatever color it was, probably not white but it seemed like white, functioned as white, blankness to signify that anything might happen, anything good or bad was possible, the quiet and the whiteness meaning a kind of reluctance or maybe, at last, an inability to interfere. So he had gone to the zoo. Not thinking about what he was doing, it was like walking into it straight out of the elevator. So surprising that the plainest, most clinical sort of experience could grade directly into Africa, shift suddenly and naturally, the light snow and the local sparrows drifting about among the spectacular caged birds, the barks of the mandrill. The distinctions were softened. He's dozing off now; the edge of a dream. He places his coffee mug and his glasses on the side table and drops the paper on the floor. He should turn up the thermostat a little, but he'd rather be motionless, drift off in the slight chill. The pale yellow has gone, and now there are just the blue flowers. How long do they last, he wonders. What would they be like in the snow?

• • •

Mosquitoes again or cicadas. He doesn't want to wake up. It's chilly all around him, but if he doesn't move he'll stay warm, a boundary of warmth right next to him if he can stay asleep. A dream of animals, dogs and cats—a menagerie in his house, his backyard. Dogs and cats and cicadas and something else rattling, making too much noise; a fearful racket like rattling and barking, then the awful baboon face suddenly close-up, shrieking him awake with a jerk. He's in the recliner. It takes a second to remember. He can't focus yet, doesn't have his glasses. The noise continues, intermittent rattling and squeaking not as loud as he dreamed. Straight ahead at the glass door. He doesn't move at first; he's paralyzed by the imminence of it—all pale yellow, a field of pale yellow or a curtain, overwhelming and impossible to reconcile immediately. A rattling and squeaking and something spoken—inaudible. He begins to see it; he was trying to focus past it, but it's right there; she's standing at the door knocking at it, causing it to rattle and squeak on its tracks; more like pushing, it looks like, with her open palm every few seconds. He reaches for his glasses slowly, without turning his head, like reaching for binoculars or a gun. She seems so large against the glass door, backlit, a yellow glow around her edges where the light comes through the housecoat. Like some animal one is accustomed to seeing only faintly, at a distance, suddenly confronted, enormous, reared up on its hind legs. She's looking down at him, right into his eyes, and saying something—it seems to be the same thing over and over—and every now and then jostling the glass door with the palm of her hand. He's unable to move. Why does she keep doing that? She can see he's awake. Somehow it's actually difficult to move; he has trouble getting a grip on the wooden lever to raise the recliner. He's got it all the way back, his feet toward the glass door. He's terribly exposed. He wonders how long she's been there. He tucks his robe around him, then with one hand gives the lever a tug while jerking his body forward and bending his legs against the elevated footrest. This practically launches him into a standing position no more than a couple of feet from the woman on the other side of the glass, who immediately shifts to a conversational mode unconcerned with the barrier. "Oh, Mr. Delabano," she says, flattening the second *a*, then something about her sister and the flowers—this close, he can hear her pretty well through the glass as long as she's facing him, but when she turns and gestures she fades out, so he catches it in waves; he thinks of the birds that used to fly into the glass occasionally until his wife put up a large decal of a cat's face, the ghostly adhesive residue of which is still visible and still working as far as he can tell except in the present instance. "Century plants," she says, fixed on him now, "my sister says they are"; she must have come in the gate on the other side, walked around the front of the house to find a way in. "They're not very tall but they're blooming and it's wonderful; they almost never do—every hundred years or sometimes not at all; not at all sometimes," and here she turns to look back at the flowers and he loses it again except for "wonderful" a couple of times. She's perfectly happy for him not to open the door. She needs him to stand up, but that's it, nothing else—this, he senses, is just what's required, exactly right. If he were to open the door it might get out of control; she might panic and start flapping around the house or something. He should wait. Presently it will conclude, he suspects, as long as he does nothing exciting, avoids kicking it into some higher gear. ". . . the little book about the century plant," she's facing him again; he's getting a sort of book report. Her hands are clasped in front of her—finished gesturing apparently—like the hands of a schoolgirl making a presentation, her eyes so large and far apart as if gazing over an audience, past the lights toward something in general, really into it now and sure of the situation, his passiveness beyond the glass. "Such pictures," she's saying, "and so many very good ones, pastel and gouache; we think some were gouache but so delicate the way they emerged from the gray pages, highlighted, whitened like those wonderful Renaissance drawings, and just one page a night, just one every night till he finished—so exciting, we wanted to peek, but he'd hold the book so we couldn't and we really didn't want to, it was so exciting every night to see how it looked, how the little boy grew up and older and older but the century plant never bloomed; he could only imagine it one way or another, every page with a different one, every night a different flower in his imagination until he's simply too old and it was so sad; it was too much for us and we couldn't bear to look at it again . . ." At this point she drifts off into a whisper; she's lowered her eyes, running down now perhaps, still talking, although he can no longer hear what she says. He can hear the refrigerator humming, and every now and then a gust of wind and the buzzing of the weather stripping at the front door. If he closed his eyes, there would be no way to tell she was there. He imagines, for some reason, she is heavily perfumed—that she's whispering through clouds of scent, and if he opened the door he'd be enveloped in it. The pale, thin skin of her face is like waxed or oiled paper, as if, for many years, she had applied to it, on a regular basis, away from the sun which would cause evaporation, some fragrance or scented lotion whose aromatic volatiles have combined with the tissue, rendered it translucent—her eyelids so thin she must see light through them like oiled paper windows in houses long ago, frosted glass, white curtains. And densely perfumed, he imagines. Some strange trade-off having been accomplished: opacity for scent. She's stopped talking now but is still holding that position—eyes lowered, hands clasped in front. Has she closed her eyes? He can't tell, looking down at her. Is she really standing there now, silently facing his glass door with her eyes closed? Maybe he can back away. He glances behind him; he doesn't want to trip or make a noise, but when he turns back she's looking at him without speaking. She gives him one of those competent, automatic smiles that self-assured people know how to produce for strangers on the street whose glance they have engaged for just a moment too long, and automatically he returns it as she turns and disappears around the east side of the house. He waits until he thinks he hears the clink of the gate latch, then slides open the glass door and steps outside. He's quite surprised. The air is still for the moment but there's nothing. Not even the slightest fragrance. Nothing at all except the faint smell of smoke.

• • •

"Century plants," says the nurseryman on the other end of the line. "There's nobody that stocks them as far as I know; I had to chuck the last ones I had."

"Why is that?" asks Mr. Delabano.

"Just no market anymore; outdoor cactus and stuff like that went out of fashion. You can probably find one someplace, but I couldn't tell you where."

"Are there problems with gophers?"

"Where? You mean here?"

"No, with century plants. Do gophers like them?"

"You'd have to ask the gophers, I guess; I sure don't know. I never heard anybody say anything—can you hold on just a minute?" Mr. Delabano can hear the cash register, loading instructions for a birdbath. Maybe he should get a birdbath, except what if the birds wouldn't come? He's on the kitchen phone and he can see the four plants from here. They're not century plants. He thinks he knows what century plants are, and they're not like these. The flowers seem to be spreading open even more. They're stiffer and their centers more intensely red. He can see the red from the window now.

"Yeah, is there anything else?"

"Can you tell me what a century plant looks like?"

"What, the whole thing?"

"Yes, the plant and the flower," says Mr. Delabano, thinking he should have waited a couple of days for his rose man to get back from vacation.

"Well, the flowers aren't much, but you know what a yucca looks like?"

"Yes," says Mr. Delabano, not entirely sure.

"It looks like that but bigger, and when it's ready to bloom, a real long spike with side branches like a big coat rack or a TV antenna stuck in the ground. Think that'll do it?"

"Yes, thanks very much," says Mr. Delabano, still looking out the window at the blue flowers swaying in the wind on their springy stalks, winking red occasionally when they bob in his direction.

He turns off the coffee maker and rinses his mug in the sink. Then he gets a lemon from the refrigerator and plops the entire thing into the disposal. It makes an awful noise at first but grinds down to a hum in a few seconds. It's a trick his wife used when the smell got too bad. Now the sink smells like lemons.

But the rest of the house seems to have acquired an odor, he decides, walking in with the mail, most of which gets tossed into the unexamined pile accumulating on the wing chair by the front door. He suspects it's time for a general housecleaning, although he hates to do it; it saddens him inexplicably. Especially the sound of the vacuum cleaner. He opens the front door and then the one to the patio, letting the breeze flow through to the back. Maybe just an airing out, he thinks. And a few cut roses. He gets his jacket and his pruners, but back in the kitchen he finds himself immobile, his garden gloves in his hand, sitting at the table and looking out the open door at the flowers, feeling the breeze pour through the house and listening to the clothes dryer dinging away like a radiation leak.

SHARON OLDS

Emily Dickinson's Writing Table in Her Bedroom at the Homestead, Amherst, Mass.

The chair next to her writing table
is the chair my parents tied me to
that day. Not the same chair,
but a cousin of it,
a Hitchcock from Connecticut,
factory beside sluice gates
through which shad leap, rubefacted
with roe. My cervical vertebra
feels the peneblum. My swayback sways
away from the lower bar, and I can almost
still feel, with my buttocks, the maze
of glazed string in the seat. My wrists
do not remember being tied
to the struts rising from the seat, it makes me
uneasy to try to remember that.
But I remember the alphabet soup she fed me,
the pleasure of being spoon-fed, I wanted
to read each dense message as if it were
falling, intelligible manna. When I was
alone in the room I would drift . . . I had never
been without pencil or paper—no scissors,
no Scotch tape. I would sing, sometimes,
loaf-shaped quatrains from the hymnal, but when someone
approached I'd be silent. When my father came in,
I wonder what it was like for him
to come into a room with his child tied to a chair in it,

I think he liked it, I think it felt
right to him, he had great faith in me.
I would be a chair that grew up
and spoke well and went to his college.
I was the maple they tapped, troughed,
I was their Druid, they trusted me, they
knew if there was to be sweetness ever come
out of that house, it would have to come from me.

The Necklace

At the worst of the depression, one moment in the office,
suddenly my necklace shifted,
flowed across some high ribs
and sank down along the top of one breast
as if a creature had got into my shirt,
yet I felt its will-lessness, caress
of matter only—whipper or snapper,
milk or garter, just the vertebrae,
the spine which had taken its coccyx in its jaw
around my throat's equator and now
stirred on the plates of the mortal. And these were
the pearls from my mother, as if she slithered
along me to say, Come away from your father,
that ploughed bed is a grave, come away,
come away—as if these drops of her milk,
aged and polished to a gem hardness,
spoke in some oyster Braille on my chest
near my own breast, suckler singing
to suckler, anti-Circe my mother
led me away from that trough with a soft
raking, over me, of her gentlest whip—just that
wobble along me, earth on her axis,
chariot-wheel of the morning.

ABOUT THE COVER

William Christenberry, *Southern Monument VI*, 1980–91, painted wood, metal, gourds, dirt, and wire, 20 x 16 x 16 in.

Each cover of *Grand Street* features an actual-size detail of a chosen artwork. The entire sculpture is reproduced above. An enlarged detail from the same work appears on the title page. A portfolio of photographs by William Christenberry begins on page 81.

CONTRIBUTORS

Theodor W. Adorno (1903–1969) was a member of the Frankfurt school of critical theory. In his books—among them *Negative Dialectics, The Jargon of Authenticity, Dialectic of Enlightenment* (with Max Horkheimer), *The Authoritarian Personality, The Philosophy of Modern Music,* and *Aesthetic Theory*—he considered aesthetic, moral, and political philosophy, particularly as they were shaped by the response to Nazism and the Second World War. "Wagners Aktualität" appears in volume 16 of Adorno's *Gesammelte Schriften* (Frankfurt: Suhrkamp, 1970–86, pp. 543–64).

David Bellos has written about nineteenth-century French literature and is the translator of most of Georges Perec's work currently available in English. His biography, *Georges Perec: A Life in Words,* will be published by Godine in the spring. Bellos is Professor of French Studies at the University of Manchester, England.

Mei-Mei Berssenbrugge received a PEN WEST award for her latest book, *Empathy. Sphericity* will be published later this year by Kelsey Street Press. She lives in New Mexico with Richard Tuttle and their daughter.

Michael Biggins has translated widely from Slovene and Russian, with work recently appearing in *American Poetry Review, The Paris Review,* and *Grand Street.* He lives in Lawrence, Kansas.

Gerald Burns won the 1992 National Poetry Series with his book *Shorter Poems,* which will be issued in May by Dalkey Archive Press.

William Christenberry lives in Washington, D.C., where he teaches at the Corcoran School of Art. His sculpture and photographs have been widely exhibited throughout the United States and Europe. He is represented by the Nancy Drysdale Gallery in Washington, D.C. and by the Pace/MacGill Gallery in New York.

Seamus Deane is Professor of English and American Literature at University College, Dublin. His most recent books are *Selected Poems* (1988), *The French Enlightenment and Revolution in England 1789–1832* (1988), and *The Field Day Anthology of Irish Writing,* three volumes (1991).

CONTRIBUTORS

Richard Dove, born in Bath, England, in 1954, has published poetry in German and English and has translated various twentieth-century German poets, including Jakob van Hoddis, Alfred Lichtenstein, and Ernst Meister.

Martin Duberman is Distinguished Professor of History at CUNY and founder-director of the Center for Lesbian and Gay Studies at the CUNY Graduate School. He is the author of fifteen books, including *Black Mountain*, *Paul Robeson*, and *Cures: A Gay Man's Odyssey*. "The Night They Raided Stonewall" is an excerpt from *Stonewall*, to be published by Dutton in May.

Susan Gillespie is Vice President for Public Affairs at Bard College. Her translations have appeared in *Brahms and His World* (1990), *Mendelssohn and His World* (1991), and *Richard Strauss and His World* (1992), all published by Princeton University Press in conjunction with the Bard Music Festival.

James Haining recently settled in Portland, Oregon, where he will continue work on his Salt Lick Press and Lucky Heart Books series. He has produced Salt Lick Press projects since 1969.

Keith Haring was born in 1958 in Kutztown, Pennsylvania. His work has been included in such major exhibitions as the Venice Biennale and the Whitney Biennial, and retrospectives of his work are currently planned in Japan and Europe. Haring died in New York City in 1990.

Lyn Hejinian is the coeditor (with Barrett Watten) of *Poetics Journal* and the author of numerous books, most recently *Oxota: A Short Russian Novel* and *The Cell*. *Description,* a volume of her translations from the work of the Russian poet Arkadii Dragomoshchenko, was published by Sun and Moon Press in 1990. She is a member of the Poetics Faculty at New College of California, where she teaches poetic theory and lectures on the social contexts of writing.

Pham Thi Hoai was born in 1960 in the Thanh Hoa province of Vietnam. Her first novel was translated into French as *La Messagère de cristal* and published in 1991. She is also the author of a collection of

CONTRIBUTORS

short stories and has translated Kafka, Brecht, and Dürrenmatt into Vietnamese.

Félix Jiménez is a writer and critic. He was born in San Juan, Puerto Rico, studied comparative literature at Yale, and has written for *The Village Voice, The Nation,* the *Washington Post,* and *The Threepenny Review.* He coedited the literary journal *Aldebaran* and in 1983 received the Ateneo Puertorriqueno Prize for poetry.

Jasper Johns is one of the preeminent figures of postwar American painting. A retrospective commemorating the thirty-fifth anniversary of his legendary first exhibition of "Target" and "Flag" paintings at the Leo Castelli Gallery (New York) was recently held at the same gallery.

Rodney Jones is living this year in Mexico. His most recent book, *Transparent Gestures,* was published in 1989 by Houghton Mifflin and received the National Book Critics Circle Award in poetry.

Komar & Melamid (Vitaly Komar, b. 1943, and Alexander Melamid, b. 1945) have been working collaboratively since 1965. Their work was shown at the notorious Beljaevo outdoor exhibition (bulldozed by the KGB in 1974), as well as at the Museum of Modern Art (New York), the 1977 Venice Biennale, Documenta 8 (Kassel, Germany), and many other exhibitions. Komar & Melamid live and work in New York, where they are represented by Ronald Feldman Fine Arts.

Edvard Kocbek (1904–1981), a poet, prose writer, religious thinker, and, for a short time, statesman, remains one of the central figures of Slovenia's cultural history during the twentieth century. Some of his work has recently appeared in *The New York Review of Books.*

Andrew Kopkind is associate editor of *The Nation* and a sometime film reviewer and cultural critic.

Michael Krüger was born in Saxony in 1943 and lives in Munich. A critic, essayist, and prose writer of note, he is best known for his twelve books of poetry, including *Idylls and Illusions,* perhaps the most distinguished cycle in German since Stefan George's *Das Jahr der Seele.*

CONTRIBUTORS

Bernadette Mayer's recent books include *The Formal Field of Kissing, Sonnets,* and *A Bernadette Mayer Reader.* She leads workshops in experimental writing at the New School for Social Research and the St. Mark's Church Poetry Project. Her current projects are the Greek "love of" *(phil)* poems, *The Ethics of Sleep,* and *MIND of Hour.*

Andrew McCord's translations of the medieval Hindi poet Kabir appeared in *Grand Street* 43. He lives in New York City.

Albert Mobilio writes for *The Village Voice Literary Supplement.* His chapbook *Bendable Siege* was published last year by Red Dust Books.

Sharon Olds's most recent book is *The Father* (Knopf, 1992). She teaches at New York University and Goldwater Hospital for the physically disabled on Roosevelt Island, New York.

Georges Perec is the author of *Life: A User's Manual* and of dozens of works long and short in almost every genre, from fiction to film scripts, poetry, drama, and crosswords. He is now generally considered one of the most significant literary innovators of the twentieth century. His last novel, *53 Days,* will be published in the spring.

Andrei Platonov (1899–1951), the author in English translation of the short-story collection *The Fierce and Beautiful World* and the novels *The Foundation Pit* and *Chevengur,* is now regarded in both Russia and abroad as a master of twentieth-century Russian prose, the peer of Bulgakov and Nabokov. *Happy Moscow* was written between 1932 and 1936.

Pruitt.Early is the collaborative team of Robert Pruitt (b. 1964, Washington, D.C.) and Walter Jackson Early Jr. (b. 1963, Raleigh, North Carolina); they began exhibiting under that name in 1989. Recent solo exhibitions have been held at 303 Gallery and the Leo Castelli Gallery in New York, and APAC, Centre d'Art Contemporain, in Nevers, France. Their work was also included in the group exhibition "Post-Human," curated by Jeffrey Deitch at FAE Musée d'Art Contemporain in Lausanne, Switzerland. Pruitt and Early live in Brooklyn and are represented by 303 Gallery.

CONTRIBUTORS

Judson Rosengrant is a fellow of the Russian Research Center at Harvard University and the translator of works by Olesha, Limonov, Iskander, and Lydia Ginzburg, whose classic study of the psychological method in literature, *On Psychological Prose*, was recently published in his edition by Princeton University Press.

David Searcy lives in Dallas, where he continues to work on the novel *Ordinary Horror*, whose opening chapters are presented here. Selections from his long essay *A Trip to the Sun* have appeared in *Southwest Review, Boxcar, Temblor*, and *Raddle Moon*.

Edmund White is the author of several novels, including *A Boy's Own Story* and *The Beautiful Room is Empty*. He has just finished a biography of Jean Genet, which Knopf will publish next fall.

Minor White (1908–1976), one of the most important photographers of the postwar era, also held numerous teaching posts and wrote extensively on the art of photography. He was the cofounder and first editor of *Aperture*.

Fred Wilson was born in the Bronx in 1959. He has created installations at White Columns, the Gracie Mansion Gallery, and Metro Pictures, all in New York. He recently exhibited at the first Cairo Biennial in Egypt, and his installation "The Museum: Mixed Metaphors" is currently at the Seattle Art Museum. He will be included in the 1993 Whitney Biennial. He lives and works in New York and is represented by Metro Pictures. A forthcoming book on "Mining the Museum" is to be published by the New Press.

Peter Zinoman is a Ph.D. candidate studying Vietnamese history at Cornell University.

Statement of Ownership

Statement of Ownership, Management, and Circulation (Act of August 12, 1970: Section 3685. Title 39. United States Code). No. 1. Title of Publication: Grand Street. No. 2. Date of filing: 2-15-93. No. 3. Frequency of issue: quarterly. No. 4. Location of the known office of publication: 131 Varick Street, Room 906, New York, N.Y. 10013. No. 5. Location of the headquarters or general business offices of the publisher: 131 Varick Street, Room 906, New York, N.Y. 10013. No. 6. Name and address of publisher and editor: Jean Stein, 131 Varick Street, Room 906, New York, N.Y. 10013. No. 7. Owner: New York Foundation for the Arts, 155 Ave. of the Americas, New York, N.Y. 10013-1507. No. 8. Known bondholders, mortgagees, and other security holders owning or holding one percent or more of the total amount of bonds, mortgages, or other securities: none. No. 9. For optional completion by publishers mailing at regular rates. No. 10. Extent and nature of circulation. Average number of copies each issue during preceding twelve months. No. A. Total number of copies printed: 6,751. No. B. Paid circulation: 1. Sales through dealers and carriers, street vendors, and counter sales: 2,857. 2. Mail subscriptions: 1,361. No. C. Total paid circulation: 4,218. No. D. Free distribution by mail, carrier, or other means: 597. No. E. Total distribution: 4,815. No. F. Copies not distributed: 1. Office use, left over, unaccounted, spoiled after printing: 1,743. 2. Returned from news agents: 193. No. G. Total: 6,751. Actual number of copies of single issue published nearest to filing date: 7,000. No. 11. I certify that the statements made by me above are correct and complete. Signature of editor, publisher, business manager, or owner: Jean Stein, editor and publisher.

ILLUSTRATIONS

cover William Christenberry, *Southern Monument VI*, 1987, large format Polaroid 809 monoprint, 10 x 8 in. Courtesy of the artist, Nancy Drysdale Gallery (Washington D.C.), and Pace/MacGill Gallery (New York).

title page William Christenberry, *Southern Monument VI* (detail), 1980–91, painted wood, metal, gourds, dirt, and wire, 20 x 16 x 16 in. Courtesy of the artist and Moody Gallery (Houston).

p. 10 Minor White, *Gino Cipola*, 1940, gelatin silver print, 10 x 8 in. Courtesy of the Minor White Archive, Princeton University.

p. 21 Minor White, *Ernest Stones and Robert Bright*, 1949, gelatin silver print, 10 x 8 in. Courtesy of the Minor White Archive, Princeton University.

p. 32 Carl Emil Doepler, drawing of the Valkyries from *Götterdämmerung*, 1876. Courtesy NA/RWG (National Archiv der Richard Wagner Stiftung–Richard Wagner Gedenkstätte Bayreuth).

pp. 34, 37, 41 From Oswald Georg Bauer, *Richard Wagner*. Frankfurt am Main: Propylen Verlag, 1982.

p. 39 Courtesy NA/RWG (National Archiv der Richard Wagner Stiftung–Richard Wagner Gedenksttte Bayreuth).

p. 43 Courtesy of Lauterwasser, Überlingen/Dodehsee.

p. 46 Photograph by Sepp Bär.

p. 49 Photograph by Wilhelm Rauh. Courtesy of Festspielleitung Bayreuth.

p. 53 Photograph by Sabine Toepffer.

p. 54 Photograph by Mara Eggert.

p. 56 Courtesy of Gröringer Fotografenagentur.

p. 66 Jasper Johns, *0–9*, 1960, lithograph, $27\frac{7}{8}$ x 22 in. Courtesy of the artist, Leo Castelli Gallery (New York), and Universal Limited Art Editions (West Islip, New York).

pp. 83–85, 87–89, 91–94 William Christenberry, untitled, 1992, EK 74 photographic prints, 10 x 8 in. each. Courtesy of the artist, Nancy Drysdale Gallery (Washington, D.C.) and Pace/MacGill Gallery (New York).

p. 96 Komar & Melamid, *The Origin of Socialist Realism*, 1982–83, oil on canvas, 72 x 48 in. Collection of Ronald and Frayda Feldman, New York. Photograph by D. James Dee.

pp. 120, 129, 139 Keith Haring, *Once Upon A Time . . . . . .* , 1989, acrylic mural, Gay and Lesbian Community Center, New York.

pp. 153–69 Fred Wilson, *Mining the Museum*, 1992. Installation at the Maryland Historical Society. All objects (unless otherwise noted) are in the permanent collection of the Maryland Historical Society, Baltimore, Maryland.

pp. 153–54, 157–58 (bottom)**, 159, 161–68** Photography by Ken Schless. Photographs courtesy The New Press, New York.

p. 154 Portrait photographs of Native Americans courtesy of the Maryland Commission on Indian Affairs.

ILLUSTRATIONS

p. 155 Collection of Ricky Swann Robinson. Photograph courtesy of Ricky Swann Robinson and the Maryland Commission on Indian Affairs.

pp. 156, 158 (top), **160, 169** Photographs courtesy of the Maryland Historical Society.

p. 157 (shackles) Private collection.

p. 176 Pruitt.Early, two untitled xerographs (details), early 1990s. Courtesy of the artists and 303 Gallery (New York).

p. 178 (top to bottom) Pruitt.Early, *Painting for Teenage Boys (Tie-Dye, Bad to the Bone)* (detail), heat transfers on fabric with plastic shrinkwrap, six panels, 23 x 23 in. each; untitled xerograph from *Witty One-liners* catalogue (detail); untitled xerograph (detail). All early 1990s. Courtesy of the artists and 303 Gallery (New York).

p. 180 Pruitt.Early, two untitled xerographs (details), early 1990s. Courtesy of the artists and 303 Gallery (New York).

p. 182 (top to bottom) Pruitt.Early, *Painting for Teenage Boys (Pabst Blue Ribbon)* (detail), flag on fabric with plastic shrinkwrap, six panels, 23 x 23 in. each; *Sculpture for Teenage Boys (Pabst, Case, Nude Center)* (detail), beer cans with decals, 19 x 8 x 5 in. Both early 1990s. Courtesy of the artists and 303 Gallery (New York).

p. 184 (top to bottom) Pruitt.Early, two untitled xerographs; *Artwork for Teenage Girls, "Coming This Spring"* (detail), photographic mural and enamel on wood, 100 x 168 x 62 in. All early 1990s. Courtesy of the artists and 303 Gallery (New York).

p. 186 Pruitt.Early, *Artwork for Teenage Boys*, installation view, enamel on wood and heat transfer on fabric; untitled xerograph; *Painting for Teenage Boys (Black Denim; What's on a Man's Mind)* (detail), heat transfers on fabric with plastic shrinkwrap, six panels, 23 x 23 in. each. All early 1990s. Courtesy of the artists and 303 Gallery (New York).

p. 194 Jean-Auguste-Dominique Ingres, *Oedipus and the Sphinx*, 1808, oil on canvas, 76 x 54. Collection of the Louvre, Paris. Photograph courtesy of Giraudon/Art Resource (New York).

p. 208 Photograph by George Hixson.

p. 255 Fragment of anonymous poster from lower Manhattan, November 1992.

An Indispensable Collection

36 Edward W. Said on Jean Genet
Terry Southern & Dennis Hopper on Larry Flynt
Poems by John Ashbery, Bei Dao
Stories by Elizabeth Bishop, William T. Vollmann
Portfolios: William Eggleston, Saul Steinberg

William S. Burroughs on guns **37**
John Kenneth Galbraith on JFK's election
Poems by Clark Coolidge, Suzanne Gardinier
Stories by Pierrette Fleutiaux, Eduardo Galeano
Portfolios: *Blackboard Equations,* John McIntosh

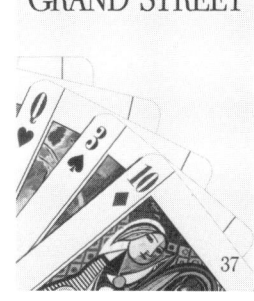

38 Kazuo Ishiguro & Kenzaburo Oe on Japanese literature
Julio Cortázar's *Hopscotch:* A Lost Chapter
Poems by Jimmy Santiago Baca, Charles Wright
Stories by Fernando Pessoa, Ben Sonnenberg
Portfolios: Linda Connor, Robert Rauschenberg

James Miller on Michel Foucault **39**
Nadine Gordimer: *Safe Houses*
Poems by Amiri Baraka, Michael Palmer
Stories by Hervé Guibert, Dubravka Ugrešić
Portfolios: *Homicide: Bugsy Siegel,* Mark di Suvero

40 Gary Giddins on Dizzy Gillespie
Toni Morrison on race and literature
Poems by Arkadii Dragomoshchenko, Tom Paulin
Stories by Yehudit Katzir, Marcel Proust
Portfolios: Gretchen Bender, Brice Marden

41 Nina Berberova on the Turgenev Library
Mary-Claire King on tracing "the disappeared"
Poems by Rae Armantrout, Eugenio Montale
Stories by Ben Okri, Kurt Schwitters
Portfolios: Louise Bourgeois, Jean Tinguely

42 An unfinished novel by Henry Green
Lawrence Weschler on Poland
Poems by Jorie Graham, Gary Snyder
Stories by Félix de Azúa, David Foster Wallace
Portfolios: Sherrie Levine, Ariane Mnouchkine–Ingmar Bergman: two productions of Euripides

43 Jamaica Kincaid on the biography of a dress
Stephen Trombley on designing death machines
Poems by Robert Creeley, Kabir
Stories by Victor Erofeyev, Christa Wolf
Portfolios: Joseph Cornell, Sue Williams

GRAND STREET *Back Issues Now Available*
Order Them While They Last

Back issues are $12.00 each ($15.00 overseas and Canada), which includes postage and handling. Please send name, address, issue number(s) and quantity. Payment must be in U.S. dollars. American Express, Mastercard, and Visa accepted; please send credit card number and expiration date.

Address orders to *Grand Street* Back Issues, 131 Varick Street, Suite 906, New York, N.Y. 10013

F·O·C·U·S·I·N·G

On Beauty Parlors
Autumn 1988

On Trains & Railroads
Summer 1989

On Poets

James Wright, Winter 1990

John Berryman, Autumn 1991

Elizabeth Bishop, Winter 1992

Setting Out—an on-going series of autobiographical essays by poets on their early days.

On Baseball
Summer 1992

Begin your subscription ($15) with any of these and receive our next three issues. Or choose our **Poetry Lovers Special**—begin a two-year subscription ($27) with our three special issues on poets. Send your check today, attention: Box 2446-A. Or call 717-337-6774 and use your VISA or MASTERCARD.

Gettysburg College / Gettysburg, PA 17325

PLOUGHSHARES

Voices From the Other Room

A Special Issue Featuring Emerging Writers

edited by

Marie Howe &
Christopher Tilghman

Ploughshares, a journal uniquely guest-edited by different poets and writers, has had a long-standing tradition of discovering and promoting new literary talent. In the spirit of that tradition, the Winter 1992–93 issue, edited by Marie Howe and Christopher Tilghman, features thirty-one poets and eight fiction writers who are at various stages of launching literary careers—some who are pure "discoveries," breaking into print for the first time, others who are on the verge of publishing a first book. The issue also introduces an enhanced, more readable design, and includes guest-editor profiles. Get this exciting issue of *Ploughshares* singly for $8.95 postpaid, or as the first of a three-issue subscription for $19. Published three times a year in quality paperback.

❏ Send me this issue of *Ploughshares* for $8.95
❏ Send me a one-year subscription, beginning with this issue, for only $19 ($24 int'l)

Name _____

Address _____

_____

Mail with check to:
Ploughshares • Emerson College
100 Beacon St. • Boston, MA 02116-1596   GRW92

JOSH BAER GALLERY

476 Broome St.
3rd Floor
New York NY
1 0 0 1 3
212-431-4774
Fax 431-3631

representing

Alan Belcher

Nancy Dwyer

Leon Golub

Carter Kustera

Annette Lemieux

Annette Messager

Lorna Simpson

Alexis Smith

Nancy Spero

Oliver Wasow

Krzysztof Wodiczko

OTHER WORLDS

A TRIP WORTH TAKING

SUBSCRIBE NOW

1 year $18 ___   2 years $32 ___

Name _____

Address _____

City _____

State _____ Zip _____

$ _____ enclosed (check/m.o.)   Bill me ___

Visa ___ Mastercard ___ Exp. Date _____

Card # _____

Signature _____

Make checks payable to *Conjunctions*
Mail to: *Conjunctions*
Bard Collogo, Annandale-on-Hudson, NY 12504

CONJUNCTIONS: 19
OTHER WORLDS
GUEST EDITED BY PETER COLE

JOHN ADAMS
ADONIS
DAVID ANTIN
JOHN ASHBERY
JOHN BARTH
DONALD BAECHLER
JOHN CAGE
PAT CALIFIA
TOM CLARK
ARTHUR A. COHEN
WILLIAM CORBETT
CID CORMAN
MARTIN EARL
BARBARA EINZIG
ELAINE EQUI
FORREST GANDER
ELI GOTTLIEB
HENRY GREEN
BARBARA GUEST
THOM GUNN
FRIEDRICH HÖLDERLIN
FANNY HOWE
EWA KURYLUK
JAMES LAUGHLIN
PHILLIP LOPATE
CHRISTOPHER MIDDLETON
NOVALIS
ALEKSEI PARSHCHIKOV
JIM POWELL
JAMES PURDY
CARL RAKOSI
PETER READING
DAVID SHAPIRO
DENNIS SILK
IAIN SINCLAIR
CHARLES STEIN
ADAM THORPE
MELISSA TOWNSEND
ELIOT WEINBERGER
MARJORIE WELISH
JOHN WIENERS

"*Conjunctions* shocks, dazzles, enchants, bores, and maddens. But what do you expect from real writing?"—*The Washington Post*

SHENANDOAH

THE WASHINGTON AND LEE UNIVERSITY REVIEW

"Full of fictional, critical, poetic and biographical splendor."
—*The New York Times Book Review*

"The best literary magazines have always endeavored to discover, accommodate, and sustain good writing . . . *Shenandoah* does all three."
— *Booklist*

"A showcase for exceptional writing."
—*The Washington Post*

AMONG OUR PAST CONTRIBUTORS:

Alice Adams	Robert Lowell
W. H. Auden	Thomas McGuane
John Berryman	Howard Nemerov
Philip Dacey	Flannery O'Connor
James Dickey	Reynolds Price
William Faulkner	David Slavitt
Jorie Graham	Jean Stafford
Seamus Heaney	Peter Taylor
John Hersey	Anne Tyler
Conrad Hilberry	John Updike
Daniel Hoffman	Eudora Welty
William Hoffman	Richard Wilbur
Maxine Kumin	Robert Wrigley

SHENANDOAH, BOX 722, LEXINGTON, VA. 24450

Name _____

Address _____

City _____ State _____ Zip _____

GS

SINGLE ISSUE: $3.50   SUBSCRIPTION: $11.00 A YEAR
($14.00 FOREIGN)